The Brothers Coen

Recent Titles in
Modern Filmmakers
Vincent LoBrutto, Series Editor

Clint Eastwood: Evolution of a Filmmaker
John H. Foote

The Brothers Coen
Unique Characters of Violence

RYAN P. DOOM

Modern Filmmakers
Vincent LoBrutto, Series Editor

PRAEGER
An Imprint of ABC-CLIO, LLC

A B C ≋ C L I O

Santa Barbara, California • Denver, Colorado • Oxford, England

Copyright 2009 by Ryan P. Doom

All rights reserved. No part of this publication may be reproduced, stored in a retrieval system, or transmitted, in any form or by any means, electronic, mechanical, photocopying, recording, or otherwise, except for the inclusion of brief quotations in a review, without prior permission in writing from the publisher.

Library of Congress Cataloging-in-Publication Data
Doom, Ryan P.
　The Brothers Coen : unique characters of violence / Ryan P. Doom.
　　p. cm. — (Modern filmmakers) (Introduction: violently original —"Murder most simple": Blood simple — "Babies, bikers, and buffoons": Raising Arizona — "The professional kill": Miller's crossing — "Life of the imaginary mind": Barton Fink — "Reinventing the circle of suicide": The Hudsucker proxy — "What's the deal with greed and wood chippers?": Fargo — "Abiding by Chandler": The big Lebowski — "Three convicts and the KKK": O brother, where art thou? — "Cutting Cain's law": The man who wasn't there — "Cruel intentions": Intolerable cruelty — "The killing joke": The ladykillers — "The unrelenting country": No country for old men — "Burning paranoia": Burn after reading.)
　Includes bibliographical references and index.
　ISBN 978-0-313-35598-1 (hard copy : alk. paper) — ISBN 978-0-313-35599-8 (ebook)
　1. Coen, Joel—Criticism and interpretation. 2. Coen, Ethan—Criticism and interpretation. 3. Violence in motion pictures. I. Title.
　PN1998.3.C6635D66 2009
　791.4302'330922—dc22　　2009033181

13　12　11　10　9　1　2　3　4　5

This book is also available on the World Wide Web as an eBook.
Visit www.abc-clio.com for details.

ABC-CLIO, LLC
130 Cremona Drive, P.O. Box 1911
Santa Barbara, California 93116-1911

This book is printed on acid-free paper ∞
Manufactured in the United States of America

Contents

Series Foreword		vii
Acknowledgments		ix
Introduction: Violently Original		xi
1	Murder Most Simple: *Blood Simple (1985)*	1
2	Babies, Bikers, and Buffoons: *Raising Arizona (1987)*	15
3	The Professional Kill: *Miller's Crossing (1990)*	27
4	Life of the Imaginary Mind: *Barton Fink (1991)*	43
5	Reinventing the Circle of Suicide: *The Hudsucker Proxy (1994)*	55
6	What's the Deal with Greed and Wood Chippers?: *Fargo (1996)*	69
7	Abiding by Chandler: *The Big Lebowski (1998)*	83
8	Three Convicts and the KKK: *O Brother, Where Art Thou? (2000)*	97
9	Cutting Cain's Law: *The Man Who Wasn't There (2001)*	111
10	Cruel Intentions: *Intolerable Cruelty (2003)*	125
11	The Killing Joke: *The Ladykillers (2004)*	137
12	The Unrelenting Country: *No Country for Old Men (2007)*	149
13	Burning Paranoia: *Burn After Reading (2008)*	163
Notes		175
Filmography		183
Academy Awards and Nominations		185
Bibliography		187
Index		193

Series Foreword

The Modern Filmmakers series focuses on a diverse group of motion picture directors who collectively demonstrate how the filmmaking process has become the definitive art and craft of the twentieth century. As we advance into the twenty-first century, we begin to examine the impact these artists have had on this influential medium.

What is a modern filmmaker? The phrase connotes a motion picture maker who is *au courant*—they make movies currently. The choices in this series are also varied to reflect the enormous potential of the cinema. Some of the directors make action movies, some entertain, some are on the cutting edge, others are political, some make us think, some are fantasists. The motion picture directors in this collection will range from highly commercial, mega-budget blockbuster directors, to those who toil in the independent low-budget field.

Gus Van Sant, Tim Burton, Charlie Kaufman, and Terry Gilliam are here, and so are Clint Eastwood and Steven Spielberg—all for many and for various reasons, but primarily because their directing skills have transitioned from the twentieth century to the first decade of the twenty-first century. Eastwood and Spielberg worked during the sixties and seventies and have grown and matured as the medium transitioned from mechanical to digital. The younger directors here may not have experienced all of those cinematic epochs themselves, but, nonetheless, they remained concerned with the limits of filmmaking: Charlie Kaufman disintegrates personal and narrative boundaries in the course of his scripts, for example, while Tim Burton probes the limits of technology to find the most successful way of bringing his intensely visual fantasies and nightmares to life.

The Modern Filmmakers series will celebrate modernity and postmodernism through each creator's vision, style of storytelling, and character presentation. The directors' personal beliefs and worldviews will be revealed through in-depth examinations of the art they have created, but brief biographies will also be provided where they appear especially relevant. These books are intended to open up new ways of thinking about some of our favorite and most important artists and entertainers.

Vincent LoBrutto
Series Editor
Modern Filmmakers

Acknowledgments

I'd first like to thank my editor, Dan Harmon, for the opportunity. He supported this project from the beginning and allowed me the chance to write in depth about not just my love for movies, but my favorite filmmakers. Thanks to Lisa and Ash at Publication Services for helping knock the book into shape. Thanks to Brian C. Seemann for knowledge and advice. He's quite a pal to help plow through my ideas (both good and bad) and various drafts (and typos). And lastly, thanks to my family, especially Patrick and Linda (my folks) for their endless support. If it wasn't for my mother's tact for words and writing or my father's fellow love and knowledge for cinema, this book would never have happened.

Introduction: Violently Original

The first time I ever watched a movie by Joel and Ethan Coen was in the late 1980s when HBO ran *Raising Arizona* in a seemingly endless loop. I was only a kid at the time, but I can still recall that goofy film and the impression it made. On the surface, the exaggerated comedic elements of Nicholas Cage's dimwitted character H.I. "Hi" McDunnough was the initial draw—with his wild hair, slow drawl, and bewildered expressions. In fact, for me certain scenes from *Raising Arizona* will always define the Coens: Hi's attempted kidnapping of one of the Arizona quintuplets; Bounty hunter Leonard Smalls grenading a rabbit and shotgunning a lizard; Hi's nighttime flight (accompanied by a yodeling and banjo score) from cops and convenience store clerks who fire weapons with reckless abandonment while dogs pursue Hi through living rooms, backyards, and alleyways. The film plays like a live-action *Looney Tunes* cartoon, but beyond the comedy, something else still connected with me.

It wasn't until years later, when the research on this book began, that I identified that unknown something as action, as violence. No matter the comedy that surrounded a scene, the violence that the Coens inflicted upon a character showed, leaving them bloodied, bruised, mentally wounded, or ultimately killed. The pain appeared real, genuine, and bona fide. The violence becomes a necessary human reaction as the stories corner them. Regardless of moral implication, characters are left with no choice but to react. Suddenly, the cartoon elements of *Raising Arizona* ceased to be as humorous. The carnage became H.I.'s reaction to tough economic times and not just slapstick. As the Coens' careers continued, the mental and physical destruction of characters, regardless of tone or genre, increased. And in the unique world of the Coen brothers, violence always finds a way to increase.

As the years passed and I transitioned from passively enjoying the movies of the Coen brothers to analyzing what their work contained, it became evident that, despite the success or failure of a film, the Coens make movies like no other filmmakers. They write, edit, produce, and direct their projects with minimal studio interference. As long as their budgets remain moderate and earn a profit, they have free reign in Hollywood, something only a handful of filmmakers (including Hitchcock, Wilder, Ford, Scorsese, Sturges, Allen, Tarantino, Polanski, Spielberg, Eastwood, and Kubrick) have ever earned. Each of these filmmakers exemplify quality, and have a unique, yet varied voice.

As the brothers' careers progressed, the name Coen became synonymous with quirky characters, inventive scripts, witty dialogue, and black humor. However, their use of vehement brutality made their work distinctive. Each of their thirteen films to date employs different violent themes: in *Blood Simple* it's murder simple; in *Raising Arizona* it's the economics of violence; in *Miller's Crossing* it's professional ethics; in *Barton Fink* it's imaginary violence; in *The Hudsucker Proxy* it's suicide; in *Fargo* it's greed; in *The Big Lebowski* it's a case of mistaken identity; in *The Man Who Wasn't There* it's reactionary violence; in *Intolerable Cruelty* it's defensive violence; in *The Ladykillers* it's necessary and accidental violence; in *No Country for Old Men* it's pure and unrelenting violence; and in *Burn After Reading* the theme is paranoia. No matter the story, no matter the genre or the tone, the Coens' presentation of savage activity is ceaseless. The violence just finds different avenues, allowing characters to justify their actions in spite of their natural disposition, setting, or situation. It drives average, ordinary people into unexplored murderous terrain.

Born and raised in Minnesota to middle class, Jewish, academic parents, Joel and Ethan existed more or less in a normal environment, making a handful of super-8 movies as kids. By the time they went to college, their future together seemed uncertain with Joel venturing off to New York University to study film and Ethan attending Princeton to major in Philosophy. But life changed when Joel helped edit a low-budget horror called *The Evil Dead* by unknown director Sam Raimi, and soon, the Coen brothers reunited to write, produce, edit, and direct their first feature, *Blood Simple*. It would establish their working relationship as Joel (listed as director) and Ethan (listed as producer) ceased being individuals and became a single entity known as the Coens. (Not until *The Ladykillers* did they share directing credits.) Far from a box-office hit, most critics recognized *Blood Simple* as a low-budget classic, a neo-noir that, depending on the critic, was either a rip-off or an ode to James M. Cain and Hitchcock. No one, however, could deny its bloody impact.

Over the course of a quarter-century career, the Coens have experienced virtually everything that Hollywood could throw. They were kings of the independent market before anyone cared about that kingdom. They made hits, they made flops, they made movies that rejected mainstream ideals, and then they made movies that embraced the very ideals they had discarded. Each of their films produces a division among critics that rivals Moses's ability to part the seas. One critic effectively summarized their plight: "I know of no other filmmakers whose work is such a puzzle, at the same time so thrilling, annoying, provocative, grating, excitingly unclassifiable, boringly predicable, fresh, and poised to shut down the cinema as we've known and loved it."[1]

Indeed, in spite of never making a sequel or reusing a character, the Coens famously recycle actors (McDormand, Turturro, Goodman, Clooney, Jenkins, Polito, Buscemi) and incorporate trivial nuances that Coen-philes love to count. Common Coen occurrences include such oddities as screaming obese people, vomit, dream sequences, powerful men behind desks, men in hats, strange haircuts, bizarre names, circular objects, unique weapons, and death. While not all remain consistent, multiple elements appear in every film. Also, the Coens revisit themes such as social class, the American dream, and the disintegration of man; and they keep most of their characters childless as the Coens avoid sex scenes in all their films minus their first. Minus sexual content, the brothers incorporate literary elements taken from a vast array of inspirations. As any budding English major knows that messages exist in all forms of literature, the Coens insert ideals and messages within each picture. Just don't tell the Coens that. They view their films as message and moral free: "None. None of them have messages. You see morals? Do we have morals?"[2]

While the Coens' voice is undeniably and violently original, the tools used to reach that style remain far from elemental. They take film clichés with plot and character stereotypes, and invent what Raymond Chandler claimed his writing rival Dashiell Hammett did best: "scenes that seemed never to have been written before."[3] The Coens write reversals of expected clichés, and write unrecognizable characters for modern sensibilities. They openly discuss doing so: "If characters talk in clichés, it's because we like clichés. You start with things that are incredibly recognizable in one form, and you play with them."[4] Nearly all their protagonists strive for abnormality and revel in it; morality, as they define it, is absent. They take basic ideals and remold the audience's initial expectations of protagonists. All their lead men can be classified as idiots, people who believe they possess more intelligence than they do: "Most of the characters in our movies are pretty unpleasant—losers or lunkheads, or both. But we're also very fond of those characters, because you don't usually see movies based around those kind of people. We're not interested in burly super-hero types."[5] They're bumbling fools always in over their heads, never able to comprehend or formulate plausible solutions. Coen characters emerge as anything but the quintessential hero. They are individuals who rarely represent a standard genre ideal: Tom Reagan, an Irish gangster void of emotion; Ed Crane, a non-existent barber with the personality of a cadaver; Marge Gunderson, a pregnant small town police chief; The Dude, a left over hippie who yearns for White Russians and bowling; Professor Dorr, an eccentric, Poe-obsessed criminal mastermind; Miles Massey, a love struck divorce attorney; Chigurh, a villain with a unique sense of ethics.

The Coens part from the standard template of stock genre characters and create ones absent of normality; their characters, put simply, emerge as unlikable, unusual, and amoral.

If Coen characters play outside the establishment, perhaps it's because of the Coens' inspirations. Every movie contains sly and obvious film and literary references, notably drawing from filmmakers (like Polanski, Kubrick, and Sturges) and a wide variety of literature, particularly crime fiction's holy trinity: Hammett, Chandler, and James M. Cain. Perhaps their admiration for classic film and literature is the reason the majority of their work lives in the past: "We tend to do period stuff because it helps make it one step removed from boring everyday reality."[6] But so far, the Coens' exploration of the past is limited to America's past, able to use regions like few other filmmakers. They appear at their best when deep into Americana, where characters don't just mirror their environment, they're a part of it. They don't feel like characters. They are people. The brothers' locations have ranged from Texas to Arizona to Mississippi to California to Minnesota to D.C. At the same time, the Coens always begin their films in the same manner with an establishing shot that predicts the type of characters to expect. The *Big Lebowski*'s tumble weed equals the floating nature of the Dude. *Fargo*'s blanket of snow reflects the coldness and purity of the residents. *Burn after Reading*'s satellite eye creates paranoia. *The Man Who Wasn't There*'s barber pole expresses the limitations of Ed Crane. Both *Blood Simple* and *No Country for Old Men*'s Texas landscape evoke clichéd tough-Texan-cowboy characteristics while *Fargo* and *Intolerable Cruelty* embody the eccentrics of the North and West. In the Coen world, characters and settings always remain fused.

Nevertheless, with all the revisionist attributes tied to their films, no element emerges as original as the Coens unique use of violence, which has created some of the most memorable, sadistic characters unleashed in Hollywood. They create villains who live by their own sense of ethics and villains who operate by their own rules—*Blood Simple*'s Loren Visser, *Raising Arizona*'s Leonard Smalls, *Miller's Crossing*'s The Dane, *Barton Fink*'s Charlie Meadows, *Fargo*'s Gaear Grimsrud, *No Country for Old Men*'s Anton Chigurh, *The Ladykiller*'s Professor Dorr. The antagonists exist on a separate plane with a disgust of civilized life and of normalcy. Only their values and beliefs matter—they are destroyers without conscience. The characters summon violence for reasons ranging from insanity to professionalism to greed, yet all share the commonality of alienation, unable to function among average people. Someone like Gaear kills without warning, evoking terror in Middle America. Everyone he executes he kills in order to protect his money, which is something Chigurh or Meadows care nothing for. In comparison, Chigurh never expresses motivation for his killings. It is just what he does.

In addition, nearly every protagonist has a doppelganger to express distinct moral obligations. From Hi and Leonard Smalls, to Moss and Chigurh, to Tom and Bernie, to Ed Crane and Big Dave, they act as the unbridled version of themselves, able to reject whatever set social standard in order to venture off into their own existence, neglecting the effects of their violence. At the same time, each film's weapon of choice always stands out—Ray's live burial; H.I.'s detonation of a grenade; Meadow's placement of a head in the box; Gaear's use of a wood chipper; Chigurh's cattle gun; Osbourne's hatchet; Leo's Tommy gun; Crane's Japanese souvenir; Walter's teeth; Wheezy Joe's inhaler; and Pickles the cat's antics. For the Coens, genres don't matter because violent characters and the tools used by those characters help to define what a Joel and Ethan Coen film is.

All this connects back to watching *Raising Arizona* on HBO as a kid. Violence, exhibited uniquely—along with distinct characters and realistic settings—carries more impact if the brutality feels real, if it's not simply exploited. When an interviewer asked about the level of violence in their films, Ethan, in the brothers' typically snarky way, responded simply, "It's called drama."[7] Violence isn't the purpose of a Coen brothers feature; it's a necessary reality.

Chandler once wrote, "Hemingway says somewhere that the good writer competes only with the dead. The good detective story writer (there must after all be a few) competes not only with all the unburied dead but with all the hosts of the living as well."[8] For the Coens, nothing seems truer. Despite a countless number of directors and films that attempt to remake, remold, reimagine past plots and characters, only the Coen brothers have carved out fascinating violent characters to combat any prior audience expectations. None of their movies duplicates their last, even if they share commonalities. Ethan once stated, "We don't generally worry about repeating ourselves. Being original and always doing the new thing is incredibly overrated."[9] Original or not, the Coens continue in the tradition of writing "scenes that seemed never to have been written before."[10]

1

Murder Most Simple

Blood Simple (1985)

"It's driving you simple."[1]

CAST: Francis McDormand (Abby), John Getz (Ray), M. Emmet Walsh (Visser), Samm-Art Williams (Meurice), and Dan Hedaya (Julian Marty).

Blood Simple. DVD. Directed by Joel Coen. Universal City, CA: Universal Studios Home Entertainment, 2001.

A man walks into a room. A ceiling fan silently swirls. He's come to see his former boss and his mistress's husband about owed money. At the desk, he finds his boss with one cowboy boot propped up on the corner of his desk. Blood pools on the wood floor. He discovers a pearl-handled pistol next to the pool. It belongs to the woman he loves, and he cannot allow for the discovery of the body. Using his jacket, he attempts to mop up the blood only to realize that cleaning a murder scene isn't easy. Murder is a dirty business. Blood isn't easily washed away; bodies don't bury themselves. The film reminds audiences that when a corpse shows up, it's a bloody mess getting rid of the thing.

This notion of the difficulty of murder creates an unspecific film, one that isn't easy to pigeonhole. Part noir, part horror, part black comedy, *Blood Simple*, which is Joel and Ethan Coen's first film, carefully balances the act of not reinventing genres or parodying them. Rather, it adopts all qualities, combining gore and tension with love and drama. The result is what Roger Ebert described as "a story in which every individual detail seems to make sense, and every individual choice seems logical, but the choices and details form a bewildering labyrinth in which there are times when even the murderers themselves don't know who they are."[2]

A "bewildering labyrinth" creates not only an interesting story, but also a study of character limits. Each character has arrived at the brink. In doing so, the Coens unwittingly begin a cycle of violence in their films, with greed and mistaken motivation driving the characters of *Blood Simple* murder simple forcing them to commit acts they never would. The film's villain explains it: "Hell, you been thinking about it so much it's driving you simple." This idea of going blood simple, propelling someone to murder, effectively drives the movie and fuses the multiple film genres and literature components. It's a tradition the Coens would continue throughout their careers as they combine various inspirations, use unusually complex characters not easily categorized nor stereotyped, and allow violence and the simple nature of man to dictate storylines. Their characters defy audience expectations and represent the opposite of what a main character should by playing outside expected social standards. They find themselves fighting their way to achieve some sort of undefined happiness. They know something is out there for them, but they just aren't sure what it is.

Blood Simple unfolds along the Texas landscape when a narration explains that nothing comes with a guarantee. Suddenly, it's night and two people, Abby and Ray, drive in the rain. Abby explains to Ray why she has left her husband, who happens to be Ray's employer. A VW Bug follows them, but speeds past as they decide to rent a motel room. They make love, and the next day private investigator Loren Visser, the driver of the VW, shares the evidence with Abby's husband, Julian Marty. Marty doesn't take the information kindly, and he fires Ray when he returns to reclaim back wages. The idea of his cheating wife drives Marty simple, leading him to hire Visser to kill them. Visser breaks in and steals Abby's pistol; however, he doesn't kill them. Instead, he doctors photographs of their death to give to Marty. Once Marty pays, Visser shoots him with Abby's pistol, and leaves the weapon behind. Ray appears to collect his owed wages, finds her gun and Marty's body, and believes Abby has shot him. He drags the supposedly deceased body to an open field—only Marty isn't dead. Ray attempts to kill him in various ways, but he can't and buries Marty alive instead. A distraught Ray attempts to return to Abby, but things have changed through their miscommunication. She's clueless about the murder, and he believes he's saved her. Abby confides in Marty's bartender, Meurice, who believes Ray has robbed the bar's vault. Visser suddenly realizes he left his lighter in Marty's office, goes there, and discovers he doesn't have the doctored photos after all. Consequently, he tracks Ray to Abby's new apartment and shoots Ray. Before Abby can escape, Visser breaks in and attempts to kill her, but Abby shoots him thinking he's Marty. It's not until Visser finally speaks that she knows it isn't her husband, leaving her in the wake of men gone murder simple.

This concept of being driven murder simple concerns all three male characters, each of which follows the laws of noir violence, allowing passion and greed to overtake them. Though it's easy to decipher the cinematic influences, the Coens' true inspiration derives from literature. Drawing on the literary world for *Blood Simple,* the Coens play with that established popular culture to create neo-noir, using existing templates and restructuring them. They recycle cliché characters and plots from various sources. Notably, *Blood Simple* borrows from two authors who heavily influenced the film noir movement that would follow them. The first is James M. Cain and his novels *Double Indemnity* and *The Postman Always Rings Twice.* These two novels set the standard for his so-called domestic noir: troubled women, wealthy husbands, and disillusioned drifters. Domestic noir perhaps best describes *Blood Simple* and its complex plot as it follows Cain's formula of an older, wealthy husband and his younger wife, who becomes entangled with a wandering loner. The two lustful lovers, the wife and the loner, eliminate the one element that stands in their way by killing the husband for love and for his money.

The problem arises with the wife, the femme fatale who has alternative motives in life without the loner. *Blood Simple* incorporates Marty as the wealthy husband, Abby as the femme fatale in constant fear, and Ray as the drifter/lover who falsely kills for love. An epidemic of communication breakdown strikes each character as they struggle to understand each other's motives. Once with Marty, who finds himself murdered twice, once by Visser for money, once by Ray for love. Another difference is evident in Visser, who murders once to prevent the deaths of two people only to be forced to kill again. The standard love triangle exists with the addition of Visser who mingles outside of that triangle, breaking from the established Cain structure. Also, rather than being unaware of the affair, Marty takes action from the beginning of the film, suspicious of all men near his wife. Instead of the two lovers conspiring to kill him, he's the one who hires the murderer. Marty immediately notices their affair, which is contrary to the common narrative build. He, not the lovers, unleashes the chaos on the new couple, who fall apart because of miscommunication about the murder. As a result, all the men decide to take fate into their own hands.

Blood Simple's men going murder simple brings forth a second literary influence. The root of the title is derived from someone who would become a well known source in the Coen world: Dashielle Hammett, the American crime writer responsible for *The Maltese Falcon, The Glass Key,* and *Red Harvest.* These works would later inspire *Miller's Crossing* and *The Big Lebowski.* In *Red Harvest,* Hammett's character, the Continental Op, effectively summarizes the Coen brothers' theme for their first film from a simple passage. Investigating corruption and surrounded by violence, the Op feels himself slowly drawn toward it. The Op states, "This damn burg's getting to me. If I don't get away soon I'll be going blood-simple like the natives."[3] The Coens effectively revive a throwaway line when P.I. Visser tells Marty that his wife's affair appears to be "driving you simple." All men experience their own simple moments as each loses their sanity as elements of greed, passion, and paranoia drive them simple. Only Abby, remaining on the outside without knowledge of the murder, keeps her sanity.

Normally, characters reveal more about themselves as a movie progresses, which leads to a satisfying conclusion, but *Blood Simple* lacks this standard dramatic structure and allows everyone to practice in miscommunication. No redemption occurs. There is no moment of clarity in which a character understands the wrongs committed. Instead, everyone's emotional state erodes, leaving Abby without answers and her world destroyed. As author Georg Seesslan explains, "In the Hitchcockian scheme of things there are, however, two missing elements in the way the suspense is constructed in *Blood Simple:* firstly, the viewer's sympathy or, failing that, pity for at least one of the characters; and secondly, the viewer's assurance that he or she know more than the protagonist."[4] Ray is left broken after dragging a man and burying him alive for a woman, only for her to reject his love through miscommunication. She believes Ray killed Marty over greed. Ray believes Abby killed Marty for freedom.

If violence is a trend in the Coens' movies, so is an establishing shot that effectively reveals the setting. *Blood Simple* opens with establishing shots of Texas: empty highways, oil fields, factories, farms, abandoned drive-in theaters. Primarily shot at night, the emptiness of the plains evokes the opposite effect of the city jungle of the average noir tale. *Blood Simple* wouldn't work outside of Texas, as the openness allows for an emptiness seldom felt in the genre. In addition, Texas adds a layer of morals and ideals specific to the region, another element the Coens revisit with each movie. The state comes with expectations, and the characters evoke those qualities, though not to the degree later accomplished with *Fargo* and *No Country for Old Men*. Likewise, their usual inclusion of social inequality is addressed when dealing with Marty. Everyone around him appears less fortunate. Visser is an eye sore and wears the same clothes throughout the movie. Ray and Meurice work beneath Marty in blue-collar roles, and Abby portrays the young housewife suddenly accustomed to having money. Anyone entering Marty's home seems impressed as they wander about staring, as he appears to have everything a man could purchase. For Marty, money solves all problems except when Ray comes to collect two weeks worth of pay. There's nothing for him to gain in the transaction, therefore, he refuses.

Another trend established in *Blood Simple* comes from the incorporation of dreams. Depending on the film, the Coens either opt for full-fledged dream sequences such as in *The Big Lebowski* or *Raising Arizona,* or the more subtle approach as in *Miller's Crossing* or *No Country for Old Men*. For *Blood Simple,* the Coens use a trick taken from countless horror films. As Abby washes her face, she hears someone enter the apartment and finds a dead Marty (despite a film flaw that she does not know her husband is dead) sitting on her bed. He professes his love for her, but knows it's a stupid thing to say. When she exclaims her love back to him, he stops her and explains she only confesses love because she's scared. He quickly changes the subject, letting her know she left her weapon behind. He tosses her compact into her hands. She awakes in a cold sweat. Some symbolism exists within the sequence, as it not only sets the stage for Ray to state the same words later, but it also introduces the compact mirror as a symbol for self-examination. Nevertheless, it's a cheap horror tactic left over from Joel's *Evil Dead* experience. They'd only use it once more, nearly twenty years later in *Intolerable Cruelty*.

A more effective tactic is employed via the Coens' use of simple violence fueled by greed and passion, which is what, perhaps, initially catches the audience's attention. Many movies have been gorier, more horrific, more intimidating, and many movies have bigger body counts (only three die here), yet *Blood Simple* delivers death in a natural fashion. The Coens employ one assault, two pistol shots, one rifle shot, one slow death through suffocation, and one stabbing. The violence appears emotionally realistic with individuals, not characters, reacting to chaos. These are gut reactions. No one, sans Marty, has time to contemplate actions—the other characters must act out of self-preservation. When Ray discovers Marty's bloody corpse, no option remains except to clean up the mess and dump the body, otherwise he risks losing his love. Once Ray drives Marty into the country and he "returns" to life, Ray cannot kill him. Ray is unable to decide whether to shoot him, run him over, or strike him with a shovel. By taking his time, it's a clear indication, that he, unlike Visser, has no stomach for murder.

In turn, both Abby and Visser kill to preserve their livelihoods. Visser, already driven murder and money simple, must now kill Ray and Abby to secure his escape. Abby ends up murdering Visser in the final act of mistaken murder. True to the nature of the genre, the violence within *Blood Simple* is anything but simple.

JULIAN MARTY:
"I'M STAYING RIGHT HERE IN HELL"

Of all *Blood Simple*'s characters, Marty represents the most complex, most flawed, and most hated because his situation forces him to act. As the owner of a sleazy bar, he exudes cliché creepiness with his greasy hair, open shirt, and gold chain. After Visser confirms the affair, he immediately attempts to pick up his bartender's date, and becomes angry at her denial. Marty has lost his wife to another man, leaving him abandoned. This should warrant sympathy, but difficulty emerges because viewers don't know about Abby and his past relationship. Viewers only know of his despair and her lust for Ray. It's never clear because of the inherent lack of communication between characters; both Marty and Abby have varying views of each other.

Abby paints Marty as a psycho, making her life unlivable. He, on the other hand, portrays her as a wandering wife, sleeping with multiple people, and always playing coy. He knows that, in order to keep such a woman, it costs: "She's an expensive piece of ass. You get a refund though if you tell me who else she's been sluicing." We never fully discern if both or neither are correct. Regardless, Marty and Abby's relationship directly correlates with the domestic noir, notably Cain's *The Postman Always Rings Twice*. Despite his strength, Marty lacks the sympathetic quality of *Postman*'s jovial husband Nick Papadakis, who takes in a drifter and provides him with both a job and opportunity. He exhibits heart, compassion, and love—every attribute absent in Marty. Marty's cowardice results in him not just hiring his own eventual hitman and isolating himself from the deed, but losing all ability to think with common sense.

Marty's introduction outlines his complex behavior. He starts with a discussion of Visser, who took multiple photographs of his wife sexually engaged. He's shocked and disgusted—not just by the evidence, but by his P.I. taking the photos. A client surprised at photos of an affair could be a cinematic first; it's a stereotype that all clients expect proof. Instead, Marty erupts at Visser, threatening beheading, which not only helps establish his disgust about the affair, but also indicates his temper. With the evidence before him, Marty is suddenly unsure how to vent his anger. He presents himself as an intimidating client, yet no one beyond Abby takes him seriously. He yearns to be a man of action, but given a chance when Ray presents himself for his owed money, Marty does not live up to that role. He can only sit outside, alone in the back of the bar with a bug zapper and a burning incinerator to keep him company.

Marty doesn't fight. Only when Ray pushes him for some sort of response does Marty acknowledge him, responding like a scorned child: "I don't particularly want to talk to you." Despite Marty's gruff exterior, he's left wanting, lacking smarts and a hardened nature. Unwilling to engage in a physical altercation, Marty launches mental warfare, effectively placing distrust in Ray's mind. He inserts doubt into Abby's love by stating, "The funniest thing to me right now is that you think she came back here for you – that's what's funny." Later, Marty continues his harassment with childish hang-up calls, establishing his dominance over the situation and creating a crack in the budding relationship. After the meeting with Ray, Marty has no recourse except to sit in his office, isolating and insulating himself. Unable to sleep, eat, or leave the bar, he just stares at a swirling ceiling fan. When Meurice walks into his office and breaks the silence to ask if he's going home, Marty answers, "I'll stay right here in hell."

At the same time, Marty isn't sure how to commit the violence he craves. He ridiculously attempts to kidnap Abby in broad daylight from Ray's home, dragging her to his car like a caveman reclaiming property. It's a disastrous attempt as Abby fights him off, leaving him retreating to rehire Visser. Marty, suffering the broken finger and humiliated by his defeat, suffers further ridicule when everyone he passes on his walk to meet Visser has a good laugh at his mangled appendage. With Visser, Marty appears bewildered. He's disgusted at his own inability to act or inflict the violence he wants. At the same time, Marty remains vague on the legality of his proposed job for Visser.

Marty cannot bring himself to spell out murder for Visser, but insists, "The more I think about it the more irritated I get." Visser, understanding the job, laughs at Marty's plight and finally states the line, "Hell, you been thinking about it so much it's driving you simple." At this point, Marty believes money will buy the trust he needs. He's isolated, lonely, distraught, and figures someone like Visser will do anything if the price is right. With Visser, his trust comes in terms of dollars, and when Visser inquires why he should trust Marty, only one response could work: "For the money." Visser does not argue the point, and by the time he shows Marty the pictures of the dead bodies, Marty cannot stomach the sight. He's the very definition of murder simple: unable to prevent a constant string of thoughts, leaving him with no alternatives but to lash out violently. Not a man of action, Marty knows that if he wants a problem solved simply, he has to pay someone to do it.

ABBY:
"I GOT LOTS OF PERSONALITY."

The ability to wield a man to kill is the basis for a film noir's femme fatale, the black widow who lures men to do deeds she has no desire to do. Femme fatales such as Lana Turner, Rita Hayworth, or Lauren Bacall ooze sexuality and make it nearly impossible for a man to turn away. Because *Blood Simple* is neo-noir, Abby appears to fit the mold of the femme fatale as she "ha[s] a tremulous sexy vulnerability that neither she nor any other Coen brother character has displayed since."[5] Vulnerability defines her. She's naïve and sexual—a deadly combination. She's a married woman who falls for a drifter and wants her husband out of the picture, but unlike her femme fatale counterparts, Abby never suggests that Ray does anything. Instead, she hints at her own desire for action, telling him within the first few moments of the movie about her .38 pearl-handled pistol that Marty gave to her on their first anniversary. Abby notes, "Figured I'd better leave before I used it on him."

In spite of her comment about murder, Abby never alludes to a future with Ray. She never suggests that life will be better if Ray disposes of Marty. Instead, her passing comment sets up the Coens' greatest ability—reversing cliché expectations. Ray has his chances to battle Marty, but he has no intention of creating a corpse. Her mention of murder allows for his involvement in the killing of Marty, even if she has no intention of doing so.

In terms of narrative, Abby personifies the most mysterious character in *Blood Simple*. We learn at the outset that she has returned from somewhere, a place we never learn. The Coens skip setting up the expected noir established love triangle between Marty, Abby, and Ray at the beginning and have her reappear, after some rift has already occurred. She returns much to the anguish of her husband. Hints arrive to explain but vanish without fruition. Marty alludes about her past adultery, but her back story, much like the emotion in the film, remains a mystery—yet another trend the Coens continue by leaving the audience to judge characters by actions instead of providing thorough backgrounds. The most we learn comes from her conversation with Ray about a psychiatric history. As they lay in his bed, Abby explains the frustration of living with Marty: "I got lots of personality. Marty always said I had too much. 'Course he was never big on personality." She reveals that he had sent her to a psychiatrist to "see if he could calm [her] down some." However, the psychiatrist found nothing wrong with her, leading Marty to fire him. No elaboration occurs, but it's clear that Marty's attempt to control his younger wife had failed.

A wounded soul, Abby drifts, according to Marty, from one man to the next in search of comfort and stability. Her preference in lovers apparently never varies: older, quiet, tough talkers. Those relationships, her choices, make her the catalyst. Even if Abby stops short of the femme fatale role, she is the person driving the men into motion by leaving Marty and landing in the waiting arms of Ray. Initially, her actions appear limited in comparison to the men. However, that changes as she becomes stronger and more independent. This is a stark contrast to the Cain domestic noir in which the women play active roles, pushing, pulling, and twisting their men, while manipulating their minds for murder. In *Blood Simple,* though, one can see Abby drift toward independence as the movie develops. She rents her own apartment where her surroundings symbolize her changing mindset. Her home with Marty is full of lush furnishings, yet the only item she removes from the house is the pearl-handled .38. By the time she rents her own apartment, the room is bare and without luxury. For the first time, she appears happy, and she is able to finally unclutter her life.

Abby might establish verbal and metaphorical changes in her life, but as the saying goes, actions speak louder than words. On the screen, she is a petite woman, thin both physically and spiritually. In spite of her appearance, Abby demonstrates an ability to defend herself as the pressure mounts. During Marty's pathetic attempt to kidnap her, Abby demonstrates that she is anything but another victim by breaking Marty's finger and kicking him in the groin. She evolves beyond the standard female victim. Usually in film, women scream, wail, and crawl their way to freedom, but Abby veers away from this cliché. She accepts the situation and acts.

At the film's conclusion, when she arrives home at her new apartment to find a nervous Ray demanding she turn off the lights, she complies only for a moment. She flips the switch on, not caring what someone might see, and confronts Ray. She refuses to allow another man to dictate her life. However, Abby fails to realize that she and Ray experience miscommunication once again. Earlier, Meurice warned Abby of Ray's instability after Meurice had listened to a phone message Marty left, setting up Ray for the missing money used to hire Visser. And as she and Ray cannot disclose the meaning of their disagreements, a rifle solves the communication problems, killing Ray. Frightened, Abby keeps her composure and refuses to be broken even as she battles Visser in another case of mistaken communication. Ray never had the opportunity to discuss Marty's death. In turn, Abby believes Marty is still alive and now hunts her. Understandably distraught, she defends herself and resorts to using the very weapon she claimed she would use: her pearl-handled .38. She shoots, even if the man she kills is not her husband.

RAY:
"I ALWAYS LIKED YOU"

As the classic loner, a drifting, love-seeking fool from the world of Cain, Ray might possess a home and a job, but he lacks direction, bartending at a strip club. This lack of ambition and motivation creates the modern drifter, because having characters wander from town to town no longer applies in the modern era. Despite his lack of fortitude, Ray holds pride and honor. Like Marty, he imagines himself a tough customer without visible emotion. No matter the situation, he remains calm and collected, and he keeps everything simple. His confrontation with Marty is matter of fact and devoid of initial drama. Ray concludes that a fist fight would solve their disagreement over Abby—a simple reaction. The very notion of returning to work for money validates Ray's simplistic nature, not caring nor worrying about the wrath of Marty.

Ray and Abby's affair starts *Blood Simple,* and like the classic drifter, Ray falls for the married woman. He has had his eye on her and attempts to disregard any of her marital drama: "Listen, I ain't a marriage counselor. [. . .] But I like you. I always liked you." He attempts to reveal a moral standpoint by saying there is little purpose in starting anything; however, he falls to temptation moments later in a seedy motel. Ray, in terms of the genre, cannot fight fate. His kind always plummets for the unattainable woman, a woman out of his league. With Cain's story revised to make Marty the one who desires murder, Ray is left cleaning the reversed mess as a supposed savior like *Double Indemnity's* Walter Huff, who worried about his own love says, "I couldn't think of anything but Lola, a lot of cops around her, maybe beating her up, trying to make her spill something that she knows no more about than the man in the moon."[6] Ray commits no murder, but he does not hesitate to act to save Abby from herself. He falls into the unknowing genre trap, a trap of miscommunication that leads to his fate as the drifter/lover. He has gone love simple, unable to see beyond their affair. Suddenly, Ray is capable of burying a body.

Ray invokes the second form of violence within *Blood Simple*. He is willing to bury Marty alive if it will protect Abby and win her love. He murders for the passion of a woman—a common element of noir that kicks off an impressive nearly 20 minute sequence without dialogue in which Ray's ethics are challenged upon discovering the seemingly lifeless body of Marty at the bar behind his desk with one boot up on his desk and a pile of blood below him. Ray understands the situation when he finds Abby's pearl-handled .38 on the floor; he knows the woman he loves has taken matters into her own hands. He never wavers in cleaning up the mess. In *Psycho*, Norman Bates finds mopping up blood difficult, but Ray lacks a mop or even basic cleaning supplies, and he must use his own jacket for the pool of blood. He soaks it up, but the blood drips, leaving a bigger mess.

Effectively unsettling, the scene creates a sense of fear not just for Ray, but for the audience. Meurice had arrived moments before at the bar, playing Neil Diamond ("Four Seasons" in the Director's Cut) at the jukebox. Regardless of the potential of being caught in a room with a bloody corpse, Ray discovers the meaning of the phrase "dead weight" in the limp Marty. He drags the body to the car, throws the rags in the incinerator, and drives away prepared to bury Marty. The sequence draws similarities from various films, notably Hitchcock's *Torn Curtain* as the ease of death never is as simple as it should be. Ray soon discerns that notion when he pulls off to the side of the road to dump the body. Marty is actually alive and tries to crawl to safety on the isolated highway. In turn, Ray ends up having to drag Marty back to the car, hoping to finish loading him before the arrival of an oncoming semi (a scene the Coens later perfected in *Fargo*. The situation and the results differed, but the isolated setting and the potential threat of discovery works to different effects in both films). Ray must now contemplate numerous ways of killing Marty, none of which he can stomach. In the end, he can only bury the problem by throwing dirt over Marty.

Ray might have saved Abby from her own supposed slop, but the incident leaves Ray a changed man. Guilt, suspicion, lust, paranoia, and the blood on his hands become too much. He calls Abby the next morning for a cryptic conversation, during which both talk around a subject unknown to the other person. Their exchange sums up their relationship. Both hold different ideas about each other and engage in miscommunication. When Ray finally sees Abby the next morning, their misunderstanding peaks. Ray, believing he has taken care of her bloody mess, cannot understand why she plays coy. He presses her and once again they dance around the issue: "What're you talking about, Ray? I haven't done anything funny." Marty's mental warfare returns as she proclaims her innocence, and for the first time, Ray doubts his love for Abby. In the end, Ray is defeated like all Cain characters, killed without knowing the truth. The simple act of love overtakes Ray and causes him to kill for a woman who never asked him to kill. Chased by Visser, Ray finally ventures to his last place of refuge, Abby's apartment. He waits in the dark only to die as a result of misinformation.

LOREN VISSER, P.I:
"IDNAT WILD?"

Private investigators are traditionally notorious for being scavengers, unethical men who'll go to any lengths to complete a job. A long list of comparable examples exists, such as Sam Spade, Phillip Marlowe, the Continental Op, Jake Gittes, and Mike Hammer. These characters are the poster boys for the industry—they are heartless, witty, mean spirited, yet honorable. Their word equals their bond because it is their livelihood. On the surface, Loren Visser fits right in, not venturing too far from the family tree of Hammett's Sam Spade, who Hammett describes as looking "rather pleasantly like a blond satan."[7] Any hero, any man of honor who resembles the Prince of Darkness clearly lacks a strong moral standing. And, though Spade remained true to his word, he still manipulated, deceived, and abused at will. Visser isn't any different.

Overweight and sweaty, Visser's never without a cowboy hat or his yellow leisure suit, perhaps an indication of his cowardly nature. He drives a tortured VW Bug, defining the sleazy sleuth with his less than stellar ethics: he works only at night and he's willing to do a job if it pays. He specializes in divorce work, sickly enjoying the job as he tracks the cheating couple. At times, he even calls them, pretending to be the husband: "Having a good time?" When he later tosses the photos of the affair on Marty's desk and Marty stares at them with disgust, Visser seems surprised. Typically, private eyes attempt to comfort clients, but Visser revels in his discoveries. He is a private eye without a moral compass—even as he reveals their sexual appetite. He can't seem to comprehend when Marty doesn't see the humor in it.

Nevertheless, Visser possesses a hidden wrinkle when compared to other great detectives. He's a sleuth willing to go beyond his advertised work for the right situation. By stepping over that mythical line, Visser allows himself to go simple for the promise of money. Whatever normal train of thought he maintained before evaporates when the dollar amount, $10,000, surfaces. He's able to justify murder if he's only killing one who yearns for death in the first place. However, as Visser discovers, murder never is simple, and for him to enjoy his monetary reward, he must eliminate anyone standing in his way. And, in his now simple mind, Ray and Abby represent that obstacle. Morally, illegal activity does not bother him. For him to survive in his line of work, he and his clients need level heads. No doubt, Visser has seen many married men and women go simple as their brains continually recycle the same negative thoughts.

For Visser, murder appears as a new venture. When he arrives at Ray's house to complete the job, the viewer may interpret the scene in a number of ways. Perhaps Visser came to the house knowing all along that he'd attempt to frame Abby by planting her gun. Perhaps he changed his mind upon arriving at the house. Initially, he seemed focused on the job with Abby's gun in hand as he crept toward the bedroom. But when he hears a noise, he stops. In that moment, the audience can see his brain calculate the odds and decide that one murder sounds better than two murders. But why did he venture to complete the job with his own weapon? Why would he not use his rifle and shoot them through the massive bedroom window?

Nevertheless, the failed job means he broke his private eye bond with Marty to perform a double-cross, something that makes him feel uncomfortable. After he shows Marty the false-murder pictures to send him dashing to vomit in the bathroom, Visser appears shaken for the first time. Suddenly alone in Marty's office, he stubs out his cigarette and wipes his hands frantically on his pants. Verbally, he would never admit such panic, and he resorts to his best weapon: talking. He reveals who he has become: "I must've gone money simple. This kind of murder . . . it's too damn risky." Risky or not, the moment Marty slides the money across the desk, Visser falls victim to his own simple nature, shooting Marty in the chest. He holds his gun in place for a few beats and sits in shock at his own actions to ensure Marty is dead. The way he saw it, murdering two people left one witness, where instead he could kill one more person, earn the same fee, and leave no storyteller. Even with the money, he broke the only level of honor all previous literary detectives before him personified; he didn't just kill for money, he broke a contract with a client. The death of Marty due to Visser's greed represents the first and certainly not the last of many Coen casualties.

Once Visser tastes murder, he ceases his detective role. In the final battle between him and Abby, horror elements are evoked as Visser keeps on coming, despite a knife through the hand. He punches through sheetrock to remove the blade, momentarily transforming into the unstoppable monster instead of a joking private eye. This final confrontation is where all miscommunication comes full circle: Abby and Ray are at odds over different ideas and Visser is in pursuit of them with the belief they know his identity. He initially opts for a sniper approach, shooting Ray from an opposing rooftop, removing himself somewhat from the violence until Abby outwits him. They never see each other, and each believes that the other possesses potentially compromising power and information. Instead of a verbal confrontation, they continue their characters' avoidance inclinations and act against the unknown. Because Abby believed Visser was Marty, all her anger and frustration toward him allowed her to standup and defend herself.

As a cowboy detective, Visser is also the representation of Texas in *Blood Simple*. Even as an antagonist, Visser provides the early narration, giving the audience an understanding about the nature of Texas amid the barren landscape. He states that the world is full of complainers, but that nothing is attached with a guarantee. He draws comparisons to the Pope, president, and any man of the year, believing that anything can go wrong: "Now in Russia, they got it mapped out so that everyone pulls for everyone else—that's the theory, anyway. But what I know about is Texas. And down here... you're on your own."

The introduction alludes to hopelessness, fate, and the individual nature of Texas, which underlines Visser and the other characters. They're all in hell, and Visser's a lone wolf left to his own devices to operate freely. He creates an oxymoron by complaining about complainers since complaints drive his business. Regardless, author Georg Seesslen explains, "Voiceovers or flashbacks lead to structural clarity at best, not to analytical explanations. Instead of being a confession, in this instance the construction becomes a confirmation of moral equanimity, a laconicism of complete failure."[8] Effective film noir utilizes narration to fill in the gaps, such as in *Sunset Boulevard* or *The Killing*. The voice-over allows the film to provide a proper setup to explain the motivation of the characters to the audience. Yet *Blood Simple* uses it as an introduction to the setting, to imply that the characters and the story will be ordinary. They're Texans—they're capable of love, jealousy, and mistakes just like everyone else.

Visser is awarded the final sequence. As he lies dying on the bathroom floor, he can't help but laugh as Abby believes Marty chased her, leaving him the chance to deliver one final joke. Visser smirks at his own wit, but suddenly his expression changes. He glances upward at the pipes of the bathroom sink. Condensation builds. A single drop gathers, ready to fall. And below, Visser, dying from the gunshot, expresses fear for the first time.

* * *

Blood Simple placed Joel and Ethan Coen on the cinema map during a period where independent films lacked modern outlets. It established not only their individualistic credentials, but defined them as filmmakers with their own style and voice. And, though no one could predict that they would rarely deviate from the method utilized in this film, the template for all future Coen films was set. Their movies would vary in plot, style, and character, but basic attributes would remain.

Critically, *Blood Simple* would start another trend, dividing the critical viewpoints. Ebert hailed the Coens' first film, stating, "It is violent, unrelenting, absurd, and fiendishly clever. There is a cliché I never use: 'Not for the squeamish.' But let me put it this way. *Blood Simple* may make you squeam."[9] On the other hand, in one considerably harsh review, Stephen Harvey of *Film Comment* admits of the film's success in festivals worldwide and praised it himself in some regards, but gave it one star, stating, "More of this vacant virtuosity is what the American screen can't get enough of, and emphatically doesn't need."[10] He argued against the clichéd nature of the material as characters appeared "gleaned from Prof. Lawrence Kasdan's Film Noir 101 course." Regardless, it's interesting that the Coens never stopped using cliché material. It makes one wonder what Mr. Harvey thought of their later works, all of which found inspiration from supposed dry wells.

2

Babies, Bikers, and Buffoons

Raising Arizona (1987)

"I couldn't help thinking that a brighter future lay ahead."[1]

CAST: Nicholas Cage (H.I. McDunnough), Holly Hunter (Edwina "Ed" McDunnough), Trey Wilson (Nathan Arizona), John Goodman (Gale Snoats), William Forsythe (Evelle Snoats), Tex Cobb (Leonard Smalls), Sam McMurray (Glen), and Frances McDormand (Dot).

Raising Arizona. Directed by Joel Coen. Beverly Hills, CA: 20th Century Fox Entertainment, 1987.

A man walks up to the clerk at a convenience store wearing pantyhose over his head. Beneath one arm, he cradles diapers. The other arm points a pistol, and he states, "I'll be taking these Huggies and whatever cash you got." The clerk, instead of complying, brandishes a cannon and doesn't hesitate to unload on the would-be thief as he escapes. In turn, the thief's waiting wife speeds away, leaving him running through streets, alleys, and houses as he avoids bullets, police, and a legion of dogs. The situation reads like a lame joke, but it best summarizes the plight of *Raising Arizona*'s H.I. McDunnough—a luckless, dimwitted, petty criminal incapable of accomplishing the most basic task, let alone robbing a gas station, or raising a child.

That scene in particular serves as mainstream America's proper introduction to the Coen Brothers. Their first film, *Blood Simple,* incorporates simple violence—the natural humanistic reaction to greed and love. Their second feature takes a distinct left turn by focusing on the disillusion of the American dream, the eroding family, and the use of economic violence as a vehicle to express the characters' frustrations within that world. Along with economically influenced violence, *Raising Arizona* examines the failed

American family and the lost American dream, for which all a man desires is a wife, a job, and a family to raise. All the McDunnoughs need is a baby to complete their family. The universal theme of the ticking marital clock takes center stage as characters battle with their own nature, attempting to break free from destined paths with little luck.

Despite *Blood Simple's* success within film circuits, independent movies during the early eighties still had insufficient outlets to reach mass audiences. However, the Coens succeeded in expanding their appeal with *Raising Arizona* as it caught the eye of popular culture. The Coens changed genres for their second film, escaping the confines of film noir with a quirky crime film filled with a cast of relative unknowns like Nicholas Cage, Holly Hunter, and John Goodman. If *Blood Simple* serves as the Coens' homage to noir, it seems fitting that *Raising Arizona* represents their attempt at creating a live-action *Looney Toons* cartoon. As Ethan explains, "We thought about these characters who rebound, and collide, and simply their speed of movement. We tried to refine the spirit of animation you find in pinball machines."[2] A new level of absurdity arises, echoing the Coens' 1985 collaboration with director Sam Raimi on *Crimewave*, for which they co-wrote the script. Listed as a comedy, *Raising Arizona* remains within the comforts of crime, not venturing far from the seedy characters and criminal dramatics, but its screwball comedic nature takes precedence over any ingenious mystery plot. Without question, *Raising Arizona* plays as a comedy; however, enough tragedy and true love enter into the story to raise the film above a standard slapstick adventure. Characters exhibit real troubles, real concerns, and real desires. They don't set off for misadventure, it just happens to find them.

The story begins with petty thief H.I. McDunnough who finally meets the woman of his dreams, Edwina or "Ed." He vows to go straight to win her affection. The Coens set up their tale perfectly in both plot and motivation within the first 11 minutes through a series of montages: H.I. conveys his inability to survive normally on the outside; Ed indicates her desperation to have a child because she is aging; H.I. sweeps Ed off her feet with lame jokes and vows never to treat her as her former fiancé did. He'd do right by her. They marry and attempt to have children, only to discover Ed's barren nature: "Biology and the prejudices of others conspired to keep us childless." Unflappable, Ed cooks up a scheme to kidnap a baby after the news breaks that furniture tycoon Nathan Arizona and his wife have had sextuplets. H.I. and Ed steal a child and keep the baby's name, Nathan Junior, thus completing their family. However, H.I. soon feels trapped. He's tempted back into a life of crime when two friends, Gale and Evelle Snoates, escape from prison. The escapees soon realize who the McDunnoughs' new baby is and decide to rekidnap the baby. Meanwhile, bounty hunter biker, Leonard Smalls, presents himself to Nathan Arizona, offering his services to track down his baby. Arizona refuses, but Smalls still searches for his payday, leading to a final confrontation with H.I. and Ed. H.I. battles the biker honorably, but is no match against the skilled tracker. Just before defeat, H.I. pulls a pin on a grenade strapped to Smalls, ending the fight for good. H.I. and Ed return Junior to the Arizonas without consequence, and H.I. has a dream that their future will be complete, a life fulfilled by their version of the American dream.

With the setting located in the blank landscape of Arizona, the Coens create their first true region-based film. As seen in a William Faulkner or Mark Twain novel, *Raising Arizona*'s characters reflect the area and define the story. As Joel states, "For a movie like *Raising Arizona*, I guess you can detect our admiration for Southern writers like William Faulkner and Flannery O'Connor. [. . .] As far as O'Connor is concerned, our characters haven't the same mystical obsessions as hers. Ours are terrestrial!"[3] *Raising Arizona* contains literary connections just as *Blood Simple* did, deriving content from sources like *The Strange Case of Dr. Jekyll and Mr. Hyde* and *Of Mice and Men*. Utilizing small attributes from each novel, *Raising Arizona* is set in Tempe, Arizona, instead of a city like Phoenix, where small town characteristics can surface. People can seem simple without lacking intelligence. Life moves at a slower pace and quirks appear amplified. Characters live more comfortably in their environment such as in the county lock-up. H.I., fresh from his proposal to Ed, casually greets a fellow felon being processed as if seeing him at Sunday church.

Arizona's barren region serves as an obvious metaphor for Ed's inability to conceive, the driving force of her character. Instead of living in the suburbs, deep within the city, or in a wooded environment, they reside in a dead landscape that constantly reminds her of her own nature. H.I. draws an allusion between her and his own job at Hudsucker Industries: "Even my job seemed as dry and bitter as the hot prairie wind." Their desert lifestyle secludes H.I. from temptation as if the irresistible lure of a robbery comes with each passing gas station. At home, he can solely focus on Ed and Junior. No distractions. No gas stations out the front window. Whether he can sustain this new family lifestyle or not, H.I. throws himself into the role of father to his budding family.

The very notion of H.I. attempting to secure a better tomorrow for his wife and child underscores *Raising Arizona*'s concern with the development and destruction of the American Dream. The latter explores the erosion of economics and family values, the rise of greed, and the chaos of violence created by it. Smalls represents the end of America, the entity that could destroy all. Nathan Arizona represents capitalism gone wrong. H.I. and Ed are the dying American dream, attempting to build the ideal family. They structure themselves after two models. One comes from Nathan Arizona, a boastful egomaniac who cares for his family and who the Coens show living the stereotypical American dream that H.I. yearns to create. His family represents the perfect family. The first time they're shown together at home is during H.I.'s kidnapping of their child; Nathan and his wife, Florence, sit side-by-side in easy chairs. Nathan talks business on the phone while Florence reads from *Dr. Spock's Baby and Child Care*. At the same time, Arizona exemplifies the class differences between the two couples. He's shown as the wealthy, successful businessman who never misses an opportunity to advance his business (during the media interview to offer Nathan Junior's reward, he promotes his business). They might be opposites of H.I. and Ed in every regard, but the Arizonas remain everything they hope to be.

The second example of achieving the American dream via family perfection is perhaps the most dynamic. It comes during a visit from H.I.'s boss, Glen, who arrives with his wife, Dot, and their mass of children. Glen and H.I. escape the family for a walk through the desert, and H.I., all dressed up for the occasion, removes his white dress shoes as he inquires about Glen's thoughts on marriage and family. H.I., with no family of his own and no role model, turns to the only married, stable example he knows. He asks, "Maybe it's wife, kids, family life. I mean, are you, uh, satisfied, Glen? Don't y'ever feel suffocated? Like, like there's something big pressin' down." Like the bachelor who suddenly feels the expectations of marriage bearing down on him, H.I. either looks for an excuse to leave or a message of hope. Unfortunately, Glen's decency never existed. H.I.'s expected example of a decent family man is anything but. Instead of offering encouragement, Glen proposes a wife swap. The unexpectedness of the suggestion creates a bizarre moment, but it becomes a turning point for H.I. He defends his wife's honor, despite the consequences. Knowing his job and decent lifestyle have concluded, he is forced to resort to crime once again.

H.I.'s criminal lifestyle defines the heavy economic violence throughout *Raising Arizona*, and despite tough economic times, only two characters actually commit murder. One is the rugged Smalls, who grenades a bunny and shoots a lizard to demonstrate his level of evilness. The second murderer is H.I., who apologizes to Smalls as he dangles the grenade pin he removed from Smalls's chest from his finger. For the tone to remain light, no realistic violence like in *Blood Simple* occurs. Even with Smalls exploding into unrecognizable parts, leaving only a smoldering boot behind, the incident lacks a cataclysmic feel. It is satisfying that H.I., usually unable to achieve the smallest task, defends his family from imminent danger. There's no callousness in H.I.'s final act of violence, only self-preservation to protect his family unit.

Beyond murder, two violent episodes effectively demonstrate the economic desperation: greed and the need for money. The first incident comes during the resulting brawl when Gale and Evelle kidnap Junior. Gale remains with H.I in the McDunnough's trailer, where the action escalates into exaggeration. The very idea of unleashing a man like John Goodman within a small mobile home has its own comedic value. Gale uses H.I. as a wrecking ball, destroying the manufactured home by throwing H.I. through walls, doors, and fixtures. Gale and his brother see potential profit in Nathan

Junior over any friendship with H.I., who stands little chance in defending his home against the brothers. Their need for the reward money, though, equals H.I.'s needs to preserve his family. After all, the brothers function as their own family unit. They need money to ensure their freedom just as much as the McDunnoughs.

The second incident (one of the most memorable and bizarre sequences ever filmed) involves H.I. falling into old habits and sticking up a convenience store while Ed and Junior wait in the car. Perhaps it is the violence within *Raising Arizona* that makes the film so memorable as this sequence more than any other exemplifies the Coens ability to exaggerate without losing the tone or flow. It could be argued that the Coens take a stance on gun violence because everyone seems to wield them freely and nearly all the characters arm themselves at one point. The Coens, in allowing their characters to express no thought to firing off rounds, seem to enjoy toying with the stereotypes of endless ammunition and acting without fear of repercussions as they unload throughout quiet neighborhoods. Cops and gas station attendants fire six-shooters like automatic weapons without caution. The Coens depict police leaning out of windows blasting away and clerks unloading without concern for customers. They unleash an army to stop a masked man grasping a package of stolen Huggies. It's hard to decipher if the Coens intended to make a statement with the scene, if the guns blazin' attitude satirizes America's love for gun violence in 1987 cinema (when action heroes like Stallone and Schwarzenegger ruled with unseen levels of mayhem using various weapons). Also, what H.I. steals matters. He's the classic case of stealing bread to feed his family, even if they haven't reached that point. His economic violence occurs because he has lost his job and still must provide for his family. He must utilize his best known skill even at the cost of alienating his wife. For H.I. to succeed and protect his American Dream, he willingly returns to the only job he ever enjoyed.

H.I. McDUNNOUGH/LEONARD SMALLS:
"WELL, IT AIN'T 'OZZIE AND HARRIET'"

Despite his appealing personality, H.I. is a loser, robbing lowly convenience stores as a career choice—and he's not even good at it. He's been to prison often enough to know fellow cons and booking officers on a first name basis. "Hi", as he instructs viewers to call him, never thinks much of his life or goals until he starts to fall for Ed. H.I. is a simple man who says what he means and does what he says. He takes people at their word and is conscious of avoiding violent crime. Strangely optimistic despite having no prospects, he exhibits boyish qualities and, in spite of his dopey narration, considerable charm. He speaks to the audience with deadpan wit and presents himself as an authority on a variety of subjects from politics to economics, which accent the underlying social commentary. H.I. says, "I tried to stand up and fly straight, but it wasn't easy with that sumbitch Reagan in the White House. I dunno, they say he's a decent man, so maybe his advisers are confused." Life isn't easy for him. Perhaps this is a result of Reaganomics or the job market, but it is his excuse for being a professional loser who knows of no other avenues in life.

Regardless, H.I. reflects all Coen brothers' lead characters. Despite holding a conventional value system, he is an outsider to the modern world, only holding one stable job and unable to find his place among the masses. When faced with possible release from prison, H.I. interacts with the parole board, attempting to be honest by telling them what they expect to hear. A repeat offender, H.I. struggles to understand his own actions. In prison, the psychologist questions his motivation in life. H.I. listens and allows the ideas to soak in as if he is suspended in a constant state of contemplation. Prison isn't just his physical location, but his mindset as well.[4] Unable to plan a good heist nor develop aspirations beyond robbing convenience stores, H.I. internally debates the need for stability after a prison counselor explains, "Most men your age, Hi, are getting married and raising up a family. They wouldn't accept prison as a substitute." H.I. cannot offer a retort and sits silently as if having never before contemplated the future. The notion of settling down never occurred to him, allowing his story to represent his attempt for maturation. Family life emerges as a chosen destiny, and he'll do anything to create that life.

While H.I. battles to secure a proper life for his budding family, a threat develops with the emergence of Smalls, the bounty hunter, who, according to H.I., appears to him as a vision as he drifts to sleep thinking of a positive future. Smalls is everything that can destroy his family, a terrifying, despicable "lone biker of the apocalypse. A man with all the powers of hell at his command." Smalls establishes multiple literary connections with his emergence after the kidnapping of Nathan Junior. Guilt creates a monster. Smalls represents H.I.'s ultimate nightmare, everything he cannot become. Dressed like a *Mad Max* extra, he's a mercenary, a sleazy bloodhound detective, a caricature of villains collected from everything viewers expect from the ultimate antagonist. He disappears in a flash; senses things before they happen; never smiles; and is filthy to the point his scent travels through the screen. If wounded, fire spurts from his shoulder in place of blood. Smalls is a living, breathing demon from hell, and the most dangerous, serious, and violent character who poses a damning threat. At the same time, Smalls personifies the proverbial private eye on the case. Smalls, however, is motivated by different reasons and is willing to return the child for a "fair price". If Arizona refuses, Smalls threatens by stating that either way he'll get the boy and find someone willing to pay market value. Smalls demonstrates none of the fatherly instincts that all other male characters exhibit after they encounter Nathan Junior. For Smalls, the baby isn't anything more than another payday.

Hidden beneath Smalls's eccentric qualities comes a deeper psychological theme. His sudden emergence coincides with H.I.'s dreams as if he actually created and released a demon to destroy himself and his desires. Psychologically speaking, "Hi's personal demons are embodied in the enigmatic Smalls, a perverted inflation of Hi's criminal yen."[5] Smalls equals H.I.'s doppelganger, his antithesis. H.I. foreshadows Smalls's arrival after being domesticated via marriage. One could interpret the purely evil nature of Smalls as H.I. relinquishing hidden desire: "But I feared that I myself had unleashed him for he was The Fury That Would Be." H.I.'s own fear, his buried criminal side, created an unstoppable entity, an entity that he could become without restraint. Smalls was H.I.'s very own Mr. Hyde set free to create chaos. Robert Louis Stevenson wrote about Mr. Hyde, "All human beings, as we meet them, are commingled out of good and evil: and Edward Hyde, alone, in the ranks of mankind, was pure evil [. . .]. My devil had been long caged, he came out roaring. [. . .] Hyde in danger of his life was a creature new to me: shaken with inordinate anger, strung to the pitch of murder, lusting to inflict pain."[6] H.I., now stuck in a relationship with a stolen child, has curbed his wild desires, those rebellious instincts that had dominated his life before being neutered by marriage. Smalls becomes everything H.I. yearns for, a lone biker roaming the countryside in search of bounties. He answers to no one and has not just the skills to complete a task, but the ability to strike fear and to inflict unthinkable carnage regardless of economic standing.

The final battle between H.I. and Smalls brings the conflicting personalities together. No moment ever connects them overtly, yet the revelation of their matching Mr. Horsepower (which resembles Woody Woodpecker) tattoos is coincidence, comic timing, or perhaps something else. In the end, no other character could stop Smalls. Arizona might have stood up to him, but Smalls vanishes before the completed conversation. Only H.I. can stop him. Not a killer by nature, H.I. defends his family while remaining ethically sound. Despite laying bloody and beaten on a gravel lot, he apologizes to Smalls with a whispered "I'm sorry" when he pulls the grenade pin and seals Smalls's fate. H.I. must physically destroy his alter ego in order to free himself of past desires and to secure any chance of salvaging his love for Ed and their future together.

While Smalls clearly reflects H.I.'s own mind, H.I. drifts off in a constant state of dreaming with or without his alter ego. Throughout, H.I. continually reveals his fantasies to the audience. In prison at the film's start, he lays in bed, arms folded behind his head as if entering another world. He dreams of Ed, realizing his imprisonment has separated them. But he rests assured, knowing brighter days lay ahead: "A future that was only eight to fourteen months away." Could the entire movie be a result of a lonely convict's dream? Do the Coens effectively create a dream within a dream scenario? Nearly everything H.I. experiences outside prison walls could be a dream, equated from his fears, his time watching prison TV, his false expectations, and his familiarity with movies (*Mad Max*, Westerns, and family films). Even Nathan Arizona could be from his imagination as he appears in his television ads. (It is revealed later that Arizona isn't an Arizona, but a Huffhines, which could relate to H.I.'s distrust of the "man".) Gale and Evelle represent the Western when they rob the bank, suddenly transforming from greasers into outlaws and robbing a small town bank in tan full-length road-worn dusters. Ed represents the ideal wife for his ideal family that he could have seen through countless family films. Lastly, Smalls represents the destruction of H.I.'s possible stint at a so-called normal lifestyle. Smalls embodies not just the evil nature of man, but the stereotypical biker villain.

Regardless, one aspect that does not change throughout the film is H.I. himself. Other characters behave beyond normalcy as the movie progresses, yet H.I. remains the same in every situation, right down to his fear of matrimony. His desire for Ed comes from her being the only woman he sees before entering the prison system. His mind is left with little option other than to dream of her. No matter the situation, no matter the chaos, H.I. stays the same bumbling, goofy character, unsure where he fits in his world.

Following the return of Nathan Junior to the Arizonas, H.I. has one final vision of happiness, of a perfect life with Ed as they grow old watching Nathan Junior grow from afar. In the dream, the years pass by and all their problems have eroded, leaving them living happily ever after with a houseful of McDunnough grandchildren: "This whole dream, was it wishful thinking? Was I just fleein' reality, like I know I'm liable to do? But me'n Ed, we can be good too. And it seemed real. It seemed like us." A real vision or not, it amplifies H.I.'s inclination to dream of alternate realities. If capable to envision a positive yet unachievable future with a kidnapped child, then there is little to prevent his wandering mind to conceive of a future with his booking police officer and a stolen child.

ED McDUNNOUGH:
"THIS IS A DECENT FAMILY NOW"

In terms of character, H.I. might yearn to be the man of the house, but it's clear with Ed's first appearance of snapping mug shots who would dominate the home. She's the stereotypical Southern woman: stern, forceful, supportive, and demanding when it comes to what she wants. When Ed speaks, H.I. never argues. He knows there's no use. At one point, Gale and Evelle attempt to lure H.I. out drinking instead of spending quality time with the family, but it only takes a glance from Ed to make H.I.'s decision. However, while H.I. remains unchanged from the beginning to the end of the film, Ed rides a rollercoaster of emotion. At the beginning of the story, she seems utterly unhappy snapping pictures of cons, and, after H.I. and Ed marry, Ed unravels with the knowledge that she is barren. Her hope for motherhood is destroyed.

The news story on the Arizona quintuplets changes everything as Ed and H.I. decide, "it was unfair that some should have so many while others should have so few." H.I. admits that the plan to kidnap the child was Ed's, thus she crossed the line into the criminal world, forcing her reformed husband back into the life. During the montage, H.I. admits his criminal past to an adoption agency and hopes Ed's police status would even them out as a couple, making them eligible for adoption. But as H.I. leaves crime behind, their roles reverse with Ed becoming the outlaw and H.I. resisting her plan of illegal activity. Until this moment, H.I. had seemingly never committed a crime more significant than basic store holdups. Kidnapping an infant places him in a different file, under a new category. Nonetheless, Ed crosses the abstract moral line between good and bad, police and criminal. That moral line had become blurred because of her natural motherly state. If nature would not allow Ed to create her own child, then in her mind, nature had forced her to take charge of the situation. Regardless of consequence, regardless of the harm the crime will cause others, Ed's transformation to criminal comes about without H.I.'s influence. She does not need someone like Smalls to balance her out. Instead, Mother Nature, the most powerful force available, drives her to surpass H.I.'s illegal ambitions.

Ed never second-guesses her idea, and when H.I. first attempts to steal a child and comes back empty handed, she won't have it and forces him, despite his moral objections, to return for a child. She justifies her need with the belief that "they got more'n they can handle!" She has allowed her desire for motherhood to block all normal sensibilities. Once H.I. delivers the child, Ed erupts in unbridled enthusiasm, her need for motherhood fulfilled. She's beyond herself, proclaiming immediate love. H.I.'s reaction, though slight, seems fearful, unsure of what had happened to his wife. H.I. also steals the "instructions" for the child, Dr. Spock's book. Neither of them knows about children and in H.I.'s mind, the easiest way to transition into family comes via instructions. On the other hand, Ed simply has the desire, the natural need to have a child.

With the addition of Junior to the McDunnough family, Ed has achieved her ultimate goal in creating a family. In her view, having a complete family equates to suddenly appearing as a respectable member of society and completing the American Dream. Even H.I. experiences the moment of completeness. When they first bring the baby home, H.I. immediately desires to capture the moment in a picture like any normal family would. As Ed states, "Everything decent'n normal from here on out." However, despite their desire to appear as a functional family, hints appear at its dissolution. H.I. notices a little twinkle in Junior's eye and proudly proclaims, "He's a little outlaw!" Ed dismisses it, but Gale and Evelle restate the comment later, adding to Ed's own paranoid guilt. This moment not only sparks the recollection of the crime committed, but also the fear that Junior could follow his adopted father into a life of crime. The fact that Evelle later backs up H.I.'s earlier observation by repeating the outlaw claim pushes Ed to suddenly revert to her law enforcement past, banning the Snoats from their home: "This is a decent family now." The addition of the stolen child creates, in Ed's mind, a legitimate family structure that negates all past crimes. At no point does Ed ever question H.I.'s past or attempt to uncover what made him a criminal. Once they married, she swept away all past aggressions as H.I. went into the workforce. Of course, the notion of H.I. and Ed suddenly becoming decent did not start until the final crime occurred, an unavoidable evil to create her perfect family.

That necessary evil comes full circle with the showdown between Smalls the bounty hunter and the reformed McDunnoughs. With their child in Smalls's oil-soaked hands, only Ed does not waver. H.I. attempts one-on-one combat using less than gentlemanly tactics, but Ed confronts Smalls directly. She fearlessly demands the release of the child. Along with Nathan Arizona, Ed sees through Smalls's charade and never flinches. Her pseudo-motherly instincts take over for Junior as she marches toward the biker without fear of an attack. Ed cares nothing about the economic hardships that created the situation. She only cares for her own genetic hardships. Only desires the completion of her perfect family.

THE BROTHERS GALE AND EVELLE: "WELL NOW, H.I., LOOKS LIKE YOU BEEN UP TO THE DEVIL'S BIDNIS"

A clear line exists between criminals within *Raising Arizona*. As a low-level crook, H.I. never uses live ammunition (as the film points out on various occasions) in order to ensure lighter sentences if ever caught. His illegal actions are a result of tough monetary times, not malice. On the opposite end, sit the Snoats brothers, Gale and Evelle, two career criminals with no intent to reform. They possess little ethics and have little redeeming value; however, the brothers possess a lovely, dimwitted quality that raises them above non-personality criminals like Leonard Smalls. The brothers are men of conviction, preaching ethics in spite of rejecting normal societal rules. Gale and Evelle represent not only H.I.'s past life, but constant temptation. They are a reminder of the lure of crime and the easy payday. The brothers enter into H.I.'s life early in the film, and they are his first representation of family after H.I. first contemplates the future after the counseling session. Gale and Evelle ponder the doctor's question about family life: "But sometimes your career has to come before family." Evelle adds, "Work is what's kept us happy." While comedic, their comments demonstrate H.I.'s true loneliness. Though Gale and Evelle don't have children or wives, they have each other as a family unit. H.I. must fend for himself.

Regardless, Gale and Evelle remain out of the picture until they resurface in the outside world on a dark, stormy night. The brothers emerge from the muddy ground with Gale screaming and pulling his brother out by his leg, resembling their rebirth into the world. With lightning striking and the boom of thunder, it appears they escaped hell, both literally and figuratively. As Gale bellows into the night, they seem to have escaped only to lure H.I. back to crime. H.I.'s streak of goodness ends the moment the brothers arrive at the McDunnough doorstep, as they create the classic devil versus angel scenario. Everything in his life changes with their constant temptations when they arrive and stay at their home. After they initially meet Ed, Gale immediately challenges H.I.'s manhood after Ed doesn't like the notion of escaped convicts living with them and tells them so. Gale belittles him with the ultimate relationship insult: "Gotcha on an awful short leash, don't she, H.I.?" With a near capture and near breakup of his marriage, H.I. still can't forcibly boot the brothers from his home, but Gale uses the opportunity for further temptation, informing H.I. that he has not been true to his nature. The enticement of a possible bank heist isn't enough for Gale as he also questions the stability of H.I.'s marriage, pulling H.I. back to his past, when freedom and spontaneity ruled. H.I. admits to the brothers that things have been rough with the sudden loss of his job. Evelle, true to form, again lures in his catch by telling H.I. he's still young and healthy. He asks, "What would you want with a job?" Together, the Snoats act as H.I.'s prison conscience—the mindset of the outlaw, of Smalls, and of the life H.I. had left behind. H.I. might put on dress slacks and white shoes, but he cannot defy his nature as long as he allows the past to revisit his home. They become the counterbalance to the decent life H.I. had supposedly started with Ed. They exist to question his decisions and help to underscore the existence of Smalls as "The Fury That Would Be." Without the Snoats, H.I.'s battle with a legal lifestyle would lack substance. However, with them, H.I.'s struggle for decency only becomes amplified and that much more realistic.

* * *

Few filmmakers truly attempt to reinvent themselves with each new project, and even fewer strive to chart new ground or seem willing to take risks with both story and character. The few genuine artists in Hollywood who express an individualistic voice usually appear content with rehashing established material. Quentin Tarantino, despite all his praise, never strays from his hip criminals, hipper dialogue, pop culture references, and overly blood-soaked films. Kevin Smith has attempted to venture outside his comfort area of fast, non-stop dialogue with dreadful results (see *Jersey Girl*). Woody Allen usually inserts his nerdy persona no matter the genre. Even John Carpenter, known for horror, remakes *Rio Bravo* repeatedly. The Coens might utilize familiar faces and recycle plots with constant, reoccurring themes, but each movie functions drastically differently from the next. A careful review of the Coens catalog demonstrates that variety. And *Raising Arizona* seems equated as the genesis. Released in March of 1987, the independent film grossed an impressive $22 million during its box office run.[7] It didn't place the Coens within the mainstream, but it pushed them to the edge of the cinema sandbox. *Raising Arizona*'s success can be linked to its ability to create eccentric characters and ludicrous events while still developing characters. This combination of realistic and comedic violence would develop, and the Coens would establish it as a trend from which they would not deviate.

3

The Professional Kill

Miller's Crossing (1990)

"You always take the long way around to get what you want."[1]

CAST: Gabriel Byrne (Tom Reagan), Marcia Gay Harden (Verna Bernbaum), John Turturro (Bernie Bernbaum), Jon Polito (Johnny Caspar), Albert Finney (Liam Leo O'Bannon), J.E. Freeman (The Dane), Lanny Flaherty (Terry), Olek Krupa (Tad), and Steve Buscemi (Mink).

Miller's Crossing. Directed by Joel Coen. Beverly Hills, CA: 20th Century Fox Entertainment, 1990.

It's rare that a movie's main point be delivered within the opening frame before the introduction of a single character. And in the case of the third Coen film, the point of *Miller's Crossing* is presented by a voice-over during the film's fade in; it reveals whiskey being poured into a glass, and the voice explaining a problem: "I'm talkin' about friendship. I'm talkin' about character. I'm talkin' about—hell, Leo, I ain't embarrassed to use the word—I'm talkin' about ethics." The voice is Italian crime boss, Johnny Caspar, and his ideas on how to analyze proper business conduct summarize the plight of all characters in the film. As the story unfolds, each character must decide what attributes he or she keeps or discards. These ideals—friendship, character, ethics, loyalty, and power—define those who inhabit the world of *Miller's Crossing.* And, in a crime film that's ripe with double-crosses, violence, and betrayal, maintaining ethical qualities creates characters seldom seen in any genre.

Miller's Crossing arrived in theaters during the year of the gangster, muscling against *Goodfellas, The Godfather Part III, State of Grace, King of New York,* and even Steve Martin's *My Blue Heaven.* Of those six organized crime films, only *Goodfellas* garnered mainstream appeal as it not only scored two Oscars, but it pulled in over $46 million.[2] Compared to those higher profile pictures, *Miller's Crossing* was lost in the shuffle with mixed reviews and a box office gross of just over $5 million.[3] All the movies except *Miller's Crossing* had extensive star power. Also, all the characters employed the standard criminal rise and fall of the mobster tale with thugs, bosses, floozies, guns, blood, money, and rats.

So where's the difference? The difference comes from the Coens' respect for their audience.[4] That reverence for viewers separates *Miller's Crossing*. The others, of course, respect their viewers, but don't necessarily offer the same narrative challenge. *Goodfellas,* arguably the best gangster film aside from 1972's *The Godfather,* uses standard crime narration to fill in the audience on details they could possibly fail to understand. The effective *State of Grace* imitates the basic gang epic formula as does *King of New York,* in which "a white man leads a rainbow coalition of pushers."[5] And there's not enough room to dedicate to the flaws within the final *Godfather.* Each film remains relatively obvious, allowing the crime and violence to enhance the story. All the films effectively bring audiences into the underworld lifestyle, yet *Miller's Crossing* takes a different approach. With an intricate that plot never plays straight, and characters rarely mean what they say. Sometimes the characters act without explanation, which closely follows Coen inspiration, novelist Dashiell Hammett, whose use of "crime, clues, motive analysis, suspense, solutions are secondary to a more traditional novelistic emphasis on character."[6] The Coens remove the usual stylistic narration as the movie embraces 1930s slang and speech patterns with such a rapid-fire style that characters nearly stumble over one another. It's a salute to movies like *Little Caesar, Scarface,* and *The Big Sleep,* to an era clichéd by the repetitive slew of films that followed that defined the gangster genre. The Coens, in adapting many of those classical attributes, avoid mainstream access with this approach, rewarding those willing to journey into literate, organized crime. It's not for easy digestion.

The dense plot weaves around Tom Reagan, who might just be the best criminal advisor in town. But he has problems. He's a drunk, has ever-increasing gambling debts, and carries on an affair with the boss's girlfriend, Verna Bernbaum. Despite the affair, he's a man of principle and needs control no matter the situation. He works for Liam Leo O'Bannon, the most powerful man in an unnamed Prohibition era town. They have trouble though, as Bernie Bernbaum—a man who pays for protection—has stiffed local Italian boss, Johnny Caspar, on profits for a fixed fight. Now Caspar wants Bernie dead. He asks Leo permission, which he refuses, leading to a war that leaves Caspar in control of the city. Tom, despite carrying on with Verna, sees her as a grifter who's using Leo to protect her brother Bernie. Things quickly erode when Tom informs Leo about the affair, and Leo boots him from the gang. Tom supposedly switches allegiances to Caspar, but he must kill Bernie for inclusion into Caspar's group. He tries to kill him, but allows a distraught Bernie to live. Caspar's man, the Dane, suspects a double-cross. From there, the story becomes vine-like, twisting and curving to no end as everyone attempts to gain power, look for the angle, and examine ethics. Meanwhile, Tom plays everyone. In the end, they all attempt to keep their hats, the very semblance of their being.

If the story sounds somewhat familiar, it is. Taken mainly from two Hammett novels, *The Glass Key* and *Red Harvest*, the Coens effectively fuse the two plots. They take the latter's tale of two warring gangs used in numerous films such as *Yojimbo*, *Fistful of Dollars*, *Last Man Standing*, and *The Road Warrior*, and they steal *The Glass Key*'s main character, Ned Beaumont, and his boss, Paul Madvig.[7] They give Beaumont's attributes of gambling addiction, smart tongue, and attraction to women to Tom, while staying true to the notion of recreating familiar plots in unfamiliar ways. Hammett's world was one of "urban chaos, devoid of spiritual and moral values, pervaded by viciousness and random savagely."[8] It concerned itself with the double-cross as characters speak out of both sides of their mouths with a smile and a handshake. Even the Continental Op, *Red Harvest*'s seeding sleuth, admits, "I looked most honest when I was lying."[9] It's a line Tom could have uttered at any point. *Miller's Crossing* focuses on character as the movie only allows flashes of city corruption, not an in-depth examination of it. Instead, *Miller's Crossing* examines the attributes of power, loyalty, ethics, character, and friendship.

Much like *Red Harvest*, *Miller's Crossing* takes place in a fictional city corrupt with violence and gangsters. The Coens don't even bother to name their city, which allows for some leeway in expectations. New York and Chicago carry weight, but the freedom of a fictional setting like *Red Harvest*'s Personville allows for its own continuity against well-established locales. Likewise, most crime films take place in the concrete jungle of a city using rooms, alleys, and buildings to underscore the claustrophobic environment of criminal behavior. Despite setting *Miller's Crossing* in the claustrophobic city, it uses massive, sparse rooms and sets, revoking the constriction of the asphalt jungle. The rooms become linked to specific personalities and they reflect character. Tom's apartment is spacious, perfectly decorated, and surprisingly orderly like his business life. Leo's office comes across as "a stately and manly suite appropriate to his position."[10] It echoes that of a man in charge. His opposition, Caspar, works in a tight, blue-collar office, reflecting more of a lowly P.I. atmosphere than that of an Italian mob boss. Each surrounding helps to define and dictate character.

The characters within *Miller's Crossing* differ from nearly every other Coen brothers' film as they seem more like caricatures of Hammett, Raymond Chandler, and various other noir entities than wholly original ideas like most other Coen creations. Tom is the classic dark, moody, silent lead. Verna encompasses the attributes of the common noir woman. Leo and Caspar come from a collage of gangsters, both real and fictional. No character is unfamiliar to filmgoers, yet the Coens squeeze in their own characteristics without taking the audience out of the period piece. They remold them into rounded Coen creations. Tom feels like a carbon copy of various stock criminals, but he ventures outside those stereotypical boundaries; he's deeper than the average gangster, contemplating and reflecting before pulling a trigger. Likewise, Bernie emerges as complex. He performs his role as the catalyst that sets the events into motion, the fall guy, but still rises above the stereotype. He's not exactly likeable, but he's understandable as a man trying to survive by doing what he can to work an angle. Like Tom, neither man works as a gunman and, like Verna and Caspar, they all look for an angle and play it regardless of the ramifications. *Miller's Crossing* concerns itself with ways of obtaining, working, and manipulating an angle in order to not only maintain power, but maintain a sense of loyalty, friendship, character, and ethics.

With all the power plays and the endless manipulation, the film uses a clothing accessory to express character and indicate strength: hats. Each character sports a hat at some point, and a variety of styles appear as prohibition era gangsters embraced the look as an extension of their personality. The Coens create a literary motif with the hats even if they won't admit to such: "Everybody asks us questions about the hat, and there isn't any answer really. It's not a symbol, it doesn't have any particular meaning,"[11] Joel said. Regardless of what they claim, the opening credits begin with a hat blown by the wind, floating through the middle of the woods. The Coens state, "It's an image that came to us, that we liked, and it just implanted itself. It's a kind of practical guiding thread, but there's no need to look for deep meanings."[12] Avoiding an intentional fallacy, the hat carries more weight. It can dance through the air if caught by a strong wind, but its attachment to characters suggests that it is significant. For Tom and Bernie, their hats link them together and represent their dignity, self-respect, and ethics—everything that defines them in a time before the system of gentlemanly behavior vanished, before their system became corrupt. Even in murder, they did so with a certain element of respect. The men dressed like pros and acted like it. *Miller's Crossing* maintains the professionalism as its men with hats hold power and strength. At one point, one of Leo's hooligans, Terry, socks Tom in the gut, dropping him to his knees. As Tom stands, Terry picks up Tom's hat off the ground and gives it back to him. A clear indication of character and ethics. Losing the hat, however, implies death for the character, or at least loss of self-worth. After Leo and Tom's disagreement over the initial meeting with Caspar, Leo claims he doesn't like to think. Tom responds, "Well, think about whether you should start." The line alone is self-explanatory, but as Tom says the line, he puts on his fedora. Without it, Tom—and the rest of the characters—lose everything.

In comparison to the other films released that year, the violence in *Miller's Crossing* isn't as excessive, although it contains the Coens' usual flair for two-sided violence. One side has the comedic, yet painful thrashings of Tom as nearly every character punches and kicks him. Like the classic noir detective,

Tom receives beating after beating, but never complains or stammers. He takes a punch for one reason: He's a professional and knows it's all for business. At one point, one of Caspar's men prepares to attack Tom. Tom signals for the man to wait so he can remove his jacket. In self-defense, Tom strikes the man with a chair, and the man acts shocked by the unexpected action. The man runs away like a frightened child to inform others. On the other side, the gang violence is graphic and unsettling. The unnamed city had been rather peaceful with Leo in charge, but the moment Leo denies Caspar the hit on Bernie, the bloodshed begins. Initially, the violence is implied until the discovery of Leo's thug, Rugs Daniel, by a boy and his dog in an alley. From there, it escalates as Leo sends in the police to hammer Caspar's men, and Caspar quickly responds with a hit on Leo. As a result, police and thugs have shootouts in the street.

In one of the more bizarre scenes, Leo enjoys a cigar as "Danny Boy" plays softly in the background. The smell of smoke alarms him, and he glances at the pistol on his nightstand. He snubs out his cigar just as two men burst into the room, spraying Tommy guns. The old man dives beneath his bed, shooting one of the assassins. He grabs the dead man's gun, leaps out of the window as flames erupt, and riddles the other assassin from outside. The assailants' getaway car speeds off as O'Bannon, dressed in his satin robe and slippers, rattles the Tommy gun once more. The car veers off into a tree, catches fire, and then he places his cigar back in his mouth. The body count rises with this sequence, and violence breaks out with frequency. In contrast, the Dane exhibits why others fear him with his attack on Verna. He not only threatens her, but shoots two of Leo's men without hesitation. With Dane's promise not to kill him, one of the men lives long enough to reveal information about Leo. When Dane shoots him, it reveals everything viewers need to know about his ethics and character. Another scene (featuring Coen collaborator Sam Raimi) illustrates the chaos and savagery of the era as a mass of police open fire on a gang hideout. When the shooting halts and a gangster stumbles out waving a white flag, Raimi's two-pistoled policeman guns the man down before anyone utters a word. His fellow officers react to the slaying by sharing a chuckle at watching the dead mobster twitch on the ground. By the end of the third act, blood flows freely with the brutal deaths of the Dane by Caspar, Caspar by Bernie, and Bernie by Tom. Each case of violence becomes increasingly unprofessional as the paranoia and the double-crosses mount. The notion of loyalty and ethics evaporate when characters start looking out for themselves instead of the organization.

TOM REAGAN:
"YOU DO THINGS FOR A REASON"

Tom Reagan, much like the violence in the film, comes divided in two. There's business Tom: calm under fire and always doing what's best for the company. Then there's social Tom: drunk, addicted to gambling, and unable to control his desires. Regardless, Tom is the man Caspar defines at the start of the movie; he is a man of friendship, character, and ethics, as he goes beyond what Leo requires of him. No matter what transpires, Tom remains loyal to Leo. Everyone treats Tom with respect and dignity except the Dane, who lacks those very qualities. Outside the business world, Tom cannot function. If alienated from a structured environment like the one Leo and Caspar offer, he would not survive because he doesn't display the yearning for power that the others do. At the same time, since Tom exists without this trait it enhances his ability to conduct good, effective business. A key example occurs during the first scene in the film when Leo decides to deny Caspar's request for killing Bernie because of Leo's lust for Verna. Tom tells Leo to think about what protecting Bernie will get them. And by saving him, how will offending Caspar hurt them. Tom understands ego will not win a war no matter how strong loyalties remain. He has no desire to make himself appear stronger in someone else's eyes. He only cares for the bottom line.

In spite of Tom's strong ethics, he possesses few redeeming qualities and he's not a man of action. He is effectively the anti-hero of the hardboiled stories with his drunkenness, constant beatings, and insistent gambling, but he does not fall into a blue-collar category. Tom doesn't get dirty, avoiding actual work at all costs. He is like a boardroom executive a step removed from all employees, unable to operate any equipment, but able to fire anyone and judge what's best for the corporation. Caspar effectively describes Tom's position: "You're the man behind the man who whispers in the man's ear." He plays behind the scenes; he's never forced to demonstrate muscle, and he allows his principles to talk as everything equals business. Whether it's meeting with Bernie or Caspar, he adds little beyond what's relevant to the business discussion (as both Caspar and Bernie quickly learn). They attempt small talk, but realize the futility: "I get it," Bernie says, "Get to the point." Regardless, Tom always remains a man of honor and dignity, accomplishing feats on his own terms, no matter the consequences.

Early in *Miller's Crossing*, Leo and Tom discuss Tom's illicit gambling habit and ever-increasing debt. It's not something most men in his position would worry about as a powerful gangster's right hand man, but for Tom, he cannot permit someone else to pay for his vises, stating that he pays his own debt. His own pride and ego prevent him from allowing someone else to undig his own grave. Tom's gambling worsens throughout the film, adding to his continuous debt, but he expresses no fear of the potential violence that could come his way. While he pleads with Leo to take his advice in the prevention of war, he accepts no advice from anyone else as nearly every character attempts to wean him from gambling. Unable to stop, he relies on the luck of cards, chancing a win. Leo, Bernie, and Caspar all make efforts to win his favor by erasing his debt, but Tom realizes that creates an owed favor. It means he cannot handle his own affairs, which is something he cannot afford. Even when beaten outside his home by bookie thugs, the bookies show remorse in the lashing, as Tom understands and explains no hard feelings exist. Their business utilizes violence and he understands that.

Business keeps Tom motivated and focused, and despite his lax attitude, he's much like H.I. from *Raising Arizona,* torn by his dual nature. With little self-control outside that structured world, he is unorganized, dangerous, and without thought. This duality is shown through Verna, who aside from gambling, acts as the only element of Tom's personal life. Her sexual pull, her danger is more than he can handle. He knows he's breaking Leo's trust by sleeping with her, but to him, Verna's use of Leo to protect her brother means Tom could view their affair as a way to monitor her activities and plans. Whatever distance he keeps isn't enough as Verna acts as the only person who verges on explaining and examining Tom's actions. She probes him with questions, attempting to understand his reasoning. Near the conclusion when Verna confronts him at gunpoint and demands how he could give up her brother, Tom explains that offering Bernie meant squaring things for Leo. A confused Verna had recalled Tom stating he didn't care about Leo, leaving Tom to respond, "I said we were through. It's not the same thing." His actions and thought processes baffle not only the characters of *Miller's Crossing,* but the audience as well. He presents himself as the man with the plan even as he unravels with a drink, a card, or a woman in his hand. If it's a decision that does not affect anyone else, Tom proceeds without any thought of personal harm. He simply acts and deals with the consequences. But if affecting his loyalties or business, nothing he does comes without careful analysis.

This dual nature explains his aptitude for self-analyzing: "Tom's ability to question himself perhaps more than anything else distinguishes his character. The most starkly rational human being is the only one capable of seeing that his actions often defy reasonable explanation."[13] One could suggest that Tom, in a reflective state, outlines the confusing plot on which the film embarks. This is a possible conclusion, but Tom appears deeper than that. He's a man who plays with luck, knowing how to play the right card at the right moment, just not for monetary gain. He dually considers not only a course of action, but the results of those actions. Part of Tom's character comes from his dry, witty answers that he supplies to any situation. But he doesn't always have such quick retorts. When Verna corners him for an answer to the mess he created, Tom cannot supply a proper response. He is only able to repeat the question and stare off into the night: "What did I want?" At the end of the film, he delivers a rhetorical question to Leo, asking him if he always understands why he does what he does. Whether Tom admits it or not, he possesses the fortitude to contemplate future actions—a luxury few other characters have. In the scene after he first sleeps with Verna, Tom focuses on his hat on a dresser. He smokes in bed, studying it. Nothing is said, no dramatics happen, but Tom cannot stop glaring at the image of his respect, his ethics, his character. His hat embodies and reflects every action he commits.

Like all characters in Coen films (especially H.I. in *Raising Arizona*), Tom experiences dreams with tremendous impact. Throughout, Tom has nightmares that involve the loss of his hat. The Coens slip the actual dream of his fedora tumbling through the woods during the opening credits, thus not overtly highlighting its importance as opening credits typically are overlooked. However, clues immediately appear following the credits as Tad the bartender wakes Tom after a drunken gambling binge during which he gambled away not only his money, but his hat as well. Upon waking, his first question in regards to an obvious rough night of gambling is, "Where's my hat?" Despite an evening of excessive gambling and drinking, he never concerns himself with the amount lost. He is only concerned about the loss of his hat. Tom apparently experiences the dream several times; he wakes up next to Verna one night and mumbles about it. She attempts to analyze it and foretell that he, like all people, would chase the hat and never be able to catch it. Tom, as usual, remains stoic and distant, able to maintain his composure no matter the situation. The notion of following a hat suggests normal human behavior. He explains, "Only a fool chases his hat."

Throughout the film, Tom ponders his various actions and ideals, but one moment he never reflects on comes from his lone erosion of professional ideals. The scene occurs during the telling and dramatic marching of Bernie into the woods of Miller's Crossing. If anything, the scene effectively defines the two most important characters and shows their authentic nature. Tom knows killing Bernie will save countless others, but Bernie, falling to his knees and begging without self-respect, succeeds in changing Tom's mind. In initially giving up Bernie to Caspar, Tom had no idea that his hand would be forced to save himself. In every other situation, Tom remained a step removed from violence. Now, Caspar had forced a gun into his hand. Tom must take Bernie into the woods and kill him to ensure he's now with Caspar. Forced into a violent situation, Tom chose to do what he had done throughout his career—avoid violence and negotiate.

The change in setting as Tom walks through the woods shows him continually glancing up at the treetops and sky, perhaps recalling the previous dream. As he marches Bernie deeper into the woods, it's clear he has never committed a violent act before. He wears his collar high and his hat low, hiding behind them. The more Bernie begs and pleads, the more Tom lowers the angle of his hat, cowering behind the very object that defines him. No discussion occurs with Bernie. He never tells him to shut up until after he grants him life. He listens to Bernie's cries and internally debates the situation. Regardless of the seemingly fleeting nature of Bernie's pleas to spare his life, Bernie succeeds in finding a connection with Tom: "They can't make us different people than we are. We're not muscle, Tom." Tom never reacts and seems prepared to murder Bernie until a final plea: "You can't kill me. I'm praying to you! Look in your heart!" Here, Tom exhibits a moment of weakness, a moment of humanity. He appears genuinely disgusted with himself when he fires a shot into the woods, sparing Bernie's life. Maybe Bernie reached him, maybe Tom did not want to cross Leo's wishes, or maybe Tom had fallen for Verna and her repeated wishes to help spare Bernie's life. Tom, void of emotion, gives no indication for his motivation, but he allows a grateful Bernie to walk. Tom, for the first time, appears unsure of his actions, aimlessly instructing Bernie to blow town and never reappear. Tom seems to not even understand his own reasoning. He only knows that he needs Bernie out of his two lives—business and social—for good.

At no other point does Tom unravel. As long as business is concerned, he manipulates every character he encounters. Besides Leo, Tom uses everyone he deals with. Perhaps to some degree, he hustled Leo for an advantage, but that's unlikely as business loyalties remained with Leo. Even after sleeping with Verna, Tom still has the gall to plead with Leo to see Verna's angle in saving Bernie. Leo won't hear it. When Leo still refuses to break from Verna, Tom falls on gangland sword, ruining his own friendship to stop the war and help maintain business.

At the end of the film, Tom plays everything off as if planned, but he could not have foreseen everything that occurred. Nevertheless, Tom can play off scenarios. He, and no one else, wraps up the loose ends he created. He manipulates Caspar into killing the Dane and reunites with Bernie at the Barton Arms. Tom had thought he had influenced Bernie and Caspar into killing each other, but Bernie killed first, leaving one last loose end. Tom must pin all the murders on Bernie, and even explains that plan to him. Bernie again reaches into the well to save himself and asks Tom to once again look into his heart. In the end, with all the angles played, Tom's without a weakness. Bernie had already exploited it. For whatever humanity the Bernbaums brought out of Tom, they effectively destroyed it, leaving Tom to utter, "What heart," before shooting Bernie in the forehead at the film's end. Tom's lone moment of easing his professional ideals resulted in him insulating himself further from humanity.

BERNIE BERNBAUM:
"YOU STICK BY YOUR FAMILY"

Bernie Bernbaum represents those people working outside the gangster world: the card shark, the bookie, the hustler, the grifter. He's the outcast, a homosexual Jew wading within the established system of Italian and Irish gangs to survive on his own terms with his own ethics. He has no established loyalties–like a freelance gambling and grifting contractor. In his eyes, everything comes down to whether or not it makes business sense. It's the flop of the cards and the read. It's if a profit can be made: "It's my nature. Somebody hands me an angle, I play it." Bernie lumps family and friends together as he uses them all to his advantage, for whatever angle they offer. He cares little for his sister, and the only other person he claims connection to, Mink (the Dane's lover), winds up dead by his hand. He claims friendship with Tom, but it's a ploy, an attempt at controlling him. Bernie believes he's a slick operator, able to play without consequences and with more power than he actually holds. In many regards, Bernie acts as Tom's lesser alter ego. Both men play outside the system, and despite the violent world they live in, they're inexperienced in the physical element of their work and have little interest in that form of criminal activity. Both live for the business angle. However, the two men become separated in terms of their ethics, character, and friendship.

For someone with questionable friendship, character, and ethics, Bernie's first appearance mimics another great noir man's entrance: Harry Lime from *The Third Man*. Lime, much like Bernie, remains the topic of all conversations and arguments even though he doesn't appear until midway through the second act. This leaves the audience with preconceived notions of the character. Much the same as Lime, Bernie acts as the cause for all dilemmas. Caspar and Leo go to war over him. Verna sleeps with men who she believes can protect him. After all the characters explain their alliances with or against Bernie, he finally appears, much like Lime, beneath a cloak of darkness. Bernie surfaces in Tom's apartment, his face obscured by the shadows of the apartment. Waiting to be noticed, he sits in silence opposite Tom while Tom talks business on the phone. Initially, Bernie sells himself as an equal to Tom, yet he confuses the line between business and pleasure. Tom wants what is best for business, but Bernie wants more. He desires power and money. He wants the angle against all others, and lectures Tom over the importance of friends, character, and ethics despite the fact that Bernie possesses none of them. Simultaneously, the comparisons to Lime end there. Lime, despite selling black market goods, remained a man who fought for his life. Bernie, however, falters. He begs, he cries in the face of trouble. Like his sister, he discovers ways past Tom's impermeable shell: "What were you gonna do if you caught me? I'd just squirt a few and then you'd let me go again." It becomes Bernie's reactionary defense in place of acting out. Instead of fighting for his life, he has realized that with an emotional outburst he could sway the very man who could save his life.

While Bernie operates schemes within the underworld, the Coens insert a subtle theme of homosexuality in that world between Bernie, Mink, and the Dane. Bernie's homosexuality, though never openly discussed, becomes a deathly love triangle with Mink and the Dane. Implied hints appear throughout, and it's interesting that a film set during the 1930s would accept outright homosexuality without addressing it or banishing the individuals. The Coens discuss the subject without discussing, allowing privy viewers to understand. As long as the characters keep their personal interests under wraps, maintain business ethics, and remain loyal, the rest look the other way. It seems clear that everyone knows of their relationship as people constantly refer to Mink as the Dane's boy. Tom sees an angle in the love triangle. When trying to sway

Caspar, Tom accuses Dane of turning against him for love. Tom also talks with both Mink and Bernie about their relationship; both remain vague. Mink first explains that people have more than one friend. Bernie later verifies the affair, saying Mink was terrified that the Dane discovered they had slept together. Does all this influence the story? Does it alter the characters beyond what's seen on screen? No, but it adds another layer of context, much like anyone who's read Hemingway's "Hills Like White Elephants," which explores the subject of abortion without ever naming nor addressing the subject. Once a reader understands, the story carries much more meaning and weight. Likewise, with Bernie's sexual orientation, everything becomes that much richer. His character adds another layer of realism, and the homosexual layer only adds to his alienation. For not only is Bernie Jewish, not only a grifter, but a gay man attempting to exist in a world of mobsters.

Of all the characters in *Miller's Crossing*, Bernie chatters more than any other, and what he doesn't express verbally comes via hats. In his first appearance, Bernie sports a black bowler and wears it at a cocky angle as he sits slouched in Tom's chair. Here he's confident, without doubt, that he'll sway Tom and continue to earn and play angles despite Caspar wanting him dead. For other characters, the hat represents an extension of personality, sometimes showing mood and attitude. This is demonstrated through Tom's various placements of his fedora on his head which help express his different moods. Bernie doesn't hold enough power or self-esteem to exhibit such actions. He wears the bowler with style, but he remains unaware of the significant nature of the accessory. While Tom's fedora appears as an extension of himself, Bernie's choice in hats seems like a stylistic choice rather than a part of his being. After Bernie's supposed death and resurrection, Bernie changes both his selection of hats and seats with Tom when he revisits his apartment. Now wearing a newsy hat, Bernie displays more self-assurance and strength than at any point because of his belief in his possession of power. He controls Tom. This switching of seats not only symbolically alters power, but also creates a new, more potent Bernie persona. His new threads and appearance, along with his brimming confidence, allow him to give Tom orders for once: "I guess you didn't see the play you gave me. I mean, what'm I gonna do? If I leave, I got nothing—no money, no friends, nothing. If I stay, I got you." Tom watches and listens, unimpressed as Bernie's true nature emerges. A man unable to resist the position of power when presented to him. He's the small fry finally able to make demands and control someone of Tom's caliber. He desires to instill fear within Tom and mocks Tom's silence by asking the whereabouts of his witty responses. He wants Tom to understand that the new Bernie isn't a joke. After he leaves Tom's apartment, Tom attempts to chase him down in his underwear with a pistol to erase his lone professional mistake. Bernie, however, trips him like a seasoned tough guy to demonstrate his momentary superiority, even going as far as to laugh at Tom's expense, warning him about catching a cold.

Like any insecure man suddenly ripe with power, Bernie's new position quickly fades as a fatal flaw develops from his newfound cockiness, represented by the return of his bowler hat. Tom discovers it at the home of a less than witty boxer named Drop Johnson, who placed a significant bet on a known fixed fight. As Tom wanders around his apartment in search of information, Bernie's hat—the semblance of his arrogance—sits there, sealing Bernie's fate and bringing about the threat of death for a second time. Tom knows Bernie has returned to his old ways making plays, and Tom knows he will resurface soon. This scene represents the only time a character becomes separated from his hat. Tom might have lost his head piece gambling, but reclaiming it became top priority. For Bernie, he's unaware of the significance of his missing hat, and without it, he's without the ethics to understand the importance of his headwear.

Tom granted Bernie a second chance at life, an opportunity to free himself from a world that desired his death. Once again, Bernie's notion of friends, despite not having any, resurfaces. Bernie views friends as a device to achieve desired power, thus leading him to kill his lover, Mink, in order to remain alive. In the end, when Bernie faces death once again, the lack of angles baffles Bernie. To him, with all their enemies dead, he and Tom sit square: "We got nothing on each other! So what's in it for you?! There's no angle!" For Bernie, nothing exists beyond the angle and the play as he's unable to comprehend the notion of ethics and loyalty.

VERNA BERNBAUM: "YOU'RE A SONOFABITCH, TOM"

In the typical hardboiled story, Verna Bernbaum plays the femme fatale, the dangerously independent, strong woman who lures the main character into a seedy trap. She is sexy, manipulative, and shifty, but defining Verna is a tough task as usually the femme fatale controls all parties involved by showing a little leg. She dominates Leo by having him sacrifice peace and by breaking his loyalty with Tom in order to save Bernie. But she cannot control Tom. She beds him and presents the idea of saving Bernie, but Tom has no loyalty to her or Bernie. He views her as a threat to the business, a threat to effective decision making. Therefore, her manipulative nature pales in comparison with Tom's. She exhibits the tough, hardened exterior of the traditional noir women, but remains second class when matched against Tom. Her play to save Bernie doesn't fool him, leaving her bewildered and a lackluster femme fatale.

Tom is a character of unknowing desire, unable to pinpoint exactly what he yearns for. Even though he falls to desire by sleeping with Verna, Tom uses Verna, playing into her hand to rescue her brother. After their first night together, it is clear Verna's spell failed on Tom. That night Leo suddenly appears at Tom's apartment. With Verna waiting in bed, Tom doesn't follow through with his promise to talk about Bernie. When she asks him about it, he's frank and forward, stating that Leo should dump her like the tramp she is. Verna, angry and frustrated, throws a shoe at him. She feels used, sleeping with a man and gaining nothing in return. In the end, she falls for Tom, perhaps because he's the one man she cannot conquer. Regardless, neither can deny the obvious connection between them. Whether Tom admits it or not, he cares for her. He continues to visit her and to sleep with her, and he even initially saves Bernie for her. After all, Verna is the only person who successfully analyzes Tom. She not only examines his dreams, but summarizes his plight: "You always take the long way around to get what you want."

Verna, like *Red Harvest*'s femme fatale, Dinah Brand, is an independent woman ahead of the times, matching wits with powerful men without blinking. Tom explains to Leo that she can take care of herself even better than he can. Where others seem to quiver when the Dane appears, Verna doesn't hesitate to brandish a gun at him without flopping to the ground or caving. She has no qualms with pressing a pistol against Tom's chest. She fears no man and acts independently despite knowing possible repercussions. However, the Coens never give her an avenue to express any true emotions, so every characteristic comes from action. We know of her strong desire for family protection, but beyond that, we learn little of her. She, unlike some of the men, lacks friendship, character, and ethics. Though she wields power, it's fleeting, lasting only as long as she remains with Leo.

With her not serving the traditional role for noir women, Verna hovers in unknown territory as she emerges neither sympathetic nor completely unlikable. She engages in activities to save her family despite the fact that her brother does not share the same respect for family. She loves Bernie and will do what she can to protect him. She doesn't care that others view him as scum, and she acts in her family's best interest. While Verna disallows a negative word spoken about her brother, Bernie slanders her himself by implying that she'll sleep with anyone, and that she even attempted to lure him into the bedroom. He says, "Can you believe that—my own sister! Some crackpot idea about saving me from my friends." When Tom reminds him of Verna's defense of him, Bernie can only say, "Yeah, well, you stick by your family." Nothing is revealed about the Bernbaum family, but Tom effectively summarizes their history to Leo. She, much like her brother, cannot help her manipulative nature as her family members genetically exist as grifters. Their bloodline dictates their actions, and they cannot help themselves.

Typically, love stories end in marriage, allowing the seemingly tragic female to finally discover happiness. The Coens twist that idea, revealing that a marriage will occur, though the proposal comes from Verna to Leo before Bernie's funeral. Leo admits to such, and Tom attempts to congratulate them, but it's strained. Whether or not love existed between Tom and Verna never comes out, but the announcement expresses little joy. Perhaps it is symbolic since the scene plays out during Bernie's funeral, where only Leo,

Verna, and Tom appear. In fact, the scene represents Verna's one last chance at redemption in the eyes of the audience. The Coens retract that opportunity as, once again, Tom dominates with a final jab: "Big turnout." Verna storms off, leaving both the men alone. In turn, *Miller's Crossing* comes full circle. Tom and Leo ethically and loyally are reunited, and Verna secures the stability she had searched for all along. Her proposal to Leo suggests that her manipulative nature remains, and a femme fatale can only exist around men she can control. Tom isn't one of those men.

MILLER'S GANGSTERS: *"ARE YOU GIVING ME THE HIGH HAT?"*

A gangster tale is only as strong as its gangsters. Tom Powers in *The Public Enemy*, Michael Corelone in *The Godfather*, and Tony Soprano from *The Sopranos*, all offer something beyond the standard portrayal of the evil leader behind the massive office. More than ruthless killers, they're complex businessmen who sometimes must kill to pay the rent. In *Miller's Crossing*, perhaps the two most sympathetic and likeable characters are Leo and Caspar; they retain more positive and relatable attributes than the darker, tortured characters that populate their world. Leo and Caspar seem the most ethical, loyal, and honest of all the characters. Their word is their bond. Before the era of rats and turncoats that destroyed the mob, these men depended on ethics to keep the order. As Caspar effectively explains, "It's gettin' so a businessman can't expect no return from a fixed fight. [. . .] That's why ethics is important. It's the grease makes us get along, what separates us from the animals, beasts a burden, beasts a prey. Ethics." No one quickly agrees, but these three elements (and the unspoken elements of power and loyalty) drive the film and become the measure for each character. Leo and Caspar both struggle for power and control of the city, and believe in the same convictions, but they remain opposites. Beyond obvious differences such as being Irish and Italian, the ways they present themselves and live are oddly different.

Leo might not initially agree with Caspar's ideas, but he follows the same line. His character loosely imitates that of *The Glass Key*'s Paul Madvig, the cocky, power hungry, Black Hand. However, after Leo loses his ethics through Verna, after his loyalty and friendship with Tom subsides, his empire crumbles. Despite being older, Leo parties like a young man, sleeps with and falls for dancers, drinks soda with a straw, and remains as agile as any younger man. Leo clearly respects Tom, treating him like a son as he uses him as council. When Tom questions Leo's hold on the city when Caspar attempts to muscle up, Leo replies that he can still battle anyone in this town except for Tom. The Coens demonstrate Leo's status as top dog in two sequences. The first comes during the violence-laden attack on his home against the Tommy gun assassins. It proves, as one of Leo's lackeys later says, "The old man is still an artist with the Thompson." The second comes with his vicious and public destruction of Tom. Leo rejects Tom's advice to leave Verna as he cannot see the angle. Tom begs for his trust and threatens to leave if he doesn't receive it. Leo calls the bluff, leaving Tom no choice but to reveal his affair with Verna. In his club, Leo publicly beats Tom with gang members and club goers watching. Leo rolls up his sleeves to demonstrate that, despite his age, he remains the Irish alpha dog.

Caspar, on the other hand, is the perennial family man, even forcing his employees to give his son a shiny new penny on each occasion. He expresses his love for family and attempts to explain to Tom why family matters: "You're missin' out on a complete life. I know, kids, big deal, but still, I'm tellin' ya." An argument could suggest that Caspar is nothing more than an Italian gangster cliché, but he serves an important purpose by presenting an opposing viewpoint. His lifestyle helps to define the main missing aspect in Tom and Leo's lives: family. The Coens could have used Caspar's family against him, but again, in the world of *Miller's Crossing*, the line between family and business is clearly drawn. Only Verna mixes family and business, which results in ample punishment. For Caspar, knowing and understanding the line means everything. As he repeatedly states, it's all a matter of ethics. He wants everything to be black and white. He wants everything to make sense. Even though he attempts to lure Tom with a backdoor deal in order to solve the Bernie situation, Caspar loathes double-crosses, and he brings the most emotion to any of the characters. He's the one who noticeably feels the pain of the situation as he struggles with decision making. While Leo seems at home as the boss, Caspar immediately begins to feel the stress of being in charge of the city: "Runnin' things. It ain't all gravy." With power, Caspar can barely maintain control. He's easily frustrated and angered the moment he feels someone has given him the "high hat." Before Tom, Caspar had a right-hand man in the Dane, but he lacked the supposed ethical standard that Tom brought to the organization. The Dane, like all the characters of *Miller's Crossing* save Tom, could not separate personal from business, allowing his love for Mink and his hatred of women to cloud his judgment.

As with all men in power, both Caspar and Leo suffer from ego. Leo's ego comes not just from stubbornness, but from his lust for Verna. Leo relies too heavily on Tom to aid with his decisions, and when Tom no longer stands next to him, Leo's ego interferes. Likewise, Caspar's paranoia and belief in his own self-worth become his undoing. He seemed to survive and profit quite well when working beneath Leo, but the moment he steps out to claim power, he, like all characters except Tom, allows his own ego to negate proper decisions. The final scene in the movie demonstrates Leo's reliance on Tom as he tells Tom he'd give anything if Tom would reclaim his post. However, whatever loyalty Tom had maintained toward Leo had expired once he had made Leo's world right once again. Tom, despite all their previous success, rejects Leo's offers to rejoin his clan: "I didn't ask for that, and I don't want it." Both Leo and Caspar's ego had eroded their empires, and for Tom, that lack of proper business became the final straw with Leo. Tom had gone out on a limb to ask Leo to trust him at the beginning of the film and Leo refused. In the end, Tom would rather take his luck with the cards than to defy his friendship, his character and his ethics. The mobster world had simply become too violent for a man with those unique qualities.

* * *

Regardless of the failure at the box office, *Miller's Crossing* continues to find new life as the film ages. Initially, critics condemned the Coen style for interfering in the authentic nature of the film. Roger Ebert wrote, "This doesn't look like a gangster movie, it looks like commercial intended to look like a gangster movie. Everything is too designed. That goes for the plot and the dialogue, too. The dialogue is well-written, but it is indeed written. We admire the prose rather than the message. People make threats, and we think about how elegantly the threats are worded."[14] But with the Coen brothers' literary influence, everything should sound written and prepared. *Miller's Crossing* isn't an authentic world. It's an exaggerated violent land of fiction. The characters rely on character, friendship, and ethics to guide them, standards few people in the underworld possess. The Coens have no interest in creating something to reflect the real world, so why should they start during Prohibition?

4

Life of the Imaginary Mind

Barton Fink (1991)

"I'll show you the life of the mind."[1]

CAST: John Turturro (Barton Fink), John Goodman (Charlie Meadows), Judy Davis (Audrey Taylor), Michael Lerner (Jack Lipnik), John Mahoney (W. P. Mayhew), Tony Shalhoub (Ben Geisler), Jon Polito (Lou Breeze), and Steve Buscemi (Chet).

Barton Fink. Directed by Joel Coen. Beverly Hills, CA: 20th Century Fox Entertainment, 1991.

Barton Fink enters into a massive, once exclusive hotel lobby that now appears in a state of erosion. The chairs are empty. The elevator sits silent. No living souls wander about. No newspapers turn. No cigarette smoke dangles thickly in the air. Barton walks up to the empty front desk, puts down his bags, and rings the bell. It oddly echoes throughout the room. The sound of someone on steps emerges from beneath the floor behind the desk. A pale man holding a brush and a shoe opens a trapdoor. He closes the door and gently touches the bell with his finger to end its call. He welcomes Barton to the Hotel Earle, but the ringing of the bell does more than announce Barton's arrival. It serves as the transition into his "life of the mind" (as Barton's neighbor describes it) and the imaginary violence that erupts from it.

    The Coens lay no obvious clues to this transition, but as *Barton Fink* progresses, there's a fusion of reality and fantasy, and a digression in Barton's writing and mind. Everything that follows, both in and out of the hotel, is questionable because, as Barton's mental strength erodes, viewers must discern whether they've entered into a life of the mind, whether the film's violence is imaginary, whether certain characters exist, and whether Barton has one last great story to tell.

After the highly-stylized, intricate, and reserved *Miller's Crossing*, the Coens remained in their reverted cinematic narrative stance and ventured deeper into the psychological realm with their fourth film, *Barton Fink*. It is a movie of Coen firsts: their first non-criminal lead; their first without cinematographer Barry Sonnenfeld; their first with a singular main character. They avoid a clear genre choice for their fourth movie, borrowing elements from noir, comedy, and horror. And, in the usual Coen style, they remold those elements to create something else. *Barton Fink* integrates the cliché of the struggling writer corrupted by Hollywood with the hazards of seclusion and the dangers of the human mind—all mixed with a little crime. It all creates what *Time* critic Richard Schickel calls, "Gnomic, claustrophobic, hallucinatory, just plain weird, it is the kind of movie critics can soak up thousands of words analyzing and cinephiles can soak up at least three espressos arguing their way through."[2] On an initial viewing, accessible won't be a word often affiliated with *Barton Fink* due to slow pacing and an unsociable, inactive central character such as Barton. He does little; he attends meetings where he barely utters a phrase, he sits in his smoldering hotel room staring at a painting of a bathing beauty on a beach, he obsesses over buzzing mosquitoes and peeling wallpaper while avoiding his typewriter. Yet *Barton Fink* captivates anyone who enters into its violent mind.

The story is set in 1941 on the eve of WWII in New York City where playwright Barton finds success with his tale of simple fishmongers surviving in the modern world. It is a story of the common man. At the nudging of his agent, he soon cashes in and accepts an offer to write in Hollywood despite his own moral problems with doing so. Nevertheless, he moves to Los Angeles and resides at the vacant Hotel Earle, where his mind wanders. He becomes lost in the studio system after meeting Hollywood elite such as the president of Capitol Pictures, Jack Lipnik, and writing legend W.P. Mayhew. Instead of choosing his own project, Barton is assigned to a B wrestling picture when writer's block ensues. His mind loses focus until he meets his neighbor Charlie Meadows. From this point, the Coens venture into Barton's mind where they blur what's real and what's fiction. Still unable to write a word, Barton ends up asking Mayhew's assistant and lover, Audrey, for help. They sleep together and, when Barton awakes, he discovers Audrey dead in his own bed, murdered in a gruesome fashion. Charlie cleans up the mess and leaves soon after, asking Barton to hold onto a box for him. The police meet with Barton and reveal that the true identity of Charlie is a serial killer with a nitch for removing heads. Meanwhile, Barton finishes his script only to have it rejected by the studio system. The police confront him again, accusing him of Audrey's murder. Charlie returns home from a so-called business trip, ignites the building, kills the police, and lectures Barton on his inability to listen. The film ends with Barton on the beach with Charlie's box, and with the bathing beauty painting coming to life.

In Barton's play, *Buried Ruined Choirs*, the main character lives in a dream state, lost in his blue-collar life without direction until he finally activates his life: "I'm awake now, awake for the first time in years. Uncle Dave said it: Daylight is a dream if you've lived with your eyes closed." Like his character, Barton lives blocked off from daylight, insulating him from outside influences and from the average man he supposedly represents. He fears a move to Hollywood where he'd make money and attend parties, but that would "be cutting myself off from the wellspring of that success, from the common man." In the land of imagination and false realities, the Coens keep Barton away from anything related to Hollywood. No backlots, sets, nor actors. However, he quickly finds himself cut off from his muse. The Los Angeles setting reveals the moral facets of character—all characters appear either insane, plastic, or demons in disguise. The New York and L.A. settings enhance Barton's illusion, because both places—Broadway and Hollywood—manufacture fantasy. The entire opening sequence serves as an important symbol for what's to follow. Backstage at his play, Barton acts as the puppet master, watching his creation unfold before him. Every scene that follows revolves around "the fabrication of illusion."³ The moment Barton arrives at the hotel, his state of mind changes with his surroundings. He enters into a trance-like state, inhibited by writer's block, but blocked by something more damning—his disillusionment from the choice he's made. Barton initially resists the move, but, as his agent jokes that their might be a few average people out in Hollywood, Barton, already taking himself seriously, fails to see the humor. In his mind, he has sold out to the Hollywood factory, turning his back on his inspiration. The shift in location does change him, as he, along with his idol W.P. Mayhew, has exchanged his artistic soul in order to make a hefty paycheck for his craft.

While the different locations affect Barton, so does the distinction in social class. Barton writes for the ordinary man, but shares little commonalties because he doesn't engage in average activities. After his play's triumphant opening, a skeptical Barton isn't sure about its success. He sits with three elites—the play's producer and two rich friends—and is unable or unwilling to accept their constant adoration. As they toast to his genius, Barton remains uncomfortable with the notion, unable to socialize and identify with people so far above the class he represents. Just being there goes against his dream of creating living theater for and about the common man. On each occasion in which Barton finds himself among people of wealth, Barton can barely speak, unable to engage even in the most basic conversation. He temporarily abandons his discontent in pursuit of Hollywood money. He envisions a life changed by "making money, going to parties, meeting the big shots." Barton seems to believe that Hollywood could change him, that he'd finally become social and rise above being ordinary while remaining true to the roots of his inspirations.

The Coens, on the other hand, have never deviated from their own roots, and have always made psychological films that allow a character's actions to speak in place of words. Each movie before *Barton Fink* employed the mind to define characters, but *Barton Fink* takes it a step further by creating not just a study, but also the false violence that the psyche can create. In fact, *Barton Fink* focuses solely on the writer's thoughts because dialog throughout constantly refers to the mind and people's thoughts, feelings, and ideas. It's not just Barton and his reactions, but a discussion of the human condition with over sixty mentions of the word "head." Notably, Charlie refers to the word more than any other character, and he even announces his return to the hotel by rolling the head of the elevator man down the hall.[4]

Watching a person lose his sanity isn't a novel idea, but the Coens take a well-worn concept and cut fresh angles from it. The movie's journey into the brain and departure from the standard protagonist and narrative owes just as much to literature as it does to film. In *Barton Fink*, the psychological angle becomes the downfall of a man. This disintegration of an individual is influenced by works such as Stanley Kubrick's *The Shining*, early Roman Polanski features like *Repulsion* and *The Tenant*, along with Franz Kafka's *Metamorphosis* and Robert Louis Stevenson's *Dr. Jekyll and Mr. Hyde*. Like the characters in these works, Barton cannot avoid destiny. Granted, no one can avoid fate, but Barton cannot avoid the pull of the Earle no more than Jack Nicholson's character could escape the Overlook Hotel in *The Shining*. As writers looking for fresh perspectives and a steady paycheck, both characters find a connection the moment they step inside their respective hotels. The Coens also found stylistic inspiration in Kubrick's horror film. Long hallway shots, a ghostly butler who acts as an extension of the hotel, and the hotel's manipulation of the writer's mind are all clear influences. As Barton stands in the shadows in the Earle, the lighting for his entrance suggests fate has found him. He takes his time walking through the lobby, appearing mildly frightened by the hotel's interior as if he had never stepped into one before. The manipulation of the Earle begins the moment he rings the bell.

Wherever the Hotel Earle takes Barton, his mind and the imaginary violence it creates is the scariest place one could visit. In comparison to two of the Coen's three previous films, the violence of *Barton Fink* seems tame. A mere three on-screen deaths occur, and the impact arrives during the final act, leaving three quarters of the movie tension free. Before the deaths occur, no threat of danger appears, and it remains far from Barton's world until his arrival in California. No carnage occurs immediately at the Earle. There are only signs of his deteriorating psyche, but that changes after sleeping with Audrey. The next morning while in bed together when he smacks a mosquito on her back, the sight of flowing blood and her mutilated corpse create an unexpected transition to gore. Staying true to his character, Barton has no moment of heroism or boldness. He shrieks and sits in shock until Charlie offers to help. Barton's reaction is directly opposite to that of Ray in *Blood Simple*. Ray also stumbles upon a grisly scene, but he, unlike Barton, acts to solve the problem no matter the consequence. At least he can be sure he didn't initially kill the guy. For Barton, the death of Audrey becomes something more terrifying than he could imagine.

Whether the murder happened in Barton's head, or someone actually killed her, it remains as ambiguous as the exact moment Barton's disillusion takes hold. But one moment near the end solidifies a true turn into the life of the mind. Before Charlie's return to the hotel, a distraught Barton turns to a source of comfort: the Bible. He turns to the Book of Daniel, which reads: "And the king, Nebuchadnezzar, answered and said to the Chaldeans, I recall not my dream; if ye will not make known unto me my dream, and its interpretation, ye shall be cut in pieces, and your tents shall be made a dunghill." If a clue had ever been written out for audiences and all but highlighted on the screen, this is that moment. His psyche now projects what has seemingly occurred onto the printed page, Barton's only source of safety. As he searches for clarity in more spiritual advice, he flips to the beginning of the book only to see his play now replaces Genesis. Eventually, this leads to a surreal sequence of exaggeration, in which the worst possible, most horrific scenario Barton could imagine unfolds.

The film's final two deaths come by the hand of Charlie. As the two detectives interview Barton in his apartment, they connect the obvious clues that point to him (such as the bloodstained mattress). Suddenly, the officers complain about the heat. Charlie arrives, bringing all of Hell with him. As Charlie screams, "I'll show you the life of the mind," he leaves a trail of flames, creating an inferno. Charlie's demonic nature finally surfaces. He kills one detective and then gives the final detective a peculiar send off: "Heil, Hitler." All of Barton's hatred and anger for the police, society, and himself erupt in the form of Charlie in a Mr. Hyde-like warpath. Nothing can stop him as he marches down the hallway exhibiting full imaginary violence. Whether any of it actually occurred becomes a mute point. The potential expressive nature of Barton's psyche unleashes something more violent and terrifying than reality. The problem is in the viewer's inability to decipher what's actuality and what's imaginary.

BARTON FINK:
"WELL, I'M A WRITER, ACTUALLY"

Barton Fink is a wimp—the classic Coen loser. He's a twitchy, unsure man who allows success to go to his head despite the fact that he consciously attempts to avoid such a thing. As he gains notoriety as a writer, he avoids reading press clippings and views his sudden success as fleeting. He's unsure about his place in the world, unsure of the strength of his skills. However, only moments later, he dives into a speech about his future and the future of theatre wherein the average man dominates story lines and leaves nobility behind. Of course, Barton is a man full of ironies, desiring to represent the working man's voice, yet lacking most of these qualities. At one point, Barton attends a military dance after completing his script. As the service men reject him dancing amongst them, Barton rejects them: "I'm a writer, you monsters! I create. This is my uniform! This is how I serve the common man!"

Barton's not a man's man. He's not social. He doesn't drink to forget reality. In fact, Barton represents the opposite qualities that a main character, a proactive character, should possess. He learns nothing of himself by the end and remains inherently inactive throughout, foreshadowing the character of Ed Crane from the Coen's future film, *The Man Who Wasn't There*. In each situation Barton encounters, he takes a step back, avoiding confrontations and never engaging in an argument.

However, this isn't to say Barton isn't likeable. Awkward, goofy, uneasy, Barton is Woody Allen without the jokes. Instead, the joke usually falls on Barton as his gracelessness and uncomfortable nature result in humor at his expense. The Coens obviously enjoy making Barton the fool, leaving him constantly overmatched, underprepared, and distracted. By taking Hollywood money, his mind loses comfortable subject matter, leaving him a writer without a story from his heart. The president of Capitol Pictures, Jack Lipnik, awards him a contract, but gives him no direction or pointers. They only desire "that Barton Fink feeling." In the ultimate catch-22, Barton must write the way he writes, yet he must eliminate the very element that makes his stories Fink-ish. Hollywood has purchased Barton's mind and expect results. When in New York, Barton could disappear and mingle among ordinary people, but his position with Capitol Pictures negates that.

Barton's story and inspiration are modeled after playwright Clifford Odets, the New Yorker known for *Waiting for Lefty*, a story of the striking working class who also once trekked West. And like Odets, regardless of Hollywood status, Barton's only sense of confidence comes via his writing. Barton often states that he writes from his gut, which might help the audience understand where the writer's block comes from. He's out of his element in a genre wrestling picture, unable to grasp even the fundamentals. He turns to producer Ben Geisler, who offers little advice. Fast-talking and with little time to spare, Geisler resembles the stereotypical producer, appearing just as lost as Barton and unaware of his producer status on Barton's picture. They have lunch and Geisler only adds to Barton's insecurity by telling him to talk to another writer because it is Hollywood after all. They're everywhere. Barton, a mildly celebrated writer, discovers that in Hollywood, he is reduced to nothing more than just another hack taking a paycheck. When he finally attempts to construct a cookie-cutter wrestling story on his typewriter, he smirks when writing in his beloved fishmongers into the script. Clearly, Barton lacks the creative motivation and capability to create something new. His mind cannot move beyond his initial success, and the wrestling picture ends up being more than he can handle. The writer's block, unlike his script, continues to expand. On each occasion when he struggles with thought, his mind searches for distractions, new outlets on which to focus. Whether it's the wallpaper ungluing or the pesky mosquito, everything becomes enhanced as Barton loses his concentration. This is especially true regarding the painting of the woman at the beach. This picture becomes the center of his life, a symbol of the happiness, peace, and love he cannot obtain.

Alone in Hollywood, Barton takes Geisler's advice and seeks the comfort of another writer when he happens to run into his idol W.P. Mayhew (William Faulkner in disguise) in a restroom. Mayhew, though once great, represents the very idea Barton disgusts: the sell-out. However, meeting Mayhew provides Barton with a mentor of sorts, while also providing the film with a love interest in Mayhew's assistant, Audrey. Through Audrey, Barton asserts himself twice in the movie, both times in her defense. He is ready to come to her aid when Mayhew strikes her in a drunken rampage during their first meeting. Barton's desire for a taken woman owes to classic noir, except Barton idolizes the great Mayhew, perhaps more than Audrey. In the end, when Barton convinces Audrey to come to his rescue by helping with his script, Barton has no sexual inclination. Their roles reverse, making Barton the out-of-control, panick-stricken one, and Audrey the cool and collected one, able to solve any problem. Also, the Coens' disdain for love scenes explains Barton's sexual behavior. Audrey takes complete control, leaving Barton resembling a virginal 15-year-old with an older lover. He seems overmatched both mentally and physically, and he lies down on the bed, appearing unsure about what might occur next.

Barton's subconscious apparently did know what was to come next because when he wakes up and smacks the mosquito in the next scene, she's already dead. The mystery begins. Once it is revealed that Charlie removes the heads of his victims, a question emerges: What's in the box that Charlie asks Barton to hold after Charlie disposes of Audrey's body? In the end, after Charlie's demonic origins surface, Barton finally leaves the hotel, but not before Charlie tells Barton that the box isn't his. If the box doesn't contain Charlie's personal property, then what's in the box? The Coens offer no solution to the riddle: "Where would it get you if something that's a little bit ambiguous in the movie is made clear? It doesn't get you anywhere.[5] [. . .] We wanted to remain ambiguous until the end. But what's suggested is that the crime has been committed by Charlie."[6] If it does contain the head of Audrey, perhaps Barton cannot let go of the first woman he's ever loved. Perhaps he cannot let go of Mayhew's muse, making her his own portable muse. By film's end, when Barton sits alone on a beach with the box, the girl from the painting in his room comes alive and joins him on the sand. A second supposed muse. When the painted woman speaks to him, it's safe to assume whatever lies inside the box came from Barton's violent mind. And wherever his head took him, Barton will never come back.

CHARLIE MEADOWS:
"JESUS, PEOPLE CAN BE CRUEL"

Barton repeatedly states that he speaks for the common citizen, giving them his voice while the rest of theatrical world shuns them. However, Barton has no connection to them. The closest he comes to mingling with the Average Joe with Charlie Meadows. As a working stiff who hits the streets as a door-to-door insurance salesman, Charlie's a world-weary, hard working, underappreciated, blue-collar man. Every time he attempts to share life experiences by repeatedly telling Barton that he could do so, Barton never entertains him, cutting him off: "Sure you could! And yet many writers do everything in their power to insulate themselves from the common man." Instead, Barton focuses on his own self-indulgent mission to change theatre, and in the process, blocks his connection to his own subject. Charlie represents that section of society; he charms anyone with his genuine smile and a quick story. But times are tough for a salesman, and he increasingly finds people rude, as they are unwilling to buy "a little peace of mind" in insurance. He sees the world evolving in front of him on the eve of WWII. Nevertheless, something dark lurks within him as it's soon discovered Charlie isn't everything he claims. He's Karl 'Madman' Mundt, a notorious killer. Ethan explains, "We were obviously conscious of that warm, affable image the audience feels comfortable with [Goodman]. We exploited that expectation in order to finally turn it round. Yet, as soon as he presents himself, there's something menacing, disquieting about him."[7] The idea of a quiet killer isn't exactly a new concept, but it remains frightening that the neighbor waving hello to you everyday could be a lurking serial killer.

Regardless of Charlie's murderous ways, in Barton's head, Charlie is the only character capable of expressing himself and willing to accomplish a realistic goal. He aims to ease the pain of others, and he understands their pain: "I feel for 'em. So I try to help them out." He sees nothing wrong with killing the suffering. And, in a way, one could view him as an avenging, working-class demon. After all, he continually uses business metaphors to describe his work: "I know what if feels like, when things get all balled up at the head office. It puts you through hell, Barton. So I help people out. I just wish someone would do as much for me." For Charlie, he cannot escape the hell he created. With *Barton Fink's* imaginary violence, who Charlie actually is and what he does remains a mystery. If he's nothing more than a figment of Barton's mind, did the murders actually happen? If they did, who committed them? If Charlie emerged from Barton's psyche, Barton's frustration and inability to act erupt in much the same way as in *Raising Arizona,* when bounty hunter Leonard Smalls emerges like a devilish entity from H.I. Barton had been so passive for so long that when his mind reached a stressed breaking point, it created an outlet in Charlie, who explodes in anger at the film's end: "I'll show you the life of the mind!" He wishes to share the pain he's endured as Barton's avoidance of his tales blocks the clarity of Charlie's story; we only hear bits and pieces about the "head office," which perhaps reveals who he actually is. Charlie could be a reference to Barton's repressed and delusional mind. But if he does exist, the question becomes whether Charlie's murderous alter ego exists as well, or if he is a product of Barton.

A number of hints at Charlie's devilish qualities appear throughout the movie. The most obvious comes from the heat. Every time Charlie is near, the temperature rises. When Barton arrives at the Earle, he's dressed in an overcoat and makes no mention of the heat. When he's with Mayhew or at the studio, no one else seems affected by the smoldering temperature. Only in the Earle and around Charlie do things swelter to the point of eroding the wallpaper. As Joel explains, "The hotel had to be organically linked to the movie—it had to be the externalization of the character played by John Goodman. Sweat falls from his brow like wallpaper falls from the walls. At the end, when Goodman says he's prisoner of his own mental state, that it's like a hell, the hotel has already taken on that infernal appearance."[8] In addition, though there's evidence of life at the Earle, only Charlie, Chet, and Pete, the elevator operator, seem capable of appearing. Of them all, Charlie seems most comfortable, freely calling his room his home and returning whenever things at the "head office" cool down.

For a man who makes his living relying on the ideas and beliefs of other people, Barton seldom listens. From his agent, to his producer, to W. P. Mayhew, to Audrey, Barton has endless sources of advice and inspiration, but remains too self-obsessed in his work to hear them. Barton only listens to Charlie, the one person willing to explain things in terms Barton comprehends. At the end, when Barton asks why Charlie chose to manipulate him in Audrey's murder, Charlie's response sums up Barton's nature and his inability to listen: "You think you know about pain? You think I made your life hell? Take a look around this dump. You're just a tourist with a typewriter, Barton. I live here." It is at this point that Barton finally chooses his own path. Instead of remaining at the hotel, he collects a few of his belongings and wanders off down the long, burning hallway. He leaves behind the Earle. He leaves behind the painting. He leaves behind Charlie, who sits comfortably at home in hell.

THE HOTEL EARLE: "NEVER HEARD OF IT"

All movies create an environment that enhances the story, but sometimes, the setting evolves beyond background, transforming into a character unto its own. It lives and breathes around individuals with a personality all its own. It sweats. It cries. It creaks. The Hotel Earle transcends a simple residence and becomes a gateway that alters those who enter into it. This is obviously intended as a metaphor for the hell of Hollywood, but that's too simple an argument because Barton never gives Hollywood that chance to spit him out. The hotel manipulates Barton. It's not so much that the building is hell on earth, but it traps people through mental metamorphosis; once residents, their souls, in a sense, become trapped in the halls of the hotel. Each resident becomes just another entity occupying a room who sets his shoes out for a polish. Even the footwear suggests collectiveness between the tenants as they all wear the same styled shoe. Stylistically, the Coens were influenced by numerous sources, notably Kubrick's *The Shining*, but also Chandler and Hammett's descriptions of 1940s hotels that reek. Draped in muted pinks and fading art deco, the walls seem to ooze red and lack any warmth. Even the lobby closely reflects *The Maltese Falcon* and *Key Largo*, which helps *Barton Fink* exude the classical film qualities that clearly inspired it.

Anyone entering the Earle meets the welcoming party of Chet, the caretaker at the hotel. He emerges from a trapdoor where he cleans unseen guest shoes. Pale as a ghost, he never leaves nor suggests doing so. He claims he's the night clerk, but Barton arrives during the glow of daylight. Filled with uncomfortable enthusiasm for his job, Chet's available 24 hours a day for any need. Seemingly, he is the only living entity, and he acts as an extension of the hotel. In some regards, the moment Barton enters the Earle could be the beginning of the traditional Coen dream sequence. As Joel debates, "Some people have suggested the whole second part of the movie is only a nightmare. It certainly wasn't our intention to make it a literal bad dream, but it's true that we wanted an irrational logic. We wanted the climate of the movie to reflect the psychological state of its hero."9

The line between fiction and film-realism blur, leaving the film open for interpretation. At the same time, the hotel's elevator man, Pete, represents the lasting nature of the hotel. He appears like a living corpse, lost to the Earle, and unable to answer Barton's simple questions:

"You read the Bible, Pete?"

"Holy Bible?"

"Yeah."

"I think so. . . .Anyway, I've heard about it."

Pete is the first to give a true indication of where Barton is staying. His elevator drips with red overtones and has a small fan in the corner that looks like it is more for circulation than cooling. During Barton's ride upstairs, 6 6 6 is uttered—a rather obvious clue that, nonetheless, subtly implies that the Earle's existence is much more than just a hotel.

HOLLYWOOD:
"WRITERS COME AND GO; WE ALWAYS NEED INDIANS"

For Barton, the Hollywood experience comes with too much pressure, which helps to propel his deteriorating mental state. Barton appears confused as to how to handle success when the head of Capitol Pictures fawns over him, declaring that the writer is king and he should worship the ground on which Barton walks. It's a combination of flattery and over-exuberance that, for the Hollywood characters Barton encounters, create a combination of tribute to and mockery of the movie-making business. If Barton manages to be a passive main character, Hollywood makes up for it primarily in Lipnik, a frightening, absurd, intelligent, and loyal caricature of Hollywood heavyweights like Columbia's Harry Cohn, MGM boss Louis B. Mayer, and, most significantly, Jack Warner, the inspiration for Lipnik's sudden commission to a military Colonel by the film's end.[10] Lipnik has wardrobe whip him up a complete uniform to fill his ego as he instructs Barton to suddenly call him Colonel Lipnik. He's everything wrong and right with the industry, a man who claims to know nothing of the inner-workings of scriptwriting and relies simply on his gut to guarantee success. He believes that showmanship outweighs typical common sense.

All the Hollywood characters lack depth. While they have the usual Coen quirkiness, they lack the fullness that even Coen minor players usually possess. They only display a business side—the insanity of working and surviving in show business. After all, as Barton discovers upon the completion of his script, Lipnik, who yearned for that "Barton Fink feeling," who claimed that the writer is king, tells Barton that now his brain is the property of Capitol Pictures, and they will never produce anything he writes: "Not until you grow up a little. You ain't no writer, Fink—you're a goddamn write-off!" Whatever inspired Barton to create, whatever drove him to write about a world void of violence had been squashed by men of showmanship—men who lacked heart.

Likewise to Barton's descent, Mayhew's journey serves as a forewarning of the allure of the big screen. Much like Faulkner's own venture to Hollywood, Mayhew claims all novelists turn to the screen: "All of us undomesticated writers eventually make our way out here to the Great Salt Lick." As writers who came from outside the standard system, the Coens use both Barton and Mayhew as the model example of the cinema pit. It's "the Coens' sly retrofit of a literary historical legend: the moral and artistic debasement of renowned writers who succumbed to Hollywood's clarion call following the industry conversion to sound."[11] Writers like Odets, Nathaniel West, Faulkner, F. Scott Fitzgerald, and Raymond Chandler all made their trek west in search of steady pay in the land of the minds of imagination. The Coens take liberties with Mayhew. Actor John Mahoney might resemble Faulkner, but there's also a direct correlation between Faulkner's drinking and his hatred for what he was doing with his career. And, of course, Faulkner wrote his own material (Mayhew's lover, Audrey, perfected his). Regardless, it's difficult to deny Hollywood's impact; men of great skill and creativity saw their passion and creative drive erode under the palm trees and steady income. If a writer writes from his gut, if the life of the mind can produce violence in the

form of Charlie Meadows, then Hollywood is no place for a writer, especially one of the caliber of Barton Fink.

* * *

Upon its release, *Barton Fink* received stellar reviews and won an unprecedented three awards at Cannes Film Festival. The Coens demonstrated their careful attention to detail and an ability to move beyond petty criminals. But this newly revealed ability wasn't available to the masses as the film followed the path of *Miller's Crossing* at the box office. Nevertheless, a movie like *Barton Fink* isn't a crowd pleaser and never expected box office gold. It's an art film that demonstrated that the Coens aren't one trick artists. The brothers never revisited the life of the mind in quite the same manner in any of their other releases, but it further emphasizes the point that they remain capable of more than quirky genre homages. They can construct a demented art house film that remains true to the usual Coen attributes of exaggerated hair styles, fat men screaming, powerful men behind desks, and fantastic violence—all while doing something entirely new. But if *Barton Fink* and *Miller's Crossing* struggled to find a wide audience, it was all just a hint of what was to come as their next project became their biggest flop to date.

5

Reinventing the Circle of Suicide

The Hudsucker Proxy (1994)

"I got big ideas."[1]

CAST: Tim Robbins (Norville Barnes), Jennifer Jason Leigh (Amy Archer), Charles Durning (Waring Hudsucker), Bill Cobbs (Moses), John Mahoney (Editor), Jim True-Frost (Buzz), Bruce Campbell (Smitty), and Paul Newman (Sidney J. Mussburger).

The Hudsucker Proxy. Directed by Joel Coen. Burbank, CA: Warner Home Video, 1994.

In a boardroom, executives fill the swivel chairs as a man reads statistics from a chart. At the head of the table sits Waring Hudsucker—the president and founder of Hudsucker Industries—dressed in an expensive suit, listening with a disinterested tranquility. He clears his throat for his followers's attention, takes a final puff of his cigar, and calmly checks his pocket watch as the time nears noon. He steps up from his plush leather chair to the massive, elongated table. He stretches and then sprints for an unexpected 44 floor leap. No panic overtakes him; Hudsucker has time to wipe away something from his eye and even shoo people out of the path of his falling body. The outcome of Hudsucker's jump is never shown, but when the fat lady screams, the president's reign has ended.

The Hudsucker Proxy is more or less the Coen brothers's lightest work to date in all categories, from social commentary, to character depth, to psychology, to violence. It uses the conventions of the screwball comedy over the standard Coen crime thriller. The film focuses on the characters's search for their "big idea" in order to conquer the corporate structure. They believe that the American dream can be achieved with hard work and determination. It also produces a theme of violence through the idea of corporate suicide, which manages to emerge at the boardroom level, where men at the highest level of business view suicide as their only solution for ending the corporate lifestyle. Once you're on top, the fall to the bottom must be at least 44 floors.

For all the Coens' wit and creativity in rehashing old material in a unique manner, *The Hudsucker Proxy* resulted in a creative obstacle as a mainstream film not intended for mainstream audiences. Perhaps it has one too many movie references in what the Coens call an "industry fantasy."[2] *The Hudsucker Proxy* harkens back to the nostalgia of the golden era of cinema when Jimmy Stewart, Frank Capra, and Preston Sturges represented a positive outlook for the future. The Coens melded their sensibilities to such an extent that the movie reminds the viewer more of those older cinematic references than something unique and new. The brothers have always utilized clichéd material as an outline to yield original results. *The Hudsucker Proxy*, however, appears constructed out of used parts, a coagulation of the 1930s and 1950s with soulless characters.[3] The love interest isn't memorable. The villain appears cartoonish. The environment feels false. The story doesn't necessarily hook. Everything appears skewed as every character, every scene, and every set piece is inspired by other films. Nothing, including the invention of the hula-hoop, feels original.

Regardless of its apparent flaws, all the film's elements are used intentionally. The Coens created a movie for movie lovers, a film within a film within a film with deeper references than the average viewer recognizes. That being said, it's not that *The Hudsucker Proxy* doesn't entertain or is without unique characters; it's just a few ingredients short of their usual finished product, lacking the seamless bond of settings and complex characters. Typically, their characters are people who truly exist in their environment. However, everyone within the Hudsucker world appears to live only in the film. No one functions beyond what the audience sees. Everything from the sets, to the actors, to the dialogue, to the emotion implies exaggeration, giving the film a light tone that doesn't bother to contemplate or examine the effects of suicide. Nevertheless, *The Hudsucker Proxy* remains unique within the Coen catalog. It is a film experiment that boasts memorable scenes, memorable but unoriginal characters, and a fantastic false world where big ideas can come true.

The story takes place on the eve of 1958 when naïve Norville Barnes moves to New York to conquer big business with big ideas. Luck smiles on him when he discovers an opening at Hudsucker Industries. The moment he walks into the building, president and founder, Waring Hudsucker, exits the top floor via a window and lands on the sidewalk below. Moments later, Norville is hired as a mailroom clerk, but he isn't just a pawn without ambition. He fancies himself an inventor and shows off his prototype drawing of a circle to anyone who'll look. Without warning, a blue letter (top communication between the executives) arrives, and Norville is assigned to deliver it to Sid Mussburger, the man now in charge of the company. Norville can't pass up the opportunity to reveal his prize invention and somehow lands the position as president of the company. *The Hudsucker Proxy* becomes the sweeping saga of the rise and fall of a proxy (Norville) brought in to ruin the Hudsucker Industry stock so the chairmen can purchase the stock at bottom prices. Much to their dismay Norville's invention becomes something fantastic in the hula-hoop, and ends up saving the company. While Mussburger sets out to ruin him, reporter Amy Archer figures Norville for a fake. She goes undercover as his secretary to prove it. They fall for each other, but not before Norville falls from grace as his ideas dwindle. When he hits rock bottom by attempting suicide, time stops by the hand of the narrator/clock keeper, Moses. The ghost of Hudsucker floats down from above to enlighten Norville about the contents of the blue letter, which leaves the company to the newest employee, Norville, who still has one more invention left in him.

With minimal violence and characters that don't completely resonate with the Coens' often unique qualities, *The Hudsucker Proxy* is perhaps best interpreted as the superficial corporate environment where characters, their world, and their ambitions all appear cardboard thin. Some critics complained about this idea, but the synthetic nature of the movie creates a 1950s dream-like state during which America's consumer lust created a Golden age of consumerism, ranging from cars, to televisions, to rock and roll, to hula-hoops. It's a time often equated with innocence, purity, and optimism. Everything within the movie appears part of an artificial story written by someone like the Coens' own Barton Fink.

Each of the three main characters, void of varied humanistic characteristics, represent single ideals: Norville Barnes signifies the innocence of the times, Amy Archer symbolizes the changing of the times and emergence of the independent woman, and Sidney J. Mussburger represents big business with two capital B's. The Coens never mask the formulaic nature of the material. The audience has seen it before. When Amy first attempts to meet Norville at his favorite diner, the Coens playfully engage the audience's anticipation of their first encounter by providing narrators in the form of two cabbies suffering from indigestion. They follow the scene, providing play-by-play commentary on every cliché of an initial meeting of a forceful woman gaining the attention of a dimwitted man: "Enter the dame. There's one in every story." The Coens know the material is stale, but freely play with pigeonholed stereotypes. They cease to be realistic characters, and the directors use them as mere puppets dancing on an exaggerated New York stage.

After all, Coen characters reflect their setting. And *The Hudsucker Proxy* reflects that notion perfectly. Sets resemble exaggerated miniatures, cutouts, or wonderfully painted backdrops, and New York itself appears like a false leftover set piece from the past. Joel Coen explains, "It's very hard for us to imagine a story absent a very specific locale. You can say that about all the settings of our movies: They're certainly very specific, but not real."[4] The film's three main sets validate this claim. The Hudsucker Building, though only 44 stories tall (not including the mezzanine), appears much closer in size to the Empire State Building, a dominating structure whose massive clock controls all of New York. The Hudsucker Building always remains centered in the frame. Nothing escapes it. Inside, everything implies spaciousness beyond the mailroom where the employees from the lowest social class confirm the chaos and panic of the bottom rung. At the top of the Hudsucker building, sit two important sets. The first is Mussburger's office, as empty and void as the man himself. A massive room, it overlooks New York through the overbearing clicking hands of the Hudsucker clock. Aside from a globe in the corner (for world domination no doubt), a stock ticker, a few chairs, water for life, and a desk, his work area remains surprisingly void of work. While he discusses business over the phone, the clock creates an intimidating shadow that stretches across the length of the room, pointing to Norville as he enters the room.

The second set piece is the clock tower where Moses controls the inner workings of time. He watches over the Hudsucker people like a guardian angel in coveralls. The room, obviously inspired by Fritz Lang's *Metropolis*, takes the film into the realm of fantasy where a janitor knows and sees all. Also, the room not only signifies the lifeblood of the company, but it symbolizes the concept of time. No matter what occurs outside of that room, time continues to tick. Beyond that magical room, another location emerges as the most believable environment with the least exaggeration: the newspaper office. Sure, the expected banter between reporters erupts, and the demanding, nearly abusive editor sees story potential in Norville, the "idea man," but mostly the newspaper sequences are taken from the standard newspaper office examples in *His Girl Friday, Mr. Deeds Goes to Town, All the President's Men, Picture Snatcher,* and *Citizen Kane*. They all embody the same stereotypes and clichés, and *The Hudsucker Proxy* uses them for their expected familiar quality.

The exclusion of crime in *The Hudsucker Proxy* (except for Mussburger's stock manipulation) leaves the Coens' flair for violence considerably depleted and forces corporate suicide to emerge as the focal point. Waring Hudsucker's death is the most shocking sequence, but it lacks the expected panic and self-loathing equated with suicide. Instead, Hudsucker is at peace with himself, content with his decision. He later tells Norville that he had allowed greed to "erode my character, and dissolve my better self." Whatever dread and contempt he felt for what he had become isn't shown as he leaps off the boardroom table to the street below without so much as a goodbye to his men.

Likewise, Norville eventually attempts his own jump, though he has much different results. He's saved by the stoppage of time, which doesn't sound violent, but these final few moments do result in the second death of a character. With time stopped and the angel Hudsucker intervening in Norville's life, Moses battles for his own life against Aloysius, the bald, mute janitor who resembles an evil albino. He's Mussburger's henchman, and we soon find he has more evil aspirations as a negative force within Hudsucker. Aloysius shuts the window in a seemingly innocent mistake while Norville contemplates death on the ledge. But a shot reveals Aloysius glaring out the window, awaiting Norville's eminent fall with a sick sense of satisfaction, knowing he has sealed a man's fate. And when Moses suspends time, Aloysius checks the fuse box before realizing that only one man can stop time, leading him to confront Moses on a metal catwalk suspended midair. It's a generic battle of geriatrics, a spoof of any number of classic duels between good and evil. Neither man lashes out violently. Moses fends off Aloysius with a broom, knocking him off the catwalk to fall to his death. The sequence feels neither original nor outwardly violent with Aloysius's false teeth stopping the clock again. The cartoonish quality prevents any real emotion and any tension it could possess.

NORVILLE BARNES: *"YOU KNOW, FOR KIDS!"*

Poor Norville Barnes. He falls in line with all other Coen brother male leads as another loser, another man who believes he's far smarter than he actually is while searching for his piece of the American dream. With his wild hair, tall lankiness, utter naivety, and face of constant bewilderment, Norville wanders from one situation to the next, much like *Raising Arizona*'s H.I. McDunnough, though, without the slow-witted nature. Despite the obvious moronic evidence, H.I. describes his situations and reflects upon his life with certain intelligence; he's able to explain his actions in a literate, baffling manner through narration. Norville doesn't have the luxury of narration to present his intellectual abilities. His actions present him as the ultimate Boy Scout. He sees no wrong in others and can't envision anything beyond total success. However, his introduction comes on the 44th floor of the Hudsucker building as he contemplates suicide, his own fall to doom. The Coens leave it to Moses to create sympathy through his narration, "How'd he get so high? An' why is he feelin's so low? Is he really gonna do it—is Norville really gonna jelly up the sidewalk?" Moses refers to Norville as a story, adding to the artificial nature of *The Hudsucker Proxy*. Everything is retold by an outside source with his own interpretation on the events. And Norville, much like Barton Fink, knows nothing of violence and remains incapable of reacting to it even at the point of death. As he stands on a ledge contemplating whether or not to "jelly up the sidewalk," it helps to underscore the movie's theme of corporate violence wherein, instead of disappearing or finding a new line of work, the only answer is death.

On the other hand, the moment Norville steps off the bus from Muncie, Indiana as a recent graduate of the Muncie College of Business

Administration, his expectations seem skewed. Norville just smiles with uncertainty as a representative of the clichéd image of the 1950s, a decade during which there existed the perfect family structure and the innocence before the hippie revolution. An era before widespread corruption became commonplace. The purity of the era meets Hudsucker's slogan: "The Future is Now," and Norville radiates that idea with the wonder of a Capra movie. However, he does so without the sincerity or the heart that Capra films contained. Norville assumes that things will work out. Disappointed with no prospects for work, he stops at a diner and eats alone. Again, much like Fink, Norville cannot avoid fate. As he leaves, a newspaper sways in the wind, follows him, and blows against his leg. His own coffee stain highlighted an opportunity: "THE FUTURE IS NOW. Start building yours at Hudsucker Industries. Low pay. Long hours. NO EXPERIENCE NECESSARY." Suddenly, he's standing outside the massive building, and, as Hudsucker swan dives off the building that bears his name, Norville walks in. This is an obvious changing of the guard. For Norville's wide-eyed, dopey appearance, the Coens solidly define one element about him: motivation. Norville acts compelled, inspired by his uncomplicated idea of his drawing of a perfect circle and understanding the power of it.

No matter what trouble he encounters, he rests easy knowing the drawing will lead to success. He constantly pitches his ambiguous idea, which validates his simple-mindedness. He never explains the circled inscription, and he appears disappointed when people don't immediately understand it. They are unable to visualize the magnitude of his creation. Norville doesn't waste time before introducing this idea in the mailroom, where he encounters a kindred spirit in the form of an old man. Norville tells him, "I got big ideas!" before revealing his illustration, pulling it from his shoe as if protecting his future. "Something I developed myself. Yessir, it's my ticket upstairs." Destiny moves quickly for Norville as he's able to pitch his invention to Mussburger when he delivers the blue letter. A motivated, but nervous Norville remains the humble Boy Scout and delivers his idea to Mussburger. He remains so enthusiastic about the opportunity that he cannot see through Mussburger's scheme.

Perhaps it's Norville's slightly idiotic nature that represents America's creativity during the 1950s. The newspapers dub him "the idea man," which effectively defines Norville's youthful exuberance; he is filled with ideas and yearns for the chance to prove he is capable. In giving Norville presidential power, Mussburger easily takes advantage of his pure and sanitized Midwest values and manipulates him, thus corrupting and removing his business virginity. Beyond his inventions, Norville appears to have no business sense. He allows his charm to pass for credibility, but when forced to answer something, he parrots Mussburger's various ideas and phrases: "When you're dead, you stay dead." In fact, nearly every action he takes comes from someone else, right down to the lone attempt at violence via suicide.

The rise and fall of Norville also revolves around Buzz, the elevator operator, who symbolizes Norville's most formidable opponent. Then again, he's seemingly everyone's nemesis, berating all riders except for Mr. Mussburger whom he smartly fears. Norville meets Buzz three times, each point representing different peaks in the narrative. The first occasion is during Norville's rise to the top via elevator, the second time occurs when Norville reaches the height of his corporate power, and the final occurrence transpires once Norville has been humiliated and disgraced as he roams the streets near Hudsucker when Buzz finally strikes in revenge. Buzz never calls Norville by name ("Hiya, Buddy!") until their roles reverse when Norville begins to unravel as president. Buzz, now acting as the lowly pitchman, demonstrates a prototype for a bendable straw to Norville, the president. The moment suggests that Norville has come full circle; he becomes everything he's not. The power and pressure of the corporate lifestyle alters him beyond recognition. Disappointed, berated for his lack of creativity, and called a one-hit wonder, his ego overtakes him. Even as Norville's hula-hoop represents simplicity, Buzz's improvement on an existing product, the most basic of ideas, defines Norville's failure as an idea man and his inability to create. The very man who delivered Norville to the highest level of Hudsucker Industries had undermined him, so he fires Buzz, showing aggression for the first time. Norville isn't comfortable with the firing as, once again, he can only mimic Mussburger, telling Buzz that there's no crawling at Hudsucker Industries. The incident plays as a reenactment of Norville's own chance to pitch his big idea, although it has drastically different results.

Norville's ego had been blown out of proportion by this point. A pompous ass, Norville takes self-centeredness to new heights. After his worldwide success, Norville not only dates the most attractive models, not only hires a personal bodyguard, not only has two masseuses, but employs a live orchestra to soothe his creative mind. While all this occurs, a sculptor creates a bust of him—something only fit for dictators and people of great inspiration. Amy invades his serenity at this moment and attempts to remove the pedestal from his ego, but in Norville's mind, the ride will improve, even at the cost of losing Amy. This scene leads into a Coen dream sequence. A solid white backdrop accents the dream as Norville dances with a beautiful dancer. At first, viewers might assume this woman is Amy, but in fact, she's just a dancer. As they enjoy their solo ball, it suggests Norville's desire for sophistication and entrance into the elite social class. Of course, as Norville flutters about, it's clear that he's without grace, shuffling and stumbling while the woman moves with elegance.

Norville's dream world soon ends when violence finally finds him. Near the conclusion of the movie after the last encounter with Buzz, his life has eroded to the point of public humiliation. After being struck by Buzz, Norville is surrounded by an angry mob of Norville despisers. Drunk and disillusioned, Norville transforms into the classic monster of choice while being chased by an angry mob like Frankenstein through the snowy streets, hunching to one side as if imitating the Hunchback of Notre Dame. After he embraces fate, Norville returns to Hudsucker to retire officially from the position and from life. He exchanges his high priced suit for his lowly mailroom apron, signaling utter failure. He eventually steps out onto a ledge with the snow fluttering around him like *It's a Wonderful Life*. Norville knows nothing of violence, yet he follows the same route as Hudsucker by attempting suicide. They each act like a captain going down with the ship instead of living a life of shameful failure. He falls accidentally, but is intercepted by the angel of Waring Hudsucker, complete with white robe, harp, hovering halo and singing "They'll be Coming Around the Mountain." Hudsucker reveals that he was once like Norville, an idealistic and naïve young man, but had grown to despise the "emptiness of power and wealth. [. . .] I allowed time and age to corrupt my dreams." In turn, Hudsucker had left the company to the newest employee, Norville, whose youthful exuberance is once again ignited. Norville's life comes full circle as he rekindles his relationship with Amy, and he becomes the leader Moses predicted. "He went on to rule with wisdom and compassion," even inventing a new product out of his perfect circle: the Frisbee.

AMY ARCHER:
"I'M HAPPY ENOUGH"

The familiar character of Amy Archer comes from the newsroom environment. She is a hardnosed reporter willing to do anything to complete an assignment, and she is even willing to go undercover as a secretary in order to gain the trust of someone as naïve Norville. She never hesitates or wrestles with the moral implications of misleading him in order to gather inside information that might expose him as a fraud. After all, her introduction to the narrative comes as she storms into her editor's office with Norville's story declaring that he's a fake. The other reporters sit around the office like yes men, but only Amy possesses the gall to speak. She's proud, bold, and egotistical like Mussburger; given the opportunity, she informs anyone listening about her Pulitzer Prize. Fellow reporters even gamble on whether or not she'll mention the award. Nonetheless, Amy is the modern woman, unafraid of the man's environment of hard news and willing to battle if a story lurks nearby. As the most capable of the reporters, Amy can simultaneously juggle talking on the phone with the chief, typing a story, chatting with fellow reporter Smitty, and solving a crossword puzzle for another co-worker.

If Jennifer Jason Leigh's performance feels familiar, it should. The concept of a quick-tongued, ace female reporter is an imitation of Katharine Hepburn and Jean Arthur. In fact, her story thread is plucked from *Mr. Deeds Goes to Town*, the 1936 Capra feature in which another reporter gains the trust of an unsuspecting male. Regardless of the originality, Amy is a woman unabashed by the world. She fears no one by presenting a false front of confidence to prevent any real harm to herself. She's an investigator searching for the truth in the great tradition of newspaper movies. She's willing to battle the editor, or anyone for that matter, as she has her own big ideas. She's a character who stands up for what she believes in, whereas all others just exist, completing expected jobs and living by the Hudsucker clock that looms above.

Amy's toughness, her hardened exterior results in a flawed romance with Norville. Unlike the film's inspiration, *Mr. Deeds Goes to Town* or *His Girl Friday,* romanticism isn't top priority. Amy's love of Norville comes with the genre. It's a necessary plot inclusion used to service expectations for drama. Only Amy acts as savior to Norville. She slowly falls for him after writing the first scathing article about his rise to the top. Her love, however, only develops after she gains access to the Hudsucker Building and discovers the truth behind Norville's presidency. Staying after the building lockdown, Amy searches for information to prove Norville's fraudulent nature. She flips through his appointment calendar, finding it blank beyond the entry for Wilkie Grammar School Junior Achievers Club, now canceled. She notices a door marked "Authorized Personnel Only" and enters into an area that turns the wheels of this fabricated world of Hudsucker Industries, a massive, dark, industrial area with gears, smoke, and metal catwalks. Visually stunning, the room is the clock tower, the very entity around which *The Hudsucker Proxy* revolves, and it displays the moving pieces of the world controlled by the business watch. The Coens borrow visuals for this scene from the classic *Metropolis* and *Alice in Wonderland* as Amy glances through a keyhole into the real world to catch a glimpse of Mussburger discussing the future. But a voice catches her spying, the voice of the narrator, Moses.

Amy is only one of two characters who encounter Moses, the mechanic who must grease the wheels in order to keep things moving along. He knows Amy although they had never met, and, when Amy questions him on how he recognizes her, he replies, "Ah guess ole Moses know jes about ever'thing, leastways if it concerns Hudsuckuh." With the visual stimulation and fantasy of the scene, it serves as the first glimpse at Amy beneath her coarse exterior. The moment Moses utters her name, she seems not just surprised, but wounded that someone saw the real her. He questions her undercover work, her motivations, and her happiness. Amy, in a true moment of vulnerability, can only say, "I'm happy enough." Moses laughs at the comment and disappears in the clock, leaving Amy to repeat, "I'm plenty happy" to an empty room. Amy, perhaps the most blatantly stolen character, reveals a hint of humanity in a moment that leads to love. For the remainder of *The Hudsucker Proxy,* Amy feuds with Norville because he has changed. She tells off her editor, knowing that the board used Norville like a puppet. When she reads of his success and adventures, she wears a slight smile. She might have had a hand in leading him to lose touch with reality through excess, but she cannot stand by and watch him plummet back to obscure mediocrity.

SIDNEY J. MUSSBURGER: *"PLEXIGLAS. HAD IT INSTALLED LAST WEEK"*

Of all the characters, Mussburger is the shallowest, without compassion or emotion. He's single-minded, concerned only with dollar signs, his reputation, and the success of the business as long as it lines his pockets. Waring Hudsucker himself describes him perfectly, "Well, say what you want about the man's ethics, he's a ball-to-the-wall businessman. Beat ya anyway he can. Straight for the jugular. Very effective." Every cliché of big business finds representation through Mussburger: greed, apathy, focus, corruption, and heartlessness. He first emerges at the window seconds after Hudsucker leapt through it to commit suicide. Impressed, Mussburger calmly glances past the broken shards. He strolls back past the stunned men and finds Hudsucker's smoldering cigar in an ashtray. Mussburger cannot waste a whole Monte Cristo so he finishes smoking the cigar as if nothing had occurred.

Obviously shallow, his character embodies the epitome of corporate America, never flinching in the face of adversity when presented with a violent act. He understands the show must go on, and he never mentions that their president and founder dove off the boardroom table. Instead, he immediately brainstorms for the future. Nothing can interrupt the bottom line. Only one member of the board expresses his shock, while the rest of the men calmly discuss the event without emotion. Mussburger never attempts to question Hudsucker's motivation. "What am I, a headshrinker? Maybe the man was unhappy." A focused business leader, he has no time to mourn or ponder the decision, and instead weighs the company's options. Because Hudsucker was without an heir, the stock would go public, thus losing the board's control. As a man more concerned with his pockets than with the good of the company or bottom-dollar, Mussburger is a summation of corporate greed. He embodies all the mistrust, myths, mystery, misgivings, and maniacal nature that the public sees in the corporate world.

Mussburger's shortcomings come from his cardboard nature. He doesn't function outside the boardroom. Granted, he lives and breathes the corporate life, but he's flat and without life. He's so outlandishly evil and stereotypical that he becomes more comedic than criminal, a cartoon villain taken from every known and expected source of business greed. Effectively played by the legendary Paul Newman, his character is allowed little room to maneuver by the Coens even though he is the only character who mentions an outside life. Norville, at a party celebrating his new presidency, sits with Mussburger's wife, a wealthy, elite, overweight woman plucked from the French renaissance. He attempts to complement Mussburger about his wife, but Mussburger reveals little interest in the woman. "So they tell me," he says. At one point, Mussburger even speaks of his mother, only stating that she didn't raise her son to crumble under the first sign of adversity. Regardless of his outside influences as a character, Mussburger cannot grow, but he does allude to the recurring theme of time. Along with Hudsucker, Mussburger talks of time: "The wheel turns, the music plays, and our spin ain't over yet." He underscores that he, like all in *The Hudsucker Proxy*, revolves around the massive Hudsucker clock.

One particular scene best exemplifies Mussburger's character. It's a flashback (a method rare in the Coens' work) to a sequence explaining either his cost-cutting methods or his callousness. After Norville ruins a massive account by igniting it and throwing it through a window, Mussburger chases it through the window. Miraculously, Norville catches him by the ankles, and, in turn, Mussburger glances at his custom pants recalling when he first purchased his suit. The tailor asked if he'd like double stitching for the pants. Mussburger, however, rejected the offer. To Mussburger's luck, the tailor felt strong enough about him to give him the extra layer, thus saving his life when he dangled 44 stories above the street. He saw no purpose in spending extra money if no one would know the difference. Like an experienced executive, he knew better than to waste money on the unnecessary.

MOSES, THE CLOCK MAN: *"WELL THE FUTURE, THAT'S SOMETHING YOU CAN'T NEVER TELL ABOUT"*

Moses embodies the classic bookend narrator, opening and closing *The Hudsucker Proxy* with his brand of wisdom. He delivers the story as if relating a fairy tale in a distant New York City that looks familiar, but isn't real. From the Hudsucker clock, he's able to watch all of New York celebrate New Year's Eve. Moses, the omnipresent narrator who wields the power of God, is the first voice heard by the audience, explaining that everyone celebrating New Year's hopes to capture a moment in time. He introduces us into the world with a certain comedic value via his warm, caring, and playful voice. Despite the fact that Norville stands on the edge of a building contemplating suicide, Moses knows what's to come and does not alarm the audience. It's Moses that gives Norville empathy, introducing him as a tragic figure that the audience can find sympathy for.

Moses doesn't stray from his stereotypical character. He's derived from countless old Hollywood portrayals of African-Americans, who are supposedly of lower intelligence and unfit for high level job responsibility. He behaves gentlemanly and speaks like a clichéd, uneducated, elderly Southern black man with an "ah shucks" attitude reflecting 1958. However broken his speech is, what Moses says carries weight. How he says something might sound simple-minded, but what he says matters. Keeping Moses stereotypical comes from narrative necessity, for if he demonstrated an educated manner, then it would fail to fit the period. After all, he is a blue-collar man responsible for working, not being seen. He must grease the wheels of time to keep things moving along. As a God-like mechanic who knows all the elements within the company, only a select few know of him, and he remains invisible within the corporation (beyond his nemesis, the janitor Aloysius). As Moses explains, "I keeps the ol' circle turning—this ol' clock needs plenty o' care." Moses acts as the backbone of the company, doing the difficult labor no one desires to do.

At the same time, Moses personifies his more famous Biblical counterpart, though he leads without acknowledgement and without inspiring confidence. Instead, he comes across like a proud parent, watching his children from afar and protecting them. This is especially true with Norville. Moses protects him not just by stopping time, but through his conversation with Amy during which he defends Norville's intelligence and actions. Moses, unlike Mussburger, works for the good of Hudsucker, even if it means supporting him to the end. He alludes to knowing more about the death of Waring Hudsucker, but says that Amy "never axed me 'bout dat." In spite of Mussburger's misconception of wielding superficial powers within the boardroom, Moses possesses supernatural powers. He even breaks past the fourth dimension, looking at the camera and telling the audience, "Strictly speakin, I'm never spozed to do this, but have you a better idea?" Whom Moses could find trouble with and how he actually stops time the Coens avoid explaining. Regardless, he has the job of watching over Hudsucker like a guardian angel just as the Hudsucker clock watches over all of the city and keeps this exaggerated New York moving.

* * *

The Hudsucker Proxy marked not only the Coen's first and only attempt to leave crime behind, but also marked another milestone: their first outright flop. It performed dismally at the box office and with critics. One critic wrote that the film "qualifies as an overdesigned, fatuous bore."[5] Another referred to it as "pointlessly flashy and compulsively overloaded with references to films of the 1930s. Hudsucker isn't the real thing at all. It's just a proxy."[6] Regardless, *The Hudsucker Proxy* gave the Coens a chance to avoid the label of pure genre filmmakers, but Warner Bros still had big expectations for the film. Uber-producer, Joel Silver, who allowed them the chance to explore new ground said, "I read the script and I thought that it was the most accessible of their movies."[7] He added, "I'm not in the business to make art, I'm in it to make money to buy art."[8] Budgeted upwards of $40 million, *The Hudsucker Proxy* earned close to $3 million domestically.[9] Not exactly a smash. Despite the Coens being independent for a decade, 1994 marked the emergence of the independent film market with Quentin Tarantino's *Pulp Fiction* sweeping all expectations and changing the way Hollywood perceived work outside the studio system. Tarantino, like the Coens, remodeled familiar movie worlds by reinventing the crime genre in an homage to 1970s blaxploitation. The Coens backpedaled with their *Hudsucker* homage, one that seemed dated and considerably uncool by comparison. Suddenly, the Coens found themselves once again outside Hollywood. However, *The Hudsucker Proxy*'s failure and lack of unique violence resulted in a refocused effort on their next project: *Fargo*.

6

What's the Deal with Greed and Wood Chippers?

Fargo (1996)

"This is my deal here, Wade."[1]

CAST: Frances McDormand (Marge Gunderson), Steve Buscemi (Carl Showalter), Peter Stormare (Gaear Grimsrud), William H. Macy (Jerry Lundegaard), Harve Presnell (Wade Gustafson), Kristen Rudrud (Jean Lundegaard), John Carroll Lynch (Norm Gunderson), and Steve Park (Mike Yanagita).

Fargo. Directed by Joel Coen. Santa Monica, CA: MGM, 1996.

It's not every day that people witness a man being shoved into a wood chipper. When hero Marge Gunderson stumbles upon the film's villain, he's grinding down his partner. Only a leg remains sticking up from the device as the villain attempts to shove the limb down using a log. The surrounding snow has been dyed crimson. At this point, the violence in *Fargo* suddenly becomes much more emphasized as the greed-based violence of the male characters reaches a climax. Nearly all the men of *Fargo* evoke some form of aggression in order to protect their prospective deals that offer them each a chance to earn life-changing money. They resort to assault, kidnapping, and murder to resolve any problems that arise in their attempts to obtain the money needed to make their deals come true.

Fargo brings back the flawed kidnapping plot the Coens previously used in *Raising Arizona,* though to a much different effect. The story begins when car salesman Jerry Lundegaard (played with perfect reserve by Macy) meets low rent thugs Carl Showalter and Gaear Grimsrud at the King of Clubs, a bar in Fargo, North Dakota, to arrange the kidnapping of Jerry's wife. Immediately, the motivation doesn't add up as Carl continually probes for further details as to why a man would have his own wife kidnapped only to pay the ransom himself. With the terms finally reached, Jerry gives them a stolen tan Cutlass Ciera from his car lot, and he returns to his life in Minneapolis while Carl and Gaear soon make their own journey toward Jerry's home. Meanwhile, Jerry probes his wealthy father-in-law, Wade Gustafson, about a potential big money deal for a lot of land. When Wade finally grants him a meeting, Jerry scrambles to call off the crime only to realize he has no way of actually doing it.

Carl and Gaear snatch Jean Lundegaard midday and haul her back to their hideout near Brainerd. Carl forgets to place the temporary tags on the car and they are pulled over by the police, causing violence to erupt as Gaear murders three people in the middle of the night. Thus Marge Gunderson, Chief of Police of Brainerd, enters the scene to save the day. The notion of money overwhelms the situation as Jerry had told Wade that the ransom was for $1,000,000, not the $80,000 he told Carl and Gaear. In turn, by killing Wade during the ransom delivery, Carl collects the full million. In all, seven people wind up dead, ending with Gaear's final disposal of Carl's body in the wood chipper. The police later capture Jerry on the run in a motel, and the film closes with Marge and her husband Norm snuggling in bed and returning to their world as if nothing had occurred.

Fargo is one of those rare films in which all elements connected. The Coens risked not explaining every minute deal and trusted that the audience could connect the dots, and it paid off. They took the standard crime drama and manufactured something that defied expectations while remaining true to the convention. After all, *Fargo* is a crime drama. It has cops. It has crooks. It has violence. It has a man caught in a moral dilemma. It has the classic motive of greed and the violence that moves all great crime films. *Fargo*, however, strives to expand normal character traits. Most genre characters can be defined with generic, one-word descriptions. And on the surface, both Carl and Gaear are defined in such terms according to two prostitutes: Carl—funny looking, and Gaear—The Marlboro Man. The two women cannot formulate further descriptions, but the men appear like realistic characters, not just blindly motivated carbon copies. Each person appears wholly natural, as if existing in some corner of the world—the exact element that *The Hudsucker Proxy* lacked. Instead of being slick professionals, the criminals appear completely common and amateurish in their methods and actions. They react like authentic people, not gangsters.

Likewise, there's more to Jerry than just an unfulfilled life. Something dark lurks within him as money drives him into the underworld. While Jerry's family erodes, Marge's life represents the ideal budding family unit. During her pursuit of the murderers, she still finds time for the little things in life: constantly eating and supporting her husband's painting career. As with all Coen brother films, social commentary lurks beneath the surface. *Fargo* deals with America's desensitization to violence, people's cold nature, and society's love of TV. Moreover, it's a story of normal, northern people and their reaction to the modern world. Everyone deals with adversity in the same manner. With cold, quiet discontent. Their restricted emotions are blocked not just by their societal code, but by their parkas that insulate them from the emerging violence engulfing their area.

The parkas suggest how the northern setting defines characters and reflects their attitudes, morals, and beliefs. The Coens so effectively constructed the environment that at times it transcends a motion picture and becomes a pseudo documentary of the area. Known as docu-noir[2], this style incorporates a documentary-style with the highly stylized film noir, allowing movies to present material objectively without persuasive film techniques. Used in the early 1950s in movies such as Jules Dassin's *The Naked City* and Stanley Kubrick's *The Killing*, this technique is employed by *Fargo* when the movie opens with text that declares, "This is a true story. Events depicted in this film took place in Minnesota in 1987." Unknown to the audience, this statement is entirely false, a Coen ruse to create a sense of realism before introducing a single character. Joel reveals, "By telling the public that we took our inspiration from reality, we knew they wouldn't see the movie as just an ordinary thriller. We attempted a very different stylistic approach, tackling the subject in a very dry manner."[3] Indeed, it pulls the wool over the viewer's eyes to create a false story of truth. If the audience believes what they see actually happened, if they believe the crimes actually occurred, the characters become that much more genuine and tragic.

Characters engage in routine, mundane day-to-day activities. It's not that North Dakota is an undiscovered region, but it's a region where violence feels foreign and nothing of the sort could seemingly occur. The people of the north talk funny. They utter silly things like "Ya" with nearly every sentence. They display limited emotions, but never seem to exhibit anger. The Coens take the stereotype of "Minnesota nice" and abuse it while lovingly embracing it. Ethan explains, "Minnesota is a very polite and friendly culture, and like a lot of polite and friendly cultures, it often masks, or makes you unaware, that there are other sort of things going, sort of seething, underneath, and the juxtaposition of that sort of politeness in the culture is an interesting juxtaposition to those kinds of events."[4] The goodness, the seeming Mayberry quality of the characters reflects the stereotype attached to the small town life. They drop a snowy version of Mayberry into the modern world and unleash grisly violence to see who wins. Marge perhaps best addresses this idea at the location of the first murder when she states: "I'd be very surprised if our suspect was from Brainerd." Marge couldn't be more correct.

The opening shot reveals an apparent stark blue sky that dissolves into the stark whiteness of Fargo, unveiling emotional clues about the region. The endless snow reflects the purity with everything, from the land to the people, blanketed in white to create a supposed sheen to the characters, whose wholesome quality isn't necessarily innocent, but it evokes the perfect small town quality. When murder occurs, the distilled area immediately becomes stained. Carl's aggravation enhances this purity as he grows continually frustrated with the refined nature of the people. He mocks Jerry's northern speech patterns. He insults lot attendants who smile after he berates them. He's the outsider, unable to comprehend the Minnesota nice. At the same time, while residents sport long underwear, massive parkas, snow boots, ear warmers, and scarves, Carl wears a basic jacket. He's unprepared for the cold, unfit and awkward among the natives. He's unable to deal with the niceness or make common small talk with the people. On the other hand, Gaear survives with his Scandinavian heritage, and thus blends into the crowd. He's emotionally cold, and his mute-like presence makes him into a "seemingly lobotomized specimen of depravity with a hankering for pancakes."[5]

The snow and the cold relate to the characters's lack of emotional action as no character from Brainerd wears their feelings on their parka sleeves, so to speak. Everyone exhibits a certain level of understood politeness that no one dares to cross. Even Jerry, after discussing the ransom with Wade, after his wife has vanished, cannot help but be cordial with a restaurant cashier. He is unable to display frustration anymore than he could display rudeness. Another scene, the first of Jerry at work, displays the restricted sentiment. A man purchases a car from Jerry who presses the man for extra money. The man wants to chastise Jerry, but does his best to remain calm. Only at the final breaking point, when Jerry won't budge on the price of the finish on the car, does the man explode: "You lied to me, Mr. Lundegaard. You're a ball-faced liar. A fucking liar!" When he does, it appears to pain him, as if he's left with no alternative. Jerry emerges as the stereotypical sleazy car salesman, who after the berating, can only look down at his desk like a scorned child.

Perhaps then, the northern setting molds the actions of the men in *Fargo*. The coldness does not dull their desire for money as they all are similarly infatuated by managing their own deals. As Jerry redundantly explains, "This is my deal here!" All of the men appear inept in managing this goal. Jerry yearns for it. He needs it. Deals have consumed his and all the lives of the men of *Fargo*. After all, the deal drives the men of *Fargo*, and each man has his own method to work his own schemes. Jerry has two: the parking lot proposal with his father-in-law for $750,000 and the deal with the kidnappers for $80,000 in ransom funds. Wade, in turn, leaps at the chance to take over Jerry's deal, whether it helps his son-in-law or not. Carl and Gaear work the deal with Jerry and angle for the entire ransom once "blood has been shed." Even Marge's husband, Norm, hopes for a big deal after submitting a painting for the latest postal stamp edition. This consuming greed creates the authentic feeling derived from the men's motivation as it brings forth the sudden outbursts of violence in *Fargo*.

Compared with the majority of the crime genre, the violence within *Fargo*, though bloody and unrelenting, seems minimal because it occurs quickly and has little recourse. However, seven murders happen, each one catching viewers off guard: a state trooper, a man, a child, Wade, a parking lot attendant, Jean, and Carl. Besides murder, four instances of assault occur: Jean bites Gaear, Shep whips Carl with a belt, Wade wounds Carl with a shot to the face, and Marge shoots Gaear in the leg as he flees. Nearly all the murders happen with a gun, and everyone is slain by the hands of either Gaear (five) or Carl (two). Perhaps the most memorable sequence occurs at the cabin as Gaear watches soap operas in his long underwear. Carl bursts into the house after being shot in the face, gives Gaear a share of the ransom, declares the stolen tan Ciera his own, and refuses to pay Gaear half for it. As Carl flashes his gun to square the situation, Gaear sits calmly until Carl walks away. Then Gaear chops him down with an axe, leading to the most shocking sequence of Gaear shoving Carl into the chipper. Neither the axe strike nor the disposal of the body is shown, but the implied anarchic act creates a more violent image than the visual of the death could have. These chaotic, explosive incidents create docu-noir; the violence seems authentic because the Coens never shy from the act of death. Each violent act that erupts has realistic motivation. Everyone dies for a reason, even the innocents, because they unknowingly stand in the way of the big money deal.

JERRY LUNDEGAARD:
"A DEAL'S A DEAL"

"This is my deal here, Wade. Jean's my wife," Jerry Lundegaard demands as he debates with his father-in-law, Wade Gustafson, over the ransom amount needed to pay for his kidnapped wife. This statement, the notion of a deal to call his own, however, becomes more than a simple wrestling of wills for Jerry; it's his driving force, his motivation. After all, Jerry is a man without a life of his own. He manages Wade's car lot, yet remains without complete control. It's not his own. Jerry has a family, but Wade controls that as well, popping in unexpectedly and talking of a secured future for Jerry's wife and son, but not for Jerry. Even when negotiating with criminals, Jerry remains incapable of managing the situation. For this reason, Jerry develops into a sympathetic character. He's the ultimate everyman, working for a living with a loving wife and a nice kid at home, and he has an overbearing father-in-law who can't stay out of the Lundegaard family affairs. On each occasion when Jerry does flex fatherly muscles, something surfaces to knock him back to a lower, pedestrian place. But Jerry's dark side overtakes whatever natural balance he maintained before. His Minnesota manners remain, but he emerges an empty shell driven by greed, living with a wife and son without regard for their emotions. He exhibits no sympathy for Jean, and when Stan Grossman (Wade's right hand man) asks about Jerry's son, Scotty, after the kidnapping, Jerry looks surprised as if he had forgotten about him. The search for financial independence costs him not only his family, but his morality. Jerry only displays emotions twice, once upon his capture at the conclusion and once in an earlier instance, but in the first instance, he shows pure, raw emotion. After leaving the meeting with Wade and Stan Grossman to discuss Jerry's development plan, he finally realizes he has no money of his own, no capital to broker a massive deal. He walks across a void, blanketed parking lot with only his car waiting. He sits in his frozen car for a beat before stepping back into the cold to scrape the iced windshield. After a few passes, he succumbs to frustration in a childish tantrum, smashing the scraper against the car. His frozen emotions crack suddenly and then quickly refreeze with the realization that the iced windshield still needed completion.[6]

Fargo starts with Jerry in debt, owing an unspecified amount of cash that the Coens never reveal. In all crime stories, motivation always surfaces as the primary focus, yet here, there's little reason to reveal that information. It's not needed with the docu-noir approach to the story. It would make no difference if it were gambling, bad investments, or drugs. Revealing that information would only narrow Jerry's potential as a character. If it's known that he's a gambling junky, then the viewer expects to see him at the track or reading odds nervously with a whiskey and Coke in hand. He'd fall under the gambling trappings and transform into something beyond a family man, beyond a car salesman. Removing any preconceived notions allows for unbiased basic human reactions, and eliminates the bias of an incessant gambler or junkie. These are not the characters of a crime drama cliché. Not revealing what internally motivates Jerry adds to his realism. He has no confessional. He delivers no exposition, nor do the Coens add narration to aid his tale. Jerry simply acts. For good or bad, Jerry only does what he believes is best for overall success, to achieve his end goal. Doing so adds to the authentic approach of the story. If cameras followed these individuals around, no background information would surface. We'd only have their actions to judge.

Of all the male characters, Jerry emerges as the most tragic, most inept. More than any other character, he constantly finds himself spiraling deeper into each new situation that presents itself. From the opening scene, Jerry is continually overmatched. He's an incompetent criminal, incompetent father, and incompetent husband. This fact becomes established during the opening sequence. Once Jerry arrives at the King of Clubs in Fargo and meets the potential criminals for hire, Jerry cannot manage the deal and it's quickly established who controls whom. Carl and Gaear sit at a table with empty bottles spread across it. They've been waiting. Jerry claims the times were confused, but the pair does not buy his claim. Why should they? Jerry represents the ultimate sucker with the ultimate easy score. However, that doesn't mean Jerry isn't likeable. Ethan states, "Jerry is a poor lost soul who can't stop improvising solutions to get out of the situations he's already gotten himself into. He never stops trying everything, brimming over with activity. He's almost admirable in that respect!"[7]

Jerry's humble nature equates to a humble man who's lost his path, lost touch with what's important in life, like Waring Hudsucker who committed suicide in *The Hudsucker Proxy*. Jerry willingly sacrifices his wife and child in order to achieve not just independence from what has financially suffocated him, but independence from his father-in-law. Jerry could be equated to Willy Loman, the traveling salesman whose life never quite panned out in *Death of a Salesman*. Jerry, like Willy, cannot achieve the success he believes he's capable of. They both crave and yearn for bigger deals, for an unattainable lifestyle. They see others triumph and cannot accept their losses. Willy sees his rich neighbors, late brother, and boss succeed. Jerry must cope with his father-in-law's successes. Jerry's unspoken jealousy of Wade consumes him, as is demonstrated during Marge's first interview of Jerry. She asks if he's the owner. Embarrassed, Jerry replies he's only executive sales manager. He ensures his high ranking status before explaining the dealership is his father-in-law's.

Instead of shunning Wade, Jerry envisions using him, his companies, his money, and his connections. It's flawed logic. Inexperienced in deals, Jerry has nowhere to turn other than the one financially sound man he knows, but this man has complete control over him and consistently controls Jerry's household. Early in the film, the entire family sits for dinner and young Scotty runs off to hang out with friends before finishing his plate. Wade cannot bear this lax parenting, and he attempts to control the situation offering scenarios of what their son might be doing. Jerry avoids defending his parenting decision and moves directly into his business proposal. Jerry thinks nothing of trivial family affairs, only of the business prospect. Later, as dinner ends, Jerry again proposes the possible business deal: "I'm asking you here, Wade. This could work out real good for me and Jean and Scotty." Jerry, in a second attempt, tries to implore the future of his family. Wade's reply? "Jean and Scotty never have to worry." He feels no responsibility to further the success of his son-in-law. Like Loman, Jerry must be responsible for his own achievements, for good or bad. By not helping, Wade, like Willy's family, signed an unknown death warrant by not intervening. Perhaps if Wade had allowed the deal to succeed, he could have altered Jerry's fortunes. Jerry—unable to rise above a mediocre sales rank—has no choice but to play a joker card at all costs. This card, this deal, erodes all of Jerry's sensibilities, with nothing remaining but a new criminal career opportunity.

MARGE GUNDERSON: "AND FOR WHAT? A LITTLE BIT OF MONEY?"

Of all the Coen creations, none equal the uniqueness and true genius of Marge Gunderson, a character all her own that defies every cop film before *Fargo*. She rejects the machismo of the police drama genre in spite of her own pregnancy. Marge acts as a motherly figure, truly caring for a violent and hostile world. Most detectives, police chiefs, and beat cops appear weary from the world, unable to cope with day-to-day struggles, and ground down by the beat. Films such as *Dirty Harry, Die Hard, In the Heat of the Night, Heat, Seven, Touch of Evil,* and *The French Connection* all portray the hardnosed protagonists left unable to care. They are all lost on the mission—lost to humanity. With a non-existent social life, the job, the criminal, becomes their only focus. The bottle is usually equated as a best friend. Marge breaks that trend. She adds a level of genuine care that no film in the genre has created without sacrificing character. Easily, she could have turned into a joke, without convictions, without a code to follow. The Coen's resisted a possible bombardment of jokes about her protruding stomach or ill-fitting clothes. Instead, they allow Marge to make her own jokes about her pregnancy. She tells Jerry at their first encounter, "Mind if I sit? I'm carrying quite a load here." She never uses her pregnancy as an excuse to avoid a situation or receive sympathy. She rarely even mentions it beyond natural conversation. Yet, at no point does anyone demand she relax or sit down. None of her fellow officers comment on the issue. Marge has no wild mood swings except for her lust for food. Despite the genre, Marge represents the goodness left in the world, the power of motherhood, and her dominance over the impotent men of *Fargo*.

Modesty does not just come with Marge's fruitful appearance. Her unpretentiousness is a perfect reflection of the northern setting. Granted, her deputies might seem a little too small-townish and mildly incompetent, but that remains true to the genre. If Deputy Lou had stepped beyond those elements, it would undercut Marge's impact as a character. If everyone spoke with incredible diction and solved crimes like Sam Spade, *Fargo* would lose its realism. Besides, Marge cannot show anyone up; it's not in her nature to flaunt. Marge doesn't have an edgy partner. None of her officers exhibit testosterone. She isn't haunted by the past. Instead, she plays the motherly role of the department, encouraging officers and leading without seeming masculine or losing her femininity. Most of her male police counterparts in other crime films seclude themselves like Popeye Doyle or Martin Riggs, but Marge has a loving, stable relationship with her husband, Norm, and enjoys staying up late watching television in bed. While that doesn't sound unique, those elements in a crime genre make it incredibly different, because family structures are usually in disrepair in crime movies. It makes Marge completely average. Being a cop just happens to be her profession. It's the modernization of someone like Donna Reed (if she decided to join the local police department and became a homicide detective). No longer just a homemaker, Marge continues to carry wholesome qualities. Instead, respect and affection develop. Her closest counterpart comes from Peter Falk's *Columbo,* an efficient, unassuming detective capable of charming killers with a seemingly humble, slow-witted, yet coy personality. Marge reflects that personality, but replaces the slight gag of the rumpled trench coat and disheveled hair with her ear-flapped police hat and pregnancy. They both catch their targets off guard with unexpected politeness and sincerity. Neither is capable of matching muscle, yet neither finds themselves forced to use it.

Marge's arrival at the murder scene immediately establishes her dominance on the force. She pulls no rank or ego. Alternatively, she's greeted with a cup of coffee by Deputy Lou and the investigation begins. Though confident, a lot of guessing goes into the initial search: "I guess that's a defensive wound." Viewers never learn if Marge had ever investigated anything so vicious. The police force, with Marge Gunderson in charge, also perfectly demonstrates the cold emotional state of the environment. No one reacts with the sudden influx of death. There's no panic—no media. Everyone goes about their day with a smile and a "that's a shame" attitude. Marge perhaps sums it up best when she first arrives on the scene of the dead state trooper, frozen on the side of the road. She says, "Looks like a nice enough guy. It's a real shame." She expresses sorrow regarding the dead trooper, but remains surprisingly cold when addressing the execution of a father and daughter. Though she's the loving center of the film, she still reflects the region by remaining surprisingly emotionally disconnected from the situation. Even after inspecting the bodies, Marge is professional enough, calm enough to remember to buy night crawlers for Norm. Her life continues.

Marge eventually interacts with the press, but, despite the gruesome nature of the triple homicide, the Coens avoid splashing newspaper headlines or tuning into the six o'clock news for the viewers. Instead, this information surfaces through Mike Yanagita, who calls Marge unexpectedly in the middle of the night to tell her he saw her on TV. This leads to perhaps the oddest scene and most pathetic Coen character: Mike. They later meet for lunch at the Ramada and Mike breaks down in tears, leaving Marge speechless for the first time. The scene has no bearing on the story, but it allows Marge to act outside of the criminal story, expressing a life she once had. She's a caring person and attempts to comfort Mike even after his attempts to seduce her. The episode plays awkward and uncomfortable, but it's a necessary addition to help express that Marge is not just playing the good cop. She truly does care for her world.

Like a standard investigational, docu-noir crime movie, several sequences show Marge interviewing suspects. These dually serve as comedy and information, and display Marge's ability to control a situation. Her two interviews with Jerry at the dealership showcase the genuineness that Marge exudes, but they also display Jerry's level of amateur criminal. With every question, Jerry can only stare back, as if trying to comprehend why a cop sits across from him. Also, her two encounters with hardened convicts exhibit her natural quality. Unable to physically threaten the men, she talks like a disapproving mother. With Shep Proudfoot, a massive ex-con who works as a mechanic in Jerry's garage, she lectures and questions him, threatening discipline like a high school principal. Shep barely utters a word, but Marge never falters. Much like Columbo, she defeats opponents through conversation, locking them down and leaving them no room to maneuver.

The final few scenes of *Fargo* add a sense of realism that molds the entire story together and connects Marge's family life to her job. Loving by nature, she sees beauty in the world despite the encompassing violence. In particular, the scenes with Marge and Gaear reverse the viewer's expectations of a crime climax. Clearly, having a massively pregnant police office chase down a brutal murderer as he stuffs his partner into a wood chipper in the snow seems ripe for a clichéd confrontation. The Coens, nevertheless, present the scene without humor, never mentioning the pregnancy and avoiding sexuality completely. Marge stands firmly in opposition to him and points to her badge for clarification. Gaear, for all his blank, frightening stares, bolts at the first sign of capture. Instead of the evil villain attacking, sneering, or taunting, he can only aimlessly throw a log and run in desperation in his long underwear across a frozen pond. He's the same cold blooded killer from earlier, but when faced with capture, he resorts to natural survival instincts to escape, erasing any chance for a mano a mano battle. Remaining professional, she wounds him in the leg, not in the head or chest. It's an end without action, without a chase through snowy trees or across a shattered frozen lake. The showdown exhibits a non-climatic, but realistic ending.

As Marge drives Gaear back into Brainerd, she can't help but continue to glance in the rearview mirror at the stoic Gaear sitting handcuffed, staring blankly back at her. Marge, unfamiliar with his world, strives to understand the situation: "And for what? A little bit of money. There's more to life than a little money. Don't you know that? And here ya are. And it's a beautiful day. Well . . . I just don't understand it." She not only questions Gaear's motives, but all male characters; they're unable to separate themselves from their greed and the violence they inflict. To Marge, with her simple, authentic lifestyle, Gaear's carnage won't interfere with her lifestyle or affect the way she approaches her police work. The final scene in *Fargo* supports this point. As Marge and Norm curl up in bed and drift off to sleep together, Marge states how proud she is of Norm. After all, embodying the role of the motherly figure, she nurtures Norm's ego when his painting wins a contest to be featured on the three cent stamp. They proclaim their love for one another and focus on their developing child. Though violence erupted within her small town of Brainerd, Marge and the region did not allow it to uproot their values and morals.

Marge does not appear until 32 minutes into *Fargo,* and her character's emergence comes as a surprise because, until that point, the focus was on Jerry Lundegaard. After the brutal deaths of the state trooper and the innocent bystanders by Gaear's hand, a shot of painted ducks in Marge's warm home serves as a transition to normalcy for the audience. In the Gunderson home, crime and kidnapped wives have yet to enter, and it never does enter even after the phone rings to inform Marge of the crimes. Once awake, a reversal of roles happens. Marge is called into work early in the morning and Norm emerges as the cook, concerned that Marge might be leaving with an empty stomach. Norm remains at home to paint while his wife heads out to investigate a series of murders; the Gunderson's never discuss the crime. Norm never expresses fear for his wife. It's her job and she's good at it.

CARL AND GAEAR:
"ASK THOSE POOR SOULS UP IN BRAINERD IF A DEAL'S A DEAL!"

If characters reflect the setting of *Fargo*, then the towering statue of Paul Bunyan and Babe the Blue Ox reflect the film's criminals. The image of the legendary Bunyan, dressed in flannel and resting his mighty axe on his shoulder, carries with it not just an eerie feeling, but it emanates dual meanings. Gaear, in his near mythical silence and brutality, emerges as a character bigger than life by killing his partner with an axe and disposing of him via modern tree equipment. Also, Bunyan emits two personalities as a statue. In the daylight, he, with his mighty axe, acts as the protector of the area. At night, however, the shadows play against his strong features, creating a massive monster similar to Gaear,[8] for whom the night brings bad things. Despite the mythical connection to the Paul Bunyan statue, Carl and Gaear emerge as the catalysts, propelling the film's violence and greed. They represent a chaotic, modern America penetrating small town purity and bringing hell with them. They're unlucky, urban, two-bit common criminals set loose in Brainerd, embodying the noir city unleashed in Middle America. They create an invasion of tension and horror into a way of life they don't understand.

Carl and Gaear emerge as more than crime clichés, acting naturally and realistically even if they fall to certain common stereotypes. Carl is the slimy negotiator who believes he's smoother and more intelligent than he really is; Gaear is the enforcer, the intimidator, the brute. They work as common thugs in search of work. Both men display true emotions at times, and behave not as blood thirsty murderers, but men driven by greed in search of that one big score. Greed-based violence just happens to be a tool to complete that deal. At the same time, Carl and Gaear act like a dysfunctional family unit, and it doesn't take long to establish the inner workings of the pair. Carl, the smaller, more feminine one, does all the talking, all the leg work, all the bill paying, and all the negotiating. Gaear acts like a union husband, carrying out muscle work. He accomplishes the set goal and expects immediate compensation. They, like Jerry and Jean, lack the proper communication needed to achieve business and financial success as Carl and Gaear allow greed and ego to derail their partnership just as Jerry derailed his marriage.

Of the two, Carl represents the most realistic, a complex character unwilling to accept whatever situation in which he finds himself. In some regards, Carl and Jerry reflect each other, because Carl resembles a used car salesman, believing he can talk his way out of anything. Also, both he and Jerry find themselves suffering from abuse, continually beaten down emotionally or physically, unable to overcome simple obstacles, and unable to project a positive outcome. Each time they create an alternative path, something appears that they're incapable of enduring. Regardless, Carl commands a "sociable nature, normal appetites, a capacity for acknowledging genuine horror, and a desire to preserve, as much as possible, balance and even civility."[9] A low-life for sure, he remains relatable in every situation, even when he shoots Wade. At the beginning, when Jerry first arrives at the King of Clubs, Carl does all the talking, playing the fast-talking grifter and asking all the relevant questions the audience yearns to know: "You want us to kidnap your own wife?" Carl, using simple logic, ascertains Jerry's motivation and becomes the only character to question the morality of Jerry's plan. But why wouldn't Carl recognize this? Of all the characters in *Fargo,* Jerry and Carl most closely mirror each other. They just live different lifestyles. Neither act happy nor satisfied with their place in life, and they remain willing to do anything to escape.

Carl consistently appears to be the outsider from his dress to his mannerisms. He's the ultimate cheapskate, even arguing a four-dollar charge for scouting out a parking lot. Later, when Carl believes Jerry owes them the full $80,000 once "blood has been shed," Carl collects the ransom, kills Wade, and finds the full one million. Greed overtakes him. He could have easily given Gaear his half of the $40,000 and paid Gaear for half of the Cutlass that Gaear demanded. He refused despite having the funds by earning roughly $960,000. He won't part with it on principle. Carl believes he's a master thief and attempts to exhibit nonexistent sophistication. One scene shows Carl outside his world with Gaear when he takes an escort out to dinner. When she asks what he does for a living, he has no cover story for his line of work, avoiding the question all together and asking if she has been to the bar before "with other, uh, clients?" He's not smart enough to lie. One scene in particular effectively defines Carl. It comes after he and Gaear snatch Jean and drive toward their hideout with her in the backseat. As a state trooper pulls them over, Carl ineffectively attempts to intimidate Jean: "Let's keep still back there, lady, or we're gonna have to, you know, to shoot ya." He threatens without authority, searching for menacing words. Carl remains confident in his gift of gab. He thinks he can talk his way out of the situation, and he tells Gaear that he'll take care of the problem by attempting to bribe the trooper with 50 bucks. Seconds later, the trooper hears something and leans into the car. Then Carl witnesses the level of violence Gaear can emit when he reaches across Carl, grabs the trooper, and shoots him once in the head. Blood spackles the inside of the car. Gaear eases back into his seat without reacting, his cigarette still dangling from his lips. Carl, his face splattered in blood, is left nearly speechless at the sight. He expresses the only reaction to raw violence in the movie, uttering, "Whoa, Daddy." The movie changes after this bloody eruption when violence acts like a virus, spreading throughout the characters as greed drives them to protect their deals.

Like all classic pairings, Gaear holds opposite qualities from his partner. Near mute with a deadpan, zombie stare, he resembles the culture that surrounds him, appearing to be of Viking decent and fitting perfectly into the cold environment. His arctic emotions create an extension that reflects both the surroundings and the local people. Ethan describes him as, "an outsider in relation to the milieu, but at the same time he maintains ethnic bonds with it."[10] Most of the characters, while more jovial and friendly, display no sympathy for the victims—nothing shocks. Gaear's first display of violence that erupts with the shooting of the state trooper serves not just as an introduction to brutality, but it is one of the few times he shows annoyance. As he smokes his cigarette after the shooting, he can only chastise Carl: "You'll take care of it. Boy, you are smooth, smooth, you know." Acting like a union laborer, he cannot be bothered with cleaning up his mess. This instant ability to relax defines his killer nature, foreshadowing the Coens' return to the psychopath in *No Country for Old Men*'s Anton Chigurh. Both men kill with their own sense of ethics, but Gaear, in comparison, remains driven by greed, surpassed by Chigurh's lack of motivation in his murders.

* * *

Critic Roger Ebert states in his original review of the film, "To watch it is to experience steadily mounting delight, as you realize the filmmakers have taken enormous risks, gotten away with them and made a movie that is completely original, and as familiar as an old shoe—or a rubber soled hunting boot from Land's End, more likely."[11] Risks are an excellent way of putting it, because the Coens strive to drive each film in new directions. Here, they maintain that idea but a risk remained. The comedy could have overtaken the violence. The northern character of *Fargo* could have been used for fodder. And, even worse than that, audiences could have rejected the accents, as it's not an L.A. or New York crime drama and does not display the usual dark character nature that has come to be expected. It could be argued that the film isn't a crime drama in the first place; therefore, it can reject the conventions of the genre. But darkness happens—a reminder that the world is a tough and perverse place, even in the purity of *Fargo*.

When *Fargo* opened for American audiences in 1996, few could have predicted that a small kidnapping film set in the snowy north would have cemented the Coens' careers so soon after the box office failure that was *The Hudsucker Proxy*. At that time, the brothers were nothing more than a critical sideshow attraction of sorts. They were artists known for their amusing, inventive scripts; quirky characters; and elaborate settings. Then came *Fargo*, which gained not just national acclaim and reestablished their credibility, but gained Oscar gold as well. The film won for Best Original Screenplay, and Frances McDormand won a statue for Best Actress. The Coens manufactured something wholly original to American cinema, and it took them from their status as mere idiosyncratic, independent artists to filmmakers.

7

Abiding by Chandler

The Big Lebowski (1998)

"The Dude abides."[1]

CAST: Jeff Bridges (The Dude), John Goodman (Walter Sobchak), Julianne Moore (Maude), Steve Buscemi (Donny), David Huddleston (Jeffrey Lebowski), Philip Seymour Hoffman (Brandt), Tara Reid (Bunny), Peter Stormare (Nihilist), John Turturro (Jesus Quintana), Jon Polito (Da Fino), and Sam Elliott (The Stranger).

The Big Lebowski. Directed by Joel Coen. Universal City, CA: Universal Studios Home Entertainment, 1998.

When Jeffrey "The Dude" Lebowski returns home after writing a 69-cent check for milk at the grocery store, a pair of thugs ambush him, demanding money. No simple robbery, these men want a debt repaid that supposedly his wife owes to a local pornographer. And now he must pay. They assault and torture him, submerging his head in a urine-stained toilet until he answers. Once the thugs finally glance around Dude's home, it dawns on them that he's not the wealthy husband they seek. It seems there's another Jeffrey Lebowski out there. Before they depart, they urinate on Dude's rug, drop his bowling ball on his tiled bathroom floor, and say, "Thanks a lot, asshole."

Thus begins *The Big Lebowski* and Dude's entanglement in the mistaken violence that occurs throughout the film: he is beaten by thugs, is pushed around by chauffeurs, is knocked unconscious by art thugs, is drugged by a pornographer, has a coffee cup bounced off his forehead by the Malibu Chief of Police, is threatened with castration by nihilists, and has his vehicle utterly destroyed. Despite Dude's non-violent and subdued personality, he finds himself entangled in the world of film noir while simply trying to receive compensation for his rug. The abuse Dude suffers is his rite of passage as a detective, even if he doesn't know he's portraying one. It's a case of mistaken violence, but for Dude it doesn't matter. He can only abide by whatever comes his way, violent or not.

The Coens, for all their quirky and unique creations throughout their careers, finally created their own cult classic with *The Big Lebowski*, forging a place at "the high table of classic cult films"[2] The term *cult classic* suggests a film largely ignored by mainstream audiences, but revered by a rabid fan base who keep the movie alive and elevate it to another level. They are films that have endured while more successful box office releases have largely faded from public view. Cult classics contain an intangible quality impossible to duplicate with the proper concoction of cast, story, characters, setting, and timing—everything that *The Big Lebowski* includes. In a *Rolling Stone* article reflecting on the legend of the film, Philip Seymour Hoffman feels, "There's a freedom to *The Big Lebowski*. The Dude abides, and I think that's something people really yearn for, to be able to live their life like that."[3] Whatever the reasons, the movie slowly built a unique and dedicated fan base and became legendary with annual festivals dedicated to bowling, White Russians, and jelly slippers.[4] As seen in *Fargo*, *The Big Lebowski* taps into the common man, but instead of inheriting its greed-based violence, *The Big Lebowski* addresses the inner laziness that the common man inherently buries, and creates a hero to lead people out of their non-lazy burial grounds. But to do so, he must endure the violence of the detective genre, even if it's not meant for him.

Despite the goofy concept, *The Big Lebowski* reaffirms the Coens' ability to recycle classic material into a wholly original idea in their best exercise since *Miller's Crossing*, which found its influence from Hammett. While that film remained loyal to Hammett's work, *The Big Lebowski* represents the Coens' greatest accomplishment in recycling material to create a modernization of Chandler's classic noir novel, *The Big Sleep*. The film, without officially adapting Chandler, keeps most key elements in place with loose women, drugs, sex, and a powerful, wheelchair-bound man. The initial plot has little impact on the story; as with the conventions of the detective genre, the actual plot takes a back seat to the characters. Joel explains, "The story, if you reduced it to the plot, would seem rather ridiculous or uninteresting. And it's the same with a lot of Chandler—the plots are there to drive the characters."[5] Likewise, in remaining true to Chandler, the characters remain non-conventional. Chandler's creation, Philip Marlowe, helped define detective fiction, so it seems fitting that the Coens reconstructed that character to represent Dude, someone incapable of maintaining a job or having the discipline to follow leads, track people, or effectively intimidate with violence. This isn't the first adaptation of Marlowe. Thirty some years earlier, Robert Altman first modernized him in 1973's *The Long Goodbye*, with Elliot Gould "cast as an insouciant anti-Marlowe."[6] But in that film, Marlowe still existed as he did before, just in a new era with a new attitude. The Coens removed Marlowe's attributes and motivations all together from the noir world and placed his character within the Dude in his very own slob-noir.[7]

The Coens remain true to the notion of the average man in average settings by removing (despite a Los Angeles backdrop) *The Big Lebowski* from any recognizable hardboiled world. The film creates a restructured image of L.A., while remaining loyal to Chandler.[8] In place of a concrete jungle, thunderstorms brewing in the distance, and moody alleyways, come the thundering strikes of the bowling alley—the essence of average. In the face of tragedy, violence, or even death, the Dude and his friends always respond with, "Let's go bowling." The bowling alley is their dank bar, their seedy motel, their dark alley. The Coens present the bowling alley with a sense of beauty. It is a place that unites a variety of people with a sport where, while participating, one can smoke a cigarette and drink a beer. Higher social classes have their country clubs and golf courses, but the alley is the common man's club, a place where people can discuss the "strikes and gutters, ups and downs" of life. Crime films always show the hard streets reflecting the violence of the characters, but the bowling alleys gleam on their own.

Within this new Chandler L.A., every character in *The Big Lebowski*, vicious or not, remains haunted by a violent past, unable to escape its grasp and live freely in the modern world. *The Big Lebowski* acts a period piece of sorts, set in the early 1990s during Operation Desert Storm; it performs as a contemporary movie about people who were formed and defined by a certain period. Regardless, each character lives in a different era that has nothing to do with the cliché of modern Los Angeles. The Dude is a 1960s burnout. Walter cannot leave Vietnam behind. The other Lebowski lost his ability to walk during the Korean War, and he still despises hippies like Dude. Lebowski's daughter, Maude, lives in a faded avant-garde world. Even the nihilists cling to an idea long since dead. Each character emerges stuck in the past, unwilling or unable to change who they are or the way they live.

If characters cannot change, neither can the detective genre, which comes with the expected violence required for proper suspense. The combination of comedy and the lightly-toned mistaken violence of *The Big Lebowski* reflect the comedic sadism of *Raising Arizona;* each remains comical until a graphic conclusion. Whereas *Raising Arizona* blows up a man at the end, *The Big Lebowski* finally unleashes Walter from his restricted chain causing him to disarm the three nihilists by breaking one's ribs with a bowling ball, biting the ear off of another, and knocking the last one cold with their techno-blaring radio. If Dude rejects violence, then he must have an opposite, someone capable of violence and erratic behavior at any moment. Walter, for all his crazed conversations, never flinches when his family faces potential danger.

Up until that point, most of the violence is inflicted upon Dude (he's not immune to the detective genre). After all, a detective film without brutality would insult the tradition of bullied private eyes like Marlowe, Sam Spade, Mike Hammer, or the Continental Op, all of whom suffer at the hands of their opposition. Dude—unlike those detectives who simultaneously received and delivered punishment—cannot abide by this rule. He rejects violence in his own lazy, passive way. If he suddenly exhibited aggression, if he kicked in doors or physically fought villains, then he would cease to be the Dude.

The bad guys do their worst in a continual assault of Dude. Two of the lashings he receives result in him being knocked unconscious, producing two distinctive dream sequences. In the first one, after Dude's second rug is stolen, he soars through the air while Maude flies off on his magic rug. But he can't catch her and his rug is gone. The second dream sequence incorporates a complete Busby Berkeley-inspired dance sequence with Dude as a porno-influenced cable repair man and Maude in full Viking apparel.

Nevertheless, the violence all results from a case of mistaken identity in which everyone believes Dude is someone he's not. No matter what's exacted upon him, Dude cannot and will not subscribe to violence. Walter can, though. He exudes intimidation as he threatens a fellow bowler with a pistol, smashes another man's Corvette, verbally abuses everyone he encounters, and even throws a crippled man to the ground. Walter is the embodiment of chaos, bringing violence into the bowling alley. He's a walking misplaced threat, and, while no one mistakes Walter for a detective, his aggression, his anger, his violence is all mistaken. He's employed as Dude's muscle, even if Dude never hired him.

JEFFREY "THE DUDE" LEBOWSKI: "*ALL THE DUDE EVER WANTED WAS HIS RUG BACK*"

If *Fargo* gave audiences the Coens' most inventive character in Marge Gunderson, then the Dude emerges as their most iconic. His philosophy and lifestyle have spawned legions of fans who worship him as a role model of sorts. Not that people aspire for joblessness and laziness, but they desire his complete happiness as they see him completely content, blind to the pressures of the modern world. Opposed to violence, Dude relaxes at will and exhibits complete freedom without delivering moral judgments on what's right and wrong. He never worries about money, employment, or social status, and he only cares for bowling, White Russians, marijuana, and friends. Like all Coen leads, Dude has no definitive background beyond a loose recollection of rebellious college days and working as a roadie for Metallica. With no noticeable ambition or desire, Dude focuses all his interest in bowling, where social releases roll together: entertainment, social network, and passion. Little else matters even though the Coens never once show Dude throwing a single bowling ball.

If Dude is in fact, as the Stranger accurately narrates, "Quite possibly the laziest in Los Angeles County," then he embodies the hippie revolution, never giving in to conformity. Like all the film's characters, Dude cannot leave the past behind. As the other Jeffrey Lebowski explains to Dude, "Your revolution is over, Mr. Lebowski!" But Lebowski is wrong. The Dude continues to revolt against the system, whether he's in style or not. He rebels against stereotypical Los Angeles vanity and ego, against social expectations, against society's call for marriage and procreation, and against excess. He doesn't give a damn what someone like Lebowski thinks, and he will not lash out violently no matter what insults he incurs. Instead, he believes in and practices meditative states. At one point, he soaks in a bathtub, surrounded by candles, and smokes pot. Whale songs echo on cassette in the background. In another instance, he lays on his new, unsoiled rug, listening to a cassette of Venice Beach League Player from 1987 with complete serenity inscribed on his face. He's blind to the influence of Los Angeles fashion, because to him it doesn't matter. His car, an early seventies junker, represents anything but a status symbol. His only item for which he exhibits pride is the rug that "really tied the room together." The rug is the lone room accessory in a home completely void of such frills, except, of course, for his poster of President Nixon throwing a strike.

With Dude playing detective, whether he wants to or not, he needs someone to bounce around ideas and offer counter-points in order to be effective. Just as Sherlock Holmes has John Watson, Dude has Walter, but without the positive results. No matter how hellish Walter makes life for Dude or how often he demonstrates he's incapable of playing detective, Dude continues to confide in his massive, unpredictable, and combustible Vietnam vet friend. Dude—a pacifist from the Vietnam era—never sees the irony that comes from his relationship with Walter. Dude lived a life void of violence, but his best friend creates a chaotic tidal wave, leaving a trail of carnage in his wake.

Somehow, Dude looks at Walter's violent tendencies and asinine mistakes as if they are mere annoyances, because their bond appears unbreakable. For every occasion that Walter complicates matters, the Dude forgives him. After Donny's death at the end of the film, Dude and Walter stand by the sea and share their most revealing, intimate moment. Walter delivers the eulogy only to derail into another Vietnam tirade. As he releases Donny's ashes into the air, they blow back, covering Dude. Frustrated and disgusted, Dude demonstrates his first violent outbreak: he shoves Walter. Everything Walter had done up to that moment results in a rare flash of anger from Dude, but it immediately subsides as Walter hangs his head and whispers a simple "I'm sorry." They embrace in an awkward hug, a moment they both need even if they're unable to fully express emotions. The two men—completely opposite in every possible regard except for bowling—respect, love, and fully trust one another, despite Dude so accurately saying, "I love you, Walter, but sooner or later you're gonna have to face the fact that you're a goddamn moron!" Walter can push Dude to the brink of violence, but to actually become aggressive would violate his character.

Most passive viewers might not envision Dude as a detective even with the endless barrage of mistaken genre violence. The laziest man in Los Angeles portraying a hero isn't completely apparent to the audience, because Dude's moral fibers are the opposite of someone like Marlowe. The Coens use Chandler's novel to construct a fish-out-of-water tale, altering the audience's idea of the detective. Despite the insanity that surrounds Dude and regardless of his sudden hero status, Dude remains true to his convictions. As the Stranger narrates, "Sometimes there's a man—I won't say a hero, 'cause what's a hero? [. . .] He's the man for his time 'n place. He fits right in there. And that's the Dude, in Los Angeles." The Dude can only be himself, just as "Philip Marlowe is a man of wit and honor, common yet unusual man, a lonely and proud man, and even, in a sense, a 'man of his age.'"[9] If Dude doesn't embody those characteristics, then no character ever has. What makes *The Big Lebowski* distinctive comes from its removal of Marlowe as the knight-in-blue-suit-armor detective; Dude is not a cynical private eye in search of justice. The Coens eliminated all elements of the original as if recasting Humphrey Bogart from *The Big Sleep* with Charlie Chaplin. Dude seems far removed, like *Fargo*'s Marge Gunderson, from the standard, tough detective. While Marge at least exhibits positive sleuth qualities and demonstrates that she will pull out and use her firearm, Dude exemplifies the Coen template for non-violent, loser leads—men who refuse to mature or fully embrace the adult world. Unemployed, unmotivated, and uninterested in life, Dude has no reason to accomplish anything if it's not a league night. Even the Coens' most passive characters—such as *The Man Who Wasn't There*'s Ed Crane—display desires and ambitions. The Dude exhibits no such lust. He is a complete anomaly considering the L.A. setting.

As *The Big Lebowski* progresses, Dude's hidden detective attributes surface in various forms. He imitates not just Marlowe, but a variety of characters and methods. In particular, like Holmes's famed seven-percent cocaine solution drug addiction in times of boredom, Dude maintains a state of constant intoxication to keep his mind "limber." For Dude to function, to perform and challenge his mind, he needs a drug fix much like the literary detective great needed to keep his mind challenged. Compared to other Coen characters, Dude shares commonalities with *Miller's Crossing*'s Tom Reagan, another addicted rebel. Both remain in a constantly intoxicated state, unable to function properly without some form of libation. Neither plays within the established system, finding ways to survive despite themselves. And while violence surrounds both men, neither acts out until pushed too far (granted, Tom does kill, but only in the end in his only violent outburst). Even the true P.I. of *The Big Lebowski*, Da Fino, who's been sent to search for Bunny by her Minnesota parents, mentions, "I dig your work!" Da Fino references the plot from *Miller's Crossing* of playing one side against the other. Clearly, he had not payed close enough attention to Dude's work.

And, like Holmes or Marge, Dude is instantly recognizable by his dress, wearing a uniform of his own creation: a tattered robe, sunglasses, shorts, jelly slippers, with a White Russian in hand. He is not exactly Chandler's Marlowe who was "everything a well-dressed private detective ought to be."[10] Holmes, Marge, and Marlowe, all dress in a way that reflects their detective abilities: Holmes dresses efficiently, Marge commonly, and Marlowe, despite wearing a professional suit and tie, can't hide his hangover. The Dude's sloppy appearance balances his lackluster ability. If he had decided to alter his appearance to play detective like Walter later does, Dude would rebuff his unique sensibilities.

At no point does Dude ever declare himself a detective; nonetheless, he slowly evolves into a sleuth as he starts to uncover clues and reveal information. Initially, he exhibits detective traits without calling attention to them, as his realization of Bunny's self-kidnapping plot appears only to forward the story. After he and Walter ruin the money exchange with the kidnappers, Dude attempts to report his findings to the other Lebowski, revealing the complicated nature of the mystery. When Lebowski questions the rambling comment, Dude replies, "I'll tell you what I'm blathering about! I've got information, man—new shit has come to light. And shit, man! She kidnapped herself!" The Dude discovers his new found skill even if he's incapable of explaining it. At this point, he begins to speak in detective terms and contemplates situations. During a report to Maude, he explains the complicated nature of such a case: "Lotta ins. Lotta outs. Lotta what-have-yous. And a lotta strands to keep in my head, man." His first actual clue uncovered comes after his car and the money are stolen, leading him and Walter to interview teenager Larry Sellers. Later, while at the home of pornographer Jackie Treehorn, Dude once again attempts to play detective in what is perhaps his first true sleuth moment. When Treehorn receives a call, writes a note, and leaves the room, Dude scrambles to the phone and shades a pencil over a notepad for pertinent information. Unfortunately, his work only reveals an exaggerated drawing of a penis. Not exactly a pertinent clue. Lastly, in classical detective form, Dude recounts the mysteries of the film and reveals all his findings in a montage of events. He uncovers the sinister scheme without ever sporting a Fedora or resorting to violence for answers. Dude has Walter for that.

WALTER SOBCHAK:
"YOU'RE ENTERING A WORLD OF PAIN"

If Dude and Walter represent a dysfunctional duo, then Walter seems like the classic vulgar family member, unable to accomplish the simplest task and finding trouble without looking. He creates it. Stubborn, overbearing, and unforgiving, the trouble never bothers him personally, but it disrupts everyone around him, notably Dude. After all, every situation Dude encounters comes as a direct result of Walter, starting with the initial search for reimbursement for his ruined rug. Walter propels Dude from one scenario to the next. Regardless of the anarchy Walter brings, he acts as Dude's confidante; Walter is the one he discusses the case with and seeks advice from. Why Dude would ask someone as unstable and mentally fragile as Walter for advice remains the unanswered question, but their love/hate relationship seems to be based not just on a passion for bowling, but an unbreakable friendship that disregards any carnage created.

Walter emerges as perhaps the most disturbed and deepest character—a man haunted by his violent past, unable to move on from a number of situations that shaped his psyche. Emotionally unstable yet protective and loyal, Walter is antithetical to Dude in every respect except a few. The clearest connection between the men comes from bowling. It is their central focus in life as their lives revolve around the lanes. Dude even uses the threat of quitting the team as the ultimate bluff against Walter, something they both know they cannot afford to lose. Beyond the alley, Dude and Walter also both exhibit a lack of ego and lack of excess. They're content with life. Aside from those commonalities, they remain utter opposites. Walter, unlike Dude, works. He owns and operates his own security business. Unlike Dude's free-spirited hippie roots, Walter is uptight and irritable, unable to move beyond Vietnam—the event that most shaped Walter. Dude, in his eminent wisdom, sums up Walter's curse: "What the fuck does Vietnam have to do with anything?" No matter the situation, no matter the context, Walter inserts the war into every conversation. He cannot speak without relating the situation to his past experiences in Vietnam—as if people still protest in the streets, reminding him at every turn. Of course, Dude represents that rebellion against the war and its violence, but Walter cannot relinquish his history of service and never misses an opportunity to remind others of his service.

Scarred by the violence of war, he's also broken by a divorce, expressing regret about his inability to sustain the relationship. Walter cannot move on and continues to watch his ex-wife's dog while she vacations with her boyfriend. He even continues to practice her religion despite being raised Polish Catholic. When Dude questions this by claiming that Walter lives in the past, Walter defends his stance by outlining the tradition of the Jewish faith. Moreover, Walter exhibits the most moral and ethical standards in a film about people without ethos. Such as in the military or in religion, rules must apply whether legal or social. Walter pulls a pistol on fellow bowler, Smokey, when he crosses the line, threatening to shoot him if he doesn't mark his card properly. He also refuses to bowl on the Jewish holiday of Shabbas. In the end, during the final battle with the nihilists, their lack of order becomes their undoing as they fail to adhere to the rules of a ransom. It's Walter's sense of retribution for what's right and wrong that sends Dude for repayment of the rug in the first place.

At the same time, Walter's relationship with bowling team member, Donny, is hostile. He never allows Donny to enter a conversation, or, for that matter, to speak at all. Every point of interjection from Donny results in a, "Shut the fuck up, Donny!" or "Donny, you're out of your element!" Regardless of the abrasive conversation, he gives hints of a fatherly love toward Donny. Actor Steve Buscemi believes, "I'm not quite sure how Donny fits in there, but I do think that he's loved by these guys, and that Walter loves him like a brother, and that's why he's able to treat him so badly at times."[11] Regardless of the verbal abuse, the final battle with the nihilists demonstrates Walter's fatherly, loving side toward Donny. A fear-ridden Donny asks Walter questions, not the Dude, and looks to Walter for protection. Also, for the first time, Walter expresses care for his friend and acts as a guardian for his small soldier. He stands in front of him and Dude to reassure safety: "They won't hurt us, Donny. These men are cowards." As the battle begins, we finally understand the truth behind Walter's wrath. He is the soldier of fortune he claimed to be, able to inflict the carnage he continually threatens to unleash, even if it's all mistaken violence since neither Dude and his men nor the nihilists have anything to do with the kidnapping.

While Dude mistakenly embodies the attributes of the detective, Walter envisions himself a sleuth and savors the opportunity. At Dude's landlord's one-man show, Walter suddenly appears with eager anticipation in a suit and tie—a far cry from his usual uniform of vests, shorts, and boots—to deliver reconnaissance information about who stole Dude's car. His transition comes with the sense of adventure and enthusiasm one expects from a new detective, everything Dude lacks. Walter's excitement begins just as Dude assumes the Marlowe/Holmes-type hero. Walter dishes opinions and ideas whether or not they are beneficial, or even wanted. When trouble arises, it's Walter who beats the streets for information. It's Walter who acts as sadistic enforcer. It's Walter who conducts interviews. Alone, Dude would never have advanced in the search, but the addition of Walter as a partner creates a two-headed detective able to fully examine situations. Together, they function as one part collected, one part unchecked aggression.

In a sense, Walter's persona changes as the movie progresses, starting when he automatically includes himself as the driver/bagman. He becomes the persuasive, abusive investigator, and forces his militaristic plan on Dude while dressed like a plump Rambo complete with an Uzi in preparation for battle. As a detective, Walter seems more capable of the job considering his military background and his security company, but during their interview with Larry Sellers, Walter's attempted professionalism unravels when the teen won't answer his questions. He reverts to the explosive vet, threatening Larry that he will soon "enter a world of pain."

Despite his gruff and confrontational exterior, Walter's a lonely, pathetic individual. He has obvious, glaring flaws as a person, yet he never hesitates to remind others of theirs. However, his lack of compassion hurts his ability to operate as a pseudo-detective in some regards. He erases his memory of the botched job for which he was supposed to deliver the money immediately. When Dude asks how he'll explain the loss of the money to the Big Lebowski, Walter answers, "What exactly is the problem?" Walter refuses to take blame for his own actions even when Bunny could have been killed. The Dude sits at the lanes depressed and broken, while Walter mocks the situation via song about how they've killed that poor woman. Together, the duo solve the mystery, but separate, neither man effectively can function in their role as detective, whether they employ brutality or not.

THE LITTLE LEBOWSKIS: *"ARE YOU EMPLOYED, MR. LEBOWSKI?"*

The Big Lebowski boasts an impressive array of supporting players that not only add to the surreal nature of the film, but end up just as memorable as the Dude himself. Characters appear and disappear without thought, which again refers back to the Chandler influence. As Joel admits, "Like in a Chandler novel, the hero sets out to clear up a mystery and while doing so visits a lot of odd characters who spring up like Jack-in-the-boxes."[12] Every character in *The Big Lebowski* possesses a particular quirk that's not just intended to be comedic, but also to further the examination of Los Angeles' melting pot. Failed actors, porn stars, artists, con men, pedophiles, pacifists, loners, cowboys—Los Angeles has them all.

The family of the Big Lebowski (the other Jeffrey Lebowski) resembles that of a bad soap opera with a young, former porn star mother-in-law, a feminist, avant-garde artist daughter, and lastly Brandt, Lebowski's parrot assistant. Beyond Brandt, none of the family members interact with each other, but each affects the others' affairs. Bunny terrorizes her husband with her nymphomaniacal activities. Maude controls the family fortune despite her father's claims. Lebowski controls and manipulates the image of the family. He has allowed greed and vanity to dictate his actions; he acts like a figure head, brooding, demanding, but without any real power. Emerging as the only greed-based character, Lebowski is unable or unwilling to compromise, to leave his past life behind despite not having any money of his own. He's willing to destroy the life of another man (Dude) when the opportunity presents itself. On the other hand, Bunny, the catalyst behind everything within *The Big Lebowski*, appears to be the most stereotypical and hollow character without a redeeming quality. Even with the unveiling of her background as a runaway farm kid from Minnesota, the Coens treat the information as just another narrative twist, never explaining how she married such a man. Alternately, Maude remains just as cold and emotionless as her father. She is also the character who most reflects L.A. by hanging around video directors and practicing extreme art by flying past canvases and spraying paint on them while nude. And with so many characters living in the past, it's suitable that Maude mimics a character removed from an indistinguishable past decade. She talks with a European accent and is a woman with power, unafraid to use her assistants like goons at her will.

For a detective movie taking place in seedy L.A., *The Big Lebowski* lacks any threatening or intimidating characters such as in *The Maltese Falcon,* or even *The Big Sleep,* or someone truly sinister from *Chinatown.* The Coens avoid leaving the antagonistic role vacant, by introducing a collection of dim-witted characters all battling for the adversary position. The initial, rug-peeing thugs emit no true threat, and their boss, porn king Jackie Treehorn, only appears in one sequence in a role similar to a James Bond-villain. The story thread about Treehorn and his men remains largely incomplete. After all, once they realize there's another Lebowski, why don't they simply visit the richer man to demand the money? That leaves the Nihilists as potential antagonists. They're members of the German pop-group, Autobahn, and, even though they claim that they believe in nothing, they participate in greed-based, mistaken violence. Comical in appearance and action, they present a serious threat by supposedly kidnapping Bunny and threatening to cut off the Dude's "Johnson" if the money for her ransom is not delivered. They impose their will, breaking into Dude's home and terrorizing him by dumping a marmot into the bathtub with him. Even if the men lack the fortitude to inflict actual violence, they are effectively intimidating.

As unimpressive as the villains are, two characters with minimal screen time emerge as possibly the most effective minor characters in the form of the Stranger and bowling nemesis, Jesus Quintana. Firstly, Sam Elliott's narrating cowboy appears in two scenes, each one at the bowling alley bar. In essence, he's there as a reflection of Dude's personality: laid-back, easy-going, with his own philosophy on life. As a cowboy, he appears to be an authority on heroism. He's the type of man who could handle and dish out violence. However, the Stranger does offer one piece of advice as the only character who comments on the amount of curse words Dude uses. Secondly, because dark alleyways in *The Big Lebowski* are transformed into the wooden lanes of a bowling alley, at least one character of conflict must appear there. Despite the presence of the Dude and his team, Jesus steals every one of his three scenes, including a flashback to him as he walks door-to-door revealing his sex offender status to his neighbors. A purple-jump-suit-wearing rival to the Dude's bowling team, he not only adds Latino flair to Los Angeles, but also allows space for Turturro's eccentrics. Like Walter, he threatens others aggressively and offends them with every word he speaks. He never exhibits violence, but his words and expressions are intended to insult and coerce even if they fail.

Lastly, there's Donny, the third man in the Dude/Walter family who never gets in more than a few words before Walter crudely denies him entry into the conversation. Unlike Buscemi's character, Carl Showalter, from *Fargo* who never stopped talking, Donny's a background fixture with little more input than a potted plant. Always wandering into the middle of a conversation, he's unable to generate any of his own. Even when Donny ventures outside of the bowling alley to their interrogation of Larry Sellers, Donny's a mere observer, and, like a child, is told by Walter to wait in the car. During Walter's constant belittling of Donny, the Dude never comes to his defense; his affiliation with Donny isn't as clear. Dude rarely speaks or acknowledges him beyond a few lines. When Donny obviously notes, "Phone's ringin', Dude," Dude retorts in annoyance, "Thank you, Donny." In their family, no one bothers to include Donny, the child; he always remains the outsider to all events. When faced with violence, Donny exhibits the most realistic reactions. He's just an average guy who walks outside to find three leather-clad Germans with swords demanding money. He immediately becomes terrified and turns to the one man who could handle such potential violence—Walter. Nevertheless, not until his final scene do Dude and Walter finally take notice of Donny. One fact is known for sure: his love for bowling equals that of Walter and Dude. It encompassed his life. As a persistent strike thrower, Donny is the only bowler aside from Jesus who demonstrates his skills onscreen, and throughout the film, he never misses. Finally, when the pins don't fall in his final game, his reaction to the remaining spinning pin is one of bewilderment. He knows something appears off. After his death from a heart attack, Dude and Walter celebrate his life the only way they know how: "Aww, fuck it, Dude. Let's go bowling." They can only engage in the one activity that delivers bliss to each of them.

* * *

Released in March of 1998, *The Big Lebowski* quickly followed the path of all great cult movies by fizzling at the box office. With a budget of $15 million, it barely broke even, earning just over $17 million domestically.[13] At the time of release, no fanfare existed for the Dude and his men. Typically, critics weren't sure what to make of it. One stated "it all doesn't yield anything more than that the Coens are just messing around. And they are much funnier when they are being serious."[14] Another wrote, "Since nearly every plot twist is stupidly motivated, the audience stops following the story qua story and is reduced to watching Stupid Human Tricks."[15] Roger Ebert, usually a Coen detractor, found praise for the brothers for the second straight film, hailing it as "weirdly engaging, like its hero."[16] Regardless, when the film hit video and DVD later that year, it slowly developed an audience as fans connected with Dude's sensibilities and the chaos he encounters. Portrayed perfectly by Bridges, the Dude depicts such a simplistic lifestyle that many—if able to reject and dispel money, ambition, and love—would conduct their lives in a similar fashion. The Coens have made a career of creating unique characters of violence, and *The Big Lebowski* fully embraces that concept, delivering a movie everyone has seen before, yet one that no one has. Now, over a decade after release, *The Big Lebowski* continues to discover new life as new generations abide by the film while enjoying White Russians, robes, and an uncomplicated, non-violent life through the Coens' most beloved character to date.

8

Three Convicts and the KKK

O Brother, Where Art Thou? (2000)

"Oh Lord, I've been separated from my family for so long."[1]

CAST: George Clooney (Ulysses Everett McGill), John Turturro (Pete Hogwallop), Tim Blake Nelson (Delmar O'Donnell), John Goodman (Big Dan Teague), Holly Hunter (Penny), Chris Thomas King (Tommy Johnson), Charles Durning (Pappy O'Daniel), Ray McKinnon (Waldrip), Daniel von Bargen (Sheriff Cooley), Wayne Duvall (Homer Stokes), and Michael Badalucco (George Baby Face Nelson).

O Brother, Where Art Thou? Directed by Joel Coen. Burbank, CA: Walt Disney Video, 2000.

By the time the three escaped convicts of *O Brother, Where Art Thou?* encounter the film's villain onstage declaring that "they ain't even ol' timey," the men had endured a series of relatively unrelated events in which characters appear and vanish and storylines develop and drop. This creates a Southern tale of political campaigns, racism, power, fame, and chance encounters. The film emerges as an all-you-can-eat conglomerate: music, comedy, literature, slapstick, romance, legends, myths, and even the KKK. Compiled into a single entity, the film represents the Coens at their most inventive as they continue their tradition of redrafting previously published material. However, because they never before outwardly attribute their films to a specific inspiration, *O Brother, Where Art Thou?* marks their first admitted adaptation. They utilize the basics from Homer's *The Odyssey*, though their adaptation is far from direct. The Coens play coy: "Neither of us have read *The Odyssey*." Joel explains, "I actually read *The Iliad* in college, but *The Odyssey*, no. We read the classic comics version of it and we saw the Kirk Douglas movie of it."[2]

More of an homage than a faithful adaptation, *O Brother* includes certain characters and plucks certain characteristics and ideas from its inspiration in order to create a modern Greek tragedy, with music serving not just as a soundtrack, but as character analysis. The film jumps genres to incorporate a wide array of ideas and themes ranging from being authentically *old timey* to the continuation of oral tradition. But even with its light tone, *O Brother* still employs violence in the form of faith-based hostility. For each occurrence of brutality, the person inflicting the action believes that what he is doing is right. He justifies violence through his faith—sometimes biblical, sometimes personal. But when it erupts, each occurrence comes in episodic bursts that wrap up each individual story thread. No matter the character or situation, the conviction of faith in family, mankind, self, power, government, and in God drives all motivation and violence. If all else fails, their faith will comfort them.

Granted, the basic plot for *O Brother* doesn't sound very much like the *Odyssey*, because the convicts Everett, Pete, and Delmar break away from the chain gang in order to seek a buried treasure before the state floods its location to install a lake. But Everett's tale of a promised treasure is a lie, and the men must endure the road in order for Everett to reconnect with his estranged wife, Penelope. Along the way, their episodic adventure leads them to a blind rail man who foresees their future: from Pete's cousin who betrays them for a reward, to a river baptismal, to blues guitarist Tommy Johnson who sold his soul to the devil. The escapees, along with Johnson, record the eventual hit "I Am a Man of Constant Sorrow" as the Soggy Bottom Boys. While their song gains momentum, they cross paths with political candidates during a battle for an upcoming governor's race between governor Pappy O'Daniel and Homer Stokes, and the cons join up with famous gangster, George "Baby Face" Nelson. *The Odyssey* strands pick up once again with references to the three sirens and Cyclops in the form of Big Dan, a con artist Bible salesman. Everett finally reconvenes with Penelope, only to find she has a new love. He wins her back as the Soggy Bottom Boys finally take the stage, and Stokes reveals his role as Grand Wizard. He's ousted from the public while O'Daniel pardons the men. For Everett's family reunion to be complete, the boys must find Penelope's ring. The law finally catches up with them, and devilish Sheriff Cooley attempts to hang them only for a miracle to occur when a flood sweeps the land. The film ends with Everett once again chained, though this time to his wife and flock of children.

O Brother begins just as nearly all the Coens' films do: with an establishing shot of the landscape. And just as they had done in *Fargo* and *The Big Lebowski,* they employ trickery, toying with audience's sense of anticipation in the opening frame. *Fargo* opens with a clear sky only to become snow while *The Big Lebowski* has a tumble weed crossing through modern Los Angeles. *O Brother* opens in black and white before transitioning into a dirty tan that gives the film a dusty appearance, which reflects the Depression era and evokes a unique, old-timey look. The Mississippi Delta already allows for rich characters and environments, but as colorful as those elements appear, a great deal of the texture comes from the look of *O Brother*. Everything emerges as, for lack of a better word, genuine.

In many regards, the idea of being genuine or authentic develops as the heart of the movie leaving faith to define character and action. All elements involved, from inspirations, to characters, to actions, to music, portray themselves as something they are not. As in *Fargo*, the Coens claim that the film is based on actual events, and they employ a text to authenticate the information. Acknowledging a work as significant as *The Odyssey* adds certain credibility to the film that establishes faith among the audience (even if calling it an adaptation is ridiculous considering it only uses minor elements). *O Brother* opens with a passage from the epic poem to establish integrity: "O Muse!/Sing in me, and through me tell the story/Of that man skilled in all the ways of contending/A wanderer, harried for years on end. . ." By establishing the literary credentials of the film, it enhances the notion of oral tradition. Greek tales survived through storytelling about human tragedy. In the same respect, the characters in *O Brother* use storytelling as a part of their odyssey. Everett convinces his fellow men to escape through his tales of a buried treasure. The Soggy Bottom Boys gains popularity through word of mouth. Tommy Johnson tells the tale of selling his soul to the devil. Baby Face Nelson lives off of his persona, created by effective accounts of his escapes. Even Homer Stokes motivates and persuades the citizens of Mississippi through effective speeches. Also, the Coens give a nod to oral tradition by way of a series of montages in which Everett recites fiction by the camp fire, reenacting the characters from his tale. The Soggy Bottom Boys' performance toward the end of the film illustrates a deeper sense of storytelling as they dress for the old timey parts complete with massive, flowing beards. It all creates authenticity, not actuality, and utilizes the Greek Tragedy to play out as a 1930's style movie, which enhances the genuine quality of *O Brother*.

At various times, characters ask about the legitimism of being "old timey." Applied throughout, it surfaces most notably toward the end when Homer Stokes disrupts the Soggy Bottom Boys' performance. He screams, "These boys is not white! Hell, they ain't even ol' timey!" With their false beards and integrated band with Tommy on guitar, Stokes questions their validity as musicians, which, in turn, is probably as false as Everett's beard. Stokes's probing about the true nature of the music addresses another important element of *O Brother*. The music is perhaps the most authentic element, which carries the various tales and acts as a surrogate narrator. Songs serve as transitions from scene to scene, and each one is specifically picked to offer insight into characters and situations. Each song serves a specific purpose, connecting sequences of faith and the episodic violence.

When an interviewer asks the Coens why they placed *The Odyssey* in the rural South, Ethan could only state, "On the face of it, it's an idiotic idea, isn't it?"[3] Nevertheless, the South isn't exactly new territory for the Coen brothers after *Raising Arizona* and *Blood Simple*, but *O Brother, Where Art Thou?* moves further down the Mississippi Delta circa the Great Depression. It creates the public's perception of the rural south with only certain characters possessing the gift of intelligence, and it surrounds the characters with a snapshot of Faulkner's South (his short novel "Old Man" also seems to serve some inspiration).[4] Regardless of their claim of a single source, the brothers dice up a plethora of influences, yanking characters, pulling themes, and drafting sequences to construct an original tale.

The Coens borrow from and owe (like all chain gang films) a great debt to *I Am a Fugitive from the Chain Gang*, the 1932 masterpiece by Mervyn LeRoy. Everett might not resemble Paul Muni's character, James Allen, but his desire for freedom to reclaim his life drives both characters. They're honorable men who must survive. Likewise, the villain, Sheriff Cooley, echoes the authority figure from *Cool Hand Luke* with his stoic face and mirrored glasses. Other sequences—namely the KKK lynching celebration—resemble *The Wizard of Oz*. The very episodic nature of the film compares to something like *Forrest Gump* with its cross-cultural references and the characters' ability to stumble upon history. Everett and the boys never encounter a president, but they run into a fair share of celebrities like musician Tommy Johnson (blues legend Robert Johnson in disguise), Governor O'Daniel, and public enemy Baby Face Nelson.

Beyond *The Odyssey*, perhaps the true influence for *O Brother* comes from Preston Sturges' *Sullivan's Travels*, which is often a source of Coen inspiration and the origin of the film's title. Joel explains, "There are things in it that are very reminiscent of *Sullivan's Travels*, but in a sense I would say 'reminiscent of' instead of rip-off. In our minds, it was presumably the movie he would've made if he'd had the chance. The important movie."[5] In that film, Joel McCrea's character, John Sullivan, a rich and successful comedic director, decides he wants to create more worthy films—something to display the struggles of the Great Depression. He decides to call his movie *O Brother, Where Art Thou?*, and he embarks on a road trek to understand the real America. In doing so, he soon discovers comedies like his provide the common man with relief; they don't require reminders of the actual conditions of society to be helpful. The Coens took this message to heart with the understanding that "message films are box-office poison and that laughs put asses in the seats, so they've filmed his bleak epic as a series of antic adventures and escapes with a case of cartoonish characters."[6] The brothers know better than to preach a message, so the buffoonery, the ridiculousness of the action creates an avenue to express their ideas without the need to highlight them so that audiences can understand. The messages in *O Brother* hide in the background, allowing the comedy and the faith-based violence to drive the film.

With the inclusion of the KKK, social themes become obviously apparent, but the Coens' portrayal lampoons them as the Klan dances in unison and with utter elegance. Race, though a part of the film, largely avoids controversy. African-Americans, aside from Tommy Johnson and the blind rail man, remain part of the backdrop.[7] This is the 1930's South, so to have characters openly discuss race in civil rights terms would negate the film's authenticity. After all, the Coens viewed the movie as the "Lawrence of Arabia of Hayseed movies."[8] That mindset doesn't allow for serious topical discussion, at least not much.

The violence of *O Brother*, while comical, reflects the nature of its Greek and biblical influences. If both those sources utilized atrocity in order to emphasize a point, they would be much like *O Brother*. When the faith-based violence occurs, specific points are made. Baby Face Nelson's terror fills his depression. Big Dan cons others based on their belief in religion. Sheriff Cooley tortures men to ensure that his faith in justice is served. The wicked, abrupt violence that had dominated Coen films before is replaced mostly with slapstick, as little repercussions occur from the characters' actions. Most of the violence happens to the fugitive protagonists, each of whom are punched, whipped, or beaten. Most notably, Everett suffers the most abuse, yet all the cruelty they endure happens for faithful, if sickly, comedic purposes. Nelson, as he engages in a stereotypical police shootout, machine guns a cow for no other reason than he hates cows more than he hates cops.

When graphic violence occurs, it remains minimal, void of bloodshed even with the genuine potential threat of the noose and public lynching. The Coens barely allow such fear to linger. The worst aggression occurs to Pete at the hands of Sheriff Cooley, who whips, tortures, and threatens to hang Pete if he does not reveal the whereabouts of Delmar and Everett. The scene lacks, however, the pain of a sequence like that in *The Unforgiven*, where Gene Hackman, the sheriff, brutally tortures Morgan Freeman's cowboy character. In *O Brother*, no one ever fears for Pete's life despite the noose that's dangling from a tree branch before him. Likewise, when the KKK captures Tommy, the Coens avoid any of the common expectations of hatred and intimidation linked with lynching. Instead, the scene plays comically with the three white men in black face rescuing Tommy by posing as the KKK color guard. Nevertheless, with the biblical influence, *O Brother* maintains the brutality that one must endure to complete an odyssey. The characters must have faith. The violence, though slight in comparison to previous works, still appears in an era where brutality intimidated all.

ULYSSES EVERETT MCGILL: "I'M A DAPPER DAN MAN"

George Clooney's first Coen role finally realizes his potential as a classical Hollywood star. He evokes Cary Grant, Clark Gable, and Moe Howard in a performance that is simultaneously tender, comedic, daring, and ridiculous. He's the Moe of his Stooges, leading his band of escaped misfits on a mission of misfortune. Even as their leader, Everett fulfills the Coens' typical checklist for a lead: a loser, a social misfit playing outside the system, a rebellious grifter, a man without education striving to create an intelligent persona in order to influence those around him. Immediately after their escape, Everett declares leadership over Pete and Delmar and establishes his forced intellect: "Well, Pete, I just figured it should be the one with capacity for abstract thought."

Throughout, even if his authenticity is never established, Everett portrays himself above his social status using his quick-witted nature to control those around him. He lies to Delmar and Pete about the hidden treasure in order to escape. He lies to his wife. He lies to get their record deal. He lies to the governor. He's filled with self-importance and pride—a man above the law. His pride nearly kills them because he waits to inform Pete and Delmar about the false treasure until Pete nearly dies for it. Not a hardened con, before incarceration Everett's honest jobs came from swindling the common man by practicing law without a license, lying about his prison history, and exploiting everyone's faith in his ability to lead them to financial reward. No doubt able to converse his way out of most situations, Everett is dishonest, which again calls into question his authenticity.

Everett, like nearly all Coen lead characters, reverses a previously established literary role as he (even more than Big Dan and Penelope) closely resembles his paper-bound counterpart. Everett is *The Odyssey's* Odysseus reborn, embarking on not just his adventures, but retaining some attributes of Odysseus (the first Greek hero to evoke muscle and mental strength). The Coens, in their usual fashion, reverse the majority of Odysseus's virtues in Everett, notably strength, bravery, honor, and courage—his most important qualities. In their place, Odysseus becomes a fast-talking conman versed in neither violence nor in criminal enterprises. Everett lacks courage and emerges nearly virtueless. Ethically, Everett does not think twice about joining Baby Face Nelson on a bank heist, nor does he fret over spending the loot when Nelson wanders off depressed.

Everett's true ideals appear when he finally returns home and sees his daughters and estranged wife, Penelope. She connects another loop of *The Odyssey* as the only character who retains her name from the source material. Played by Hunter, Penny (as she's called in the film) reverses Hunter's role as Ed from *Raising Arizona,* a tough-talking, unapologetic, and demanding woman who gets what she wants. Barren before as Ed, the Coens give Penny a gaggle of children, more than anyone could handle. In spite of his dreams, Everett's return to his family is not a joyous reunion. His daughters act as if he's intruded into their lives, and they revel in pointing out that Penny is set to remarry the "bona fide" Vernon Waldrip. She left Everett because she desired a better life for her and her children, and Vernon's a man with a job and prospects: "He's bona fide! What're you?" Everett cannot allow such a desertion to take place and attempts to win her back using his wit, charm, and brains. When challenged by her new suitor, Waldrip, its clear Everett knows nothing of violence. Waldrip continually punches Everett in his face as if he's a stationary target, whereas Everett can only swing wildly. Odysseus possessed both mind and muscle; Everett clearly lacks the latter, as he's beaten senseless and banned from Woolworth's.

Without physical abilities, Everett does preserve Odysseus's brains as he explains to Big Dan, "I sense that, like me, you are endowed with the gift of gab." Everett's greatest gift comes from conversing, able to talk himself out of nearly every situation, whether it's a violent or verbal altercation. He talks to ensure others' faith in his legitimacy as an intelligent man. Everett's first onscreen words display this strength when he boards a moving train moments after escaping the chain gang. He asks the hobos if any of them are "trained in the metallurgic arts before straiten circumstances forced you into a life of aimless wanderin'?" Sounding impressive, sometimes Everett talks not only to impress, but just to hear himself. He could have just as easily asked if anyone could free him from his chains, but for Everett, getting to the point is the easy way to communicate.

Another one of Everett's borrowed characteristic equals Odysseus's main weakness: pride. Taken to the extreme, his prideful conceit for his hair underscores the Coens' obscure obsession with hair. Everett's style isn't as outlandish as H.I., or as wild as Norville Barnes, or as electric as Barton Fink, yet his follicle fixation screams of the desire to appear as a bona fide man of character no matter the situation. He perfects his hair using Dapper Dan even after realizing that the scent could lead to recapture. His pride first comes to the forefront during their stay with Pete's cousin, Wash. After having their chains freshly removed and a dinner of rotten horse meat, Everett attempts to maintain his refined nature by shaping his hair carefully with pomade. Before the cons sleep in a barn, Everett asks the deprived Wash for a hairnet to protect his perfected hair from the surroundings. Awakened to barking dogs and the possibility of capture, Everett's first thoughts focus on his pride: "Oh, my hair!" Once on the road, Everett expresses not only faith in his appearance, but faith in his specific brand of pomade, stating that he's a Dapper Dan man. Later, when he awakes near the river after the encounter with the sirens, he repeats his fear of having disheveled hair. The film develops into not only a reconnection of Everett's faith in his family and the violence that arrives from the faith of others, but the search for the proper pomade.

Much like the film itself, Everett isn't limited to *The Odyssey*. A complex man, he's without conviction and unable to lash out violently like so many Coen lead characters. All characters in *O Brother* reveal a belief in something, yet Everett's faith lies in himself, in his love for his wife and daughters, and in the quality of Dapper Dan. He doesn't believe in God, the supernatural, the system, or in miracles. He mocks anyone maintaining and expressing faith: "I guess hard times flush the chump. Everybody's lookin' for answers." As other characters search for something to adhere to in a moment of weakness, for a truth to replenish themselves, Everett openly ridicules them, utilizing his supposedly authentic intellect to discount their ideals. After Delmar's joyful discovery of God during a river baptismal, Everett derides him: "Join you two ignorant fools in a ridiculous superstition? Thank you anyway." Later, when they pick up Tommy and explain the selling of his soul, Everett remains an authority, detailing to Pete a description of the devil as if it comes from genuine experience, even though it's the universally accepted version. But Everett has no witty retort to the supernatural after Pete disappears during a night with the river sirens and Delmar claims Pete has become a toad. Everett can only state, "I'm not sure that's Pete." For the only time in the movie, he's finally at a loss for words.

Nevertheless, at the film's end, faith eventually finds Everett when the Soggy Bottom Boys face the noose at the hand of the evil Sheriff Cooley. Everett's words cannot save him, and, when death seems a reality, he drops to his knees and reduces himself to begging, causing him to reveal his hidden belief. It's a prayer not to Cooley, not for forgiveness, but to God in the face of certain doom. He prays for Tommy, Delmar, and Pete. He begs for forgiveness for his pride and sinful nature: "Please, Lord. I just want to see my daughters again. I've been separated from my family for so long. [. . .] I'm sorry I turned my back on you. Forgive me, and help us, Lord, for the sake of my family." In desperation, Everett reaches for the faith he previously derided; he needs to believe in something authentic and his faith comes full circle. A miracle arrives in his moment of need in the form of a massive flood that washes away the evil and their sins. The divine intervention echoes *The Hudsucker Proxy* because, in both films, something other worldly prevents the death of the main character. As their coffins float to the surface and all four men survive, both Pete and Delmar celebrate that God saved them. Everett rejects their perception of the situation as a miracle when he says there's "a perfectly scientific explanation for what just happened." When Pete disagrees, Everett dismisses the conversation and goes back to his usual forceful conversational technique, and he explains that any man can become desperate in a "moment of stress." Throughout, Everett expresses distrust for religion and anything abstract, but with the threat of losing everything, he does hold faith in the only authentic thing a good Southern man should trust in: God.

PETE HOGWALLOP:
"IT WAS A MOMENT OF WEAKNESS"

John Turturro's portrayal of Pete lends itself more to exaggeration than an authentic portrait of an uneducated depression-era Southerner. New York Times reviewer A.O. Scott describes the performance as "obnoxiously broad, as though he had prepared for the role by studying tapes of Cletus the Slack-Jawed Yokel"[9] from *The Simpsons*. The comment, while an accurate if not dead on description, goes for all *O Brother* characters because the Coens amplify characteristics to create exaggerated ideas of Southern people and behavior. After all, the film circles around the notion of perceived myths, the ability to spin a tale through embellishment, and the authenticity of it all. Everyone appears stretched and pulled in order to meet preconceived notions that the so-called genuine old timey feeling evoke. The characters' speech, mannerisms, and dreams all represent the poor Southerner with limited ambition. In particular, Pete (along with Delmar) recreates that mythical character. When he takes the stage in full beard with the Soggy Bottom Boys, his gestures and dance convey an authentic portrayal of a prospector or moonshiner who just moseyed in from the woods. He embodies the Coen version of the classic South, right down to his ability to yodel, which allows him to personify all attributes of the stereotype. He is old timey.

Unlike Everett, Pete's appearance conveys limited pride. Because he is shirtless with suspenders and cropped hair, he demonstrates little care for what others think, and this only enhances that backwoods image. He, unlike Everett, appears to be an authentic Mississippi man, but that's not to say Pete sails as an empty vessel. Not gifted with language like Everett, Pete displays intelligence, rational thought, and exhibits his faith several times. His clothes and speech scream backwoods, but in some regards, Pete's intelligence outweighs Everett's, who overcompensates and exaggerates his intelligence. Likewise, Pete's kin seem an exaggeration of his backwoods image. Their early stay with his cousin, Wash, also validates Pete because his family isn't just poor and uneducated, but, as farmers, they reflect the only true effects of the Depression. Every element in Wash's life has been destroyed. The cattle have died. Some of his family members have committed suicide—even his wife has vanished. Pete's family has felt the Depression in ways no other element of *O Brother* expresses. His loyalty to family can be judged by his trust in his cousin, Wash, and his resulting anger at Wash's betrayal: "Damn his eyes! My pa always said, 'Never trust a Hogwallop.'" Disgusted with his family, he still cannot allow his cousin's child to roam the countryside with felons when the boy helps them escape: "Go back home 'n' mind your pa!" Later, when Everett reveals he had stolen Wash's pocket watch, Pete revolts, suddenly shocked that someone would steal from his kin.

Best represented by his emotion, desire, morals, and dreams, Pete attempts to curb any sexual desire, but does allow his instincts to take over. For example, while driving with Everett and Delmar, Pete notices the three sirens in the river and bites his fist to withhold his sexual inclination. He bolts from the car, runs down an embankment to meet them, and falls prey to their siren song. Pete brims with desire. He just isn't sure how to express it. At the same time, Pete falls under the same banner as Delmar for following Everett blindly even though he questions Everett's leadership at the start and conclusion of the film. Pete never follows through with his desire to lead, but this desire does not express that he's without intellect, only that he is willing to follow on the faith that Everett will lead them to his promised treasure.

Everett and Delmar should have listened to Pete's warning about trusting Hogwallops. When pressed, Pete turns on his friends and reveals their plans to Sheriff Cooley. His faith in the reward wanes as violence presents itself. Granted, Cooley whipped Pete and dangled the noose before him, but Pete still cracked under pressure. The betrayal weighs heavy on Pete, and he demonstrates great regret: "It was a moment of weakness." But mostly, Pete's a man with dreams above his means. As an escaped convict with no education, he dreams of mingling with the elite, engaging in intellectual conversation as the owner of not just one, but five restaurants in the west where, as the maître d', he could dazzle clients with his rowdy past. The moment of daydreaming comes as the men lay around a camp fire, running from the law and hoping for Everett's false reward. Pete's faith in the treasure allows him to dream beyond Mississippi.

DELMAR O'DONNELL: "*COME ON IN, BOYS. THE WATER'S FINE*"

If Pete represents the hillbilly doofus, then Tim Blake Nelson's character, Delmar, rises to the level of near insult. Unintelligent, unsophisticated, uneducated, Delmar has the role of goof to Pete's doofus. Smaller both mentally and physically, Delmar has little input into the group's decisions and follows without questioning the motivation for an action. When Everett and Pete argue over leadership, Delmar adds nothing, only stating that he's with them regardless in much the same capacity as Donny from *The Big Lebowski*. Incapable of making a lone decision, he's content allowing others to do the work, and he rarely exerts himself. When he does, it's for something he believes in. Something he holds faith in. Perhaps Big Dan summarizes Delmar's character best: "You don't say much my friend, but when you do it's to the point, and I salute you for it."

With *O Brother* concerned about belief and non-belief, Delmar exudes faith, constantly finding hope despite the violence surrounding him. He never worries or expresses fear, maintaining belief that he'll be able to transform his life. He holds faith that he finds an authentic transformation when they stumble across the river baptismal. As Everett discounts the notion, Delmar races toward the river, ignoring those in line in order to seek instant salvation: "Well that's it, boys. I've been redeemed. The preacher's done warshed away all my sins and transgressions. It's the straight and narrow from here on out, and heaven everlasting's my reward!" He believes that brighter days lay ahead. Delmar's naïveté and innocence help him follow others with faith. He has a desire for something tangible, something to adhere to. Conversely, Delmar is a reactionary man. After the brief crime spree with Nelson, Delmar responds to Baby Face's energy and enthusiasm for crime, realizing the thrill of the crime. Just as he followed Everett and Pete, if Nelson had not disappeared during the night, Delmar could very well have continued with him and reverted to his sinful ways.

On multiple levels, Delmar represents the child of the family, one so pure he's never been with a woman before: "I gotta get the family farm back before I start worrying about that." For him, the idea of being with a woman equals marriage, an act that seems impossible to him despite his age. In fact, mentioning re-obtaining the family farm acknowledges his desire for the classic, stereotypical farming family. He has belief in the system and in his roots. Neither Pete nor Everett emerge as hardened thugs, but Delmar's demeanor seems more in line with a mischievous child, a grown Dennis the Menace, rather than a member of the chain gang. When Baby Face Nelson asks if any of them know how to use a Walther PPK, a clueless Delmar thinks it's a town in Mississippi. Earlier in the story, when they approach Wash's home while his son aims a rifle at them, it's Delmar who talks with the boy; he's able to speak on relative terms. He even picks up spelling tips from Wash and his son: "We gotta R-U-N-N-O-F-T, but pronto." Also, Delmar doesn't repeat phrases from someone like Everett, but from others closer to his own mental capacity.

Likewise, Delmar asks questions with the curiosity of a child and appears willing to accept anything no matter how fantastic. When confronted with an unexplainable situation, Delmar jumps to improbable conclusions, such as Pete being reduced to a toad when they awake after their rendezvous with the three sirens: "We gotta find some kind of wizard to change him back!" Delmar concedes to Everett that Pete has indeed become a toad, and they even proceed to take the boxed toad to dinner. Everett, unsure and embarrassed, cannot agree with such actions, but has no logical answer to the problem. Nonetheless, Delmar refuses to give up on his friend. He will not hide the box. This pure naïve image decreases his criminal status. Even the crime that placed him in prison seems comical and creates a humorous image of Delmar—knocking over a Piggly Wiggly. This image is a far cry from one of a hardened, escaped con.

THE OTHER BROTHERS:
"HOT DAMN, IT'S THE SOGGY BOTTOM BOYS!"

With *O Brother* exploiting the episodic story structure of the Greek tragedy, it comes with a wide array of characters. Some of these characters forge their own story strands and become worthy of analysis. Some complimentary players are Coen regulars, sliding into roles that seem familiar yet different from previous characters. In *O Brother*, Holly Hunter has a reversal of her child-bearing fortune. John Goodman, as Big Dan, once again plays an effective salesman who's not everything he claims to be. In *Barton Fink*, he portrayed Charlie Meadows, a mindful, serial-killer salesman who removes the heads of his victims to ease their pain. Here, he's a grifting Bible salesman who is not concerned about the mind, but with money. And he serves quite obviously as *The Odyssey's* Polyphemus Cyclops, fulfilling a villainous and obstructive role in order to slow and dishearten the heroes.

In terms of social commentary, the political campaign serves as an obvious way to express high level corruption, and to emphasize that politics never change. Joel says, "The political undercurrent of the movie functions primarily for dramatic purposes, because the politics are frankly pretty primitive. The bad guys are racial bigots and KKK Grand Dragons, and the good guys are the heroes of the movie."[10] The two political candidates portray basic qualities, the new versus the old. These characters represent the changing of the South. For Governor Pappy O'Daniel, it's about the future, the ability to latch onto something hot; he understands times have changed. When he and his brain trust run into The Soggy Bottom Boys outside the radio station, Pappy's son asks if he should take the time to speak to the boys. O'Daniel, in his usual fiery, abusive manner, explains, "We ain't one-at-a-timin' here. We're mass communicating.'" He recognizes a political opportunity when he hears the reaction to The Soggy Bottom Boys in concert. And though his son realizes a black man plays amongst the band, O'Daniel recognizes, "Well, I guess folks don't mind they's integrated." O'Daniel senses the changing South. He just didn't realize he'd be a part of it. Surprisingly, O'Daniel has difficulty overcoming the simple gimmicks of opponent Homer Stokes's campaign, which uses a broom (to represent sweeping change) and a little person (to represent the common man). It seems to express that citizens don't always listen to the ideas, but love a good concept. For Stokes, it's about maintaining the status quo and he portrays himself as a man of the people, fighting for the common little man. However, he clings to the previous century and appears unable to seize an opportunity to adapt. Those *little* people revolt against Stokes when he determines, "These boys is not white! Hell, they ain't even ol' timey!" By vilifying the band, he undermines not only America's love for celebrity, but also the country's ability to change. The public cares about the music of the Soggy Bottom Boys, not who plays in the band.

With Stokes representing the racist, Southern bluesman, Tommy Johnson fits into *O Brother* in two main respects. For one, he and his tale of selling his soul to the devil underscore the mythical elements that transpire. He appears at a crossroads, and he helps guide the cons to a new, prosperous destiny. Secondly, Johnson acts as the musical backbone. He's the concept behind the Soggy Bottom Boys, and he connects the typical racial divide in music.[11] His character remains in the background throughout, appearing and reappearing to service the story via music when needed. This represents the supposed African-American inferiority during the period. He always plays behind his white-counterparts and remains invisible throughout the performance for the all-white audience toward the end of the movie. He plays second fiddle to Everett and the boys, which considering the era, is authentic. Having Tommy emerge during the performance would upset the film's credibility.

Lastly comes Sheriff Cooley, the man with the dark glasses who embodies evil personified. He is a man who takes the scenario of an escaped convict so personally that he will do anything to get him back. Cooley symbolizes everything that is malevolent. The Coens take the character far enough to hint that Cooley could represent Satan himself, according to Tommy, whose description of the devil mirrors Cooley's appearance. He displays no signs of a human soul, and at the end of the film, despite the governor's acquittal, he still plans to hang the men. Everett argues this fact, only to have Cooley deny the plea: "The law? The law is a human institution." Cooley's faith lies in justice, not the law. Adding to his mythical status as Satan disguised, only a miracle stops Cooley after Everett succumbs to prayer. Cooley might not resemble a stereotypical devil, but he does reflect the Old South's authentic evil and violence. Cooley, like all the secondary characters, helps to complete an eccentric version of the Deep South without rewriting history. His use of faith-based violence to solve problems changes when the South floods the area to change itself.

* * *

In many respects, the soundtrack from *O Brother, Where Art Thou?* overshadowed the movie as it went eight times platinum and ignited a blue grass revival. Produced by T-Bone Burnett, the sound created a rare non-musical musical. Joel states, "Music is a huge part of the movie. It moves like a musical."[12] Indeed, while the Coens have always incorporated and used music as an important element in their films, *O Brother* becomes a near musical. With the help of the songs, *O Brother* became one of the Coens' biggest and most accessible films, earning $45 million at the box office.[13] Overall, critics remained, as with all their films, relatively indifferent. One critic called it "a semi-successful attempt to move in a new direction."[14] Roger Ebert, on the other hand, declared, "I had the sense of invention set adrift; of a series of bright ideas wondering why they had all been invited to the same film."[15] Regardless of critical uncertainty, *O Brother* veers into new territory while remaining quintessentially Coen. Even with the inclusion of the KKK, everything carries such a light tone that nothing appears threatening, allowing the music and the characters' faith to surface. The violence, for once, takes a back seat, yet remains prevalent through the inclusion of issues of faith.

9

Cutting Cain's Law

The Man Who Wasn't There (2001)

"The more you look, the less you know."[1]

CAST: Billy Bob Thornton (Ed Crane), Frances McDormand (Doris Crane), Michael Badalucco (Frank), Scarlett Johansson (Birdy), Jon Polito (Creighton Tolliver), Tony Shalhoub (Freddy Riedenschneider), Katherine Borowitz (Ann Nirdlinger), Richard Jenkins (Walter), and James Gandolfini (Big Dave).

The Man Who Wasn't There. Directed by Joel Coen. Universal City, CA: Universal Studios Home Entertainment, 2001.

When Big Dave asks of main character Ed Crane, "What kind of man are you?" it's not simply an insulting comment, nor a rhetorical question. Instead, it's a call for an analysis of character. As lawyer Freddy Riedenschneider later states, "The more you look, the less you know," and in *The Man Who Wasn't There*, these two phrases drive the Coen brothers' ninth picture. With the unexpected success of *O Brother, Where Art Thou?* and its complete departure from their standard presentation style, the brothers returned to their roots with the gritty world of James M. Cain. Their first film, *Blood Simple*, brought a modern take to Cain's domestic noir formula; so, fittingly enough, *The Man Who Wasn't There* is an old take on that same recipe with the usual unusual Coen sensibilities attached. It represents their ultimate tribute to film noir, a black and white tale of blackmail, murder, betrayal, adultery, desire, greed, and the bizarre.

Set in 1949, the Coens place the film in Santa Rosa, California, where Alfred Hitchcock set his *Shadow of a Doubt* and where Raymond Chandler's

Philip Marlowe was born. This location not only provides a connection to the past, but it creates the small town atmosphere in a near perfect 1950s environment—a move which indicates the Cain inspiration where everyday people find themselves astray from normality. After all, no one expects violence to erupt in Anytown, USA between an insurance salesman and a housewife, or a drifter and a restaurateur, or a barber and a clothing store manager. The emotionally driven, reactionary violence of the average man creates a connection to the audience by removing elite social status or physical distance. They're your neighbors, your own family.

The film begins with effective, dry narration by the barber, Crane, who introduces his life at the barbershop. He works alongside brother-in-law Frank and isn't happy with the position, yet makes no strides to alter his position. Conflict quickly arises with the revelation that his wife, Doris, is having an affair with her clothing store boss, Big Dave, which comes after a dinner with Big Dave and his wife, Ann Nirdlinger. Crane remains indifferent and life remains miserable until opportunity presents itself in the form of dry cleaning entrepreneur Creighton Tolliver, who stops in for a haircut after potential investor Big Dave backed out. Crane sees the idea as a way to achieve independence from Doris. The problem? Crane needs $10,000 to invest. Consequently, he decides to blackmail Big Dave over his affair with Doris. Big Dave pays, but suspects the dry cleaner and beats the truth out of him, which leads to a confrontation with Crane. A newly broke and defeated Big Dave attacks Crane, leaving Crane no choice but to murder Big Dave in self-defense. Surprisingly, the police arrest Doris for the murder after it's discovered that she, as the accountant, manipulated the company's books to swindle money. Ed Crane hires Riedenschneider, the best attorney available, to defend her. But, before the trial, a distant and silent Doris hangs herself, leaving Crane to fall for the music of a beautiful, teenaged Lolita named Birdy. He sees potential in her piano playing and attempts to secure her career. Birdy fails an audition, and on the return trip home, makes a pass at Crane, which causes a near-tragic car crash. When Crane awakes in a hospital, he's arrested for the murder of Creighton Tolliver and made into a criminal mastermind. Crane is placed on death row, and we discover (only moments before his death by electrocution) that his narration has come from a collection of confessional stories he wrote for a men's magazine.

The Coens found inspiration for this film in a most curious place: on the set of *The Hudsucker Proxy*. Among the props, the brothers discovered a vintage poster demonstrating various classic men's hairstyles.[2] With that image in mind, they chose and created the character of Crane and focused on his unimpressively ordinary life. His position as the town's barber exceeds job description. He is the barber. Nothing more. And when Big Dave asks him, "What kind of man are you?" Crane cannot respond because he truly is nothing more than the barber. His barber position doesn't just describe him, it defines him. Crane exists and functions in a simple societal role and lives a common, bland life. This average nature encompasses Cain's novels *Double Indemnity* and *The Postman Always Rings Twice*—where the common man encounters bad luck, seductive women, ironic feats of fate, and burning desire—without attempting to modernize them. Joel explains, "Cain was very much in our minds, because he was interested in crime stories that involved people in their everyday lives at work, and not about underworld figures. People who work in banks, or the insurance business, or restaurants."[3] *The Man Who Wasn't There* faithfully borrows Cain's formula and operates on timed (if sometimes slow) pacing.

At the same time, recurring ideas of modernization and underlying paranoia appear through cryptic subplots. The bizarre circled objects and UFO sounds and sightings enhance the somewhat puzzling inclusion of space ships into a murder movie. The Coens had admitted to including it to reflect the 1950s state of paranoia with the Cold War: "It's got all that modern dread, that feeling of disassociation and paranoia about what's happening in the world about you."[4] This existential dread also appears in Crane's "extraterrestrial" lifestyle in which he lives a life of alienation and separation and is unable to connect with another living soul. If it weren't for the dialogue (which reeks of Coen) and the modern cast, some might mistake the Coens' tribute for a film made in 1949.

If Riedenschneider suggests that everyone take a closer look, then the Coens wouldn't be revisionists if they didn't alter some Cain aspect because, the more one examines the story, the more its evolution becomes apparent. The Coens toy with the near-pristine image that pop culture generally attaches to the 1950s with its perfect family structure. Violence, however, lurks in the dark. The Coens mix that notion with the dissolution of the family structure, and reveal that married couples still lived miserable, daunting lives. Anyone associated with marriage (though no couple has children) in the film appears unfulfilled in both career and life. In particular, the domesticated men, such as Crane and Big Dave, appear neutered in some respect, as they all search for fulfillment as each man depends upon their wives to supply them with their career positions. Only Walter, Birdy's father, has a child. Widowed, he works independently of any family business, but he still vanishes at night to uncover his family heritage and reconnect with lost love ones.

On the other hand, the unmarried individuals, such as Frank (up until Doris's death) and Riedenschneider, appear satisfied with life. Frank's father had left the barbershop to him, "and that seemed to satisfy all of Frank's ambitions: cutting the hair and chewing the fat." Riedenschneider basks in his own self-glory, eating the best food, staying at the best hotels, wearing the best clothes. Riedenschneider is a man who truly presents himself as "the best." On the surface, no one man appears capable of violence, but when forced to react to defend their way of life, their true selves finally surface.

Thornton plays Crane as if he channeled a stoic Humphrey Bogart, but reviving Bogart isn't just a cheap ploy—it's a complete reversal of character. On the whole, Crane exists as your average noir man full of desire and in search of some unknown happiness—his American dream. Crane, though, is truly a man of few words and fewer actions; he lacks both passion and emotion. He has no need for violence. It's a risky move for the Coens because sympathizing with someone who's quiet, rarely talks, barely moves, and dislikes people becomes difficult when that person exhibits negative social traits.[5] Crane's a bore except within the hands of the Coens, remaining oddly fascinating because of his inability to act or express outward emotion. Whatever desire lurks deep inside of Crane stays there as he reveals nothing and scarcely acts, besides smoking a cigarette. He lives to exist and stare with discontent.

In other words, Big Dave's question of Crane's manhood develops validity. What type of man is he? Absent of vocal desire, he expresses no sexual drive. He's an asexual lead, a character that doesn't belong in the genre. Sexual desire and unbridled lust drives the men from noir films to reactionary violence. In *Double Indemnity*, Walter Huff loses everything falling for not just one but two women. His emotions overtake him. In *The Postman Always Rings Twice*, Frank Chambers cannot escape the sexual pull of his employer's wife, Cora, and will do anything for her. Crane's lust remains absent; he yearns for the unknown, a life separate of Doris and the barbershop. Despite Crane's non-sexual nature, the Coens surround him with wanton women: Doris oozes femininity, always dressing, undressing, taking baths, and applying perfume; Birdy alludes to Vladimir Nabokov's *Lolita*, a pretty, intelligent, piano playing teenager. Cain's stories contained a femme fatale, a woman who spins a web to lure her prey by capturing a man's heart. *The Man Who Wasn't There* has Crane already married to the femme fatale. The standard noir affair plays in the background as Doris captures her boss's heart. Crane, watching with discontent, notes, "The signs were all there plain enough—not that I was gonna prance about it, mind you. It's a free country." The Coens insert Birdy to induce a hidden passion. Her sexual nature lingers before him, but Crane rejects it. Some have suggested that Crane is a homosexual, but Tolliver makes a pass at him and Crane rejects him with the same emotion he gives anyone else. Sex doesn't drive him; he rejects this motivating component of noir men. Crane never has an affair, but his motivation to use his wife's affair creates the blackmail, the jealousy, and the reactionary violence needed to become a part of a Cain noir.

Crane's lack of action, his lack of sexual longing, creates a problem for a domestic noir. If there's no lust, there's no death. And in that case, *The Man Who Wasn't There* can hardly fall under the genre if it's violence-free. Nevertheless, the reactionary violence arrives once Crane acts, even if bloodshed never occurred to him. Instead, Big Dave carries the weight of intimidation with talk of his supposed glory, gory war days. The Coens only allow a single glimpse of his reactionary violence via his attack on Crane. After Crane offers no retort to Big Dave's accusation of being behind the blackmail, Big Dave lunges at him, throws Crane against a massive window, and chokes him with such hatred the glass cracks. In self-defense, Crane uses the small blade Big Dave claimed he stole off a dead Japanese soldier, and sticks it once in his neck. This is the lone violent act seen in the film as Big Dave's other actions appear off-screen with the discovery of Tolliver's body at the bottom of a lake. Regardless, the Coens only needed a single scene to express Big Dave's violent temper and emotional turmoil. And they only needed a single scene to demonstrate that Crane possesses the ability to act if his hand is forced.

By stabbing Big Dave in one single, wooden strike, Crane expresses his one true reaction to any situation. It was here, only moments before, that Big Dave sat across from him and asked, "What kind of man are you?" Crane, unable to respond, is not someone who takes initiative. He possesses no interest in anything until he learns about the dry cleaning business and the possibility of managing a musical career. The film, following the comedic violence of *O Brother, Where Art Thou?*, stays relatively blood free minus the Big Dave confrontation. Even when the blood does flow, it's the Hitchcock *Psycho* black and white blood, lessening the brutality's impact. All events that follow happen because of Crane's instinctual reaction, and though all characters remain driven by greed, that motivation has little effect on Crane. Violence just happens to occur and Crane responds with little more emotion than if he had just given a haircut.

ED CRANE:
"ME, I DON'T LIKE ENTERTAINING"

Introductory writing classes teach students to avoid passive characters because vivacious men (not those who observe while others acts) dictate storylines. Ed Crane moves only to smoke, and in situations that call for a reaction, Crane answers with glares, neither menacing nor sarcastic, looking off into nothingness. He offers a brief smile or occasionally nods so others know he's listening, which Thornton referred to as the Ed nod: "Ed would always just accept the most horrible things with a little tiny nod. Everything he sees he just kinda accepts."[6] The barber's world holds no interest, no passion. Of all the Coen characters, Crane perhaps represents their most singular, most tragic, and most unusual. He goes beyond passive; mute both orally and physically, the polar opposite of what a main character should be. According to Joel, "Even though there's a crime in this story, we were still interested in what this guy, who's a barber, does as a barber. We wanted to examine exactly what the day-to-day was like for a guy who gives haircut after haircut."[7] His mundane life, his dullness, become fascinating.

Crane represents the unfulfilled soul who never discovered a worthy purpose. From his marriage to his career, he regrets everything. Nothing brings happiness; nothing brings satisfaction. People surrounding him talk endlessly and express trivial joy while he remains dead to the world, invisible and alienated. One evening Crane returns home and sits on his couch for a smoke: "I sat in the house, but there was nobody there. I was a ghost. I didn't see anyone. No one saw me. I was the barber." Alone after Doris's death, Crane finally equates the loneliness in life with that of his profession.

Beyond his married family—he never reveals information about his blood family—the outside world summarizes Crane's existence with two words: the barber. Desired or not, his occupation equals his self worth; he is the barber. He claims to despise the career, yet his eyes always fall upon the haircuts of others outside the shop, glaring with a slight hint of disgust for his own actions. We first understand his plight (in terms of classification) when he and Doris attend a wedding reception and a member of Doris's family can't recall his name but remembers his profession. Big Dave, having no connection to Crane and forced into conversation after dinner, can only banter about the trademark barber smock, asking where he buys them. After Doris is arrested, Frank and Crane apply for a loan for trial money, but the banker has no interest in Crane. Frank pleads for his inclusion in the process, stating he's a fellow barber, but Frank mentions Crane's trade before he explains Crane's true status as his brother-in-law.

Riedenschneider, with his lawyer wisdom, defines Crane accurately before a jury of his peers during Crane's trial. Riedenschneider states Crane had "lost his place." That Crane was too average to do anything of the sort. Riedenschneider asks the jury to look at Crane as a modern man—nothing more than a simple barber. Masterminding a murder plot, Riedenschneider says, seemed unthinkable because of Crane's ordinary status as a barber, the simplest of occupations. Crane finds the argument insulting and his defense of being just a barber belittling. Despite Riedenschneider's attempt to discredit the simple-minded nature of the barber, his notion of "the more you look, the less you know" doomed Crane. For all Crane's hidden desires and reserved composure, doubt appeared concerning his ordinary social position. Only moments after Riedenschneider's plea, Frank disrupts the trial, punching Crane with a demand: "What kind of man are you!?" For even Frank—despite knowing his brother-in-law—could no longer define him in such simplistic terms, and he exhibits another moment of reactionary violence. He's left without recourse in defending his sister. Broken down and disillusioned, Frank cannot understand who his fellow barber has become.

Thankfully, *The Man Who Wasn't There* doesn't completely rely on the commonness of the barber trade; it incorporates narration that allows for guidance into Crane's thoughts. Crane speaks to the audience with a dry, perfectly imitated narration of Cain's *Double Indemnity* and *Postman* along with films like *Sunset Boulevard*. Noir men relay their fears and desires to the audience in a confession-like delivery. They exist day-to-day, waiting for an unknown opportunity, an unknown passion in the form of women. Like

Walter Huff from *Double Indemnity* or Joe Gillis from *Sunset Boulevard*, Crane's narration represents his lasting explanation of the events that altered his life. Unlike those films, where the confessional starts with known fates of the characters, Crane gives no insight as to his whereabouts; he doesn't reveal that he's in a jailhouse or that his narration represents the final words of a condemned man awaiting final punishment. He begins his tale at the barbershop without indication that he is a man pondering his actions on death row: "Yeah, I worked in a barbershop, but I never considered myself a barber. I stumbled into it—well, married into it, more precisely." Stumbling through life accurately depicts Crane's situation as everything in his life has been dictated to him by Doris through his profession—a profession he did not choose for satisfaction, but for convenience. Even the friends the Cranes keep come from Doris.

All that Crane cannot express verbally, he delineates to the audience, no matter how bland. But through his trivial comments, another theme emerges related to the idea of life and death. Hair is used as a metaphor and he thinks of it often. In one scene, Crane cuts a boy's hair and ponders its purpose with Frank. He thinks of the act as self-mutilation, rejecting nature. Later he recalls what an undertaker once told him, that hair keeps growing after death as Crane questions, "Is it like a plant in soil? What goes out of the soil? The soul? And when does the hair realize that it's gone?" Despite Crane's professional displeasure as the barber, only a barber could think in such follicle terms. Likewise, with the Coens' own fascination with hair throughout each of their films, perhaps only the Coens could equate follicle matters with such deep, reflective ideas.

Everything Crane considers uninteresting becomes the opposite as, the more we listen, the more we begin to understand what kind of man he is— the little things that rattle around. However, Crane's tale of intrigue falls under scrutiny once he informs the reader at the end that he writes for a men's magazine: "They're paying me five cents a word, so you'll pardon me if sometimes I've told you more than you wanted to know." This comment carries several implications. For one, magazine headlines such as "I was Abducted by Aliens" and "After Ten Years of Normal Life, I Discover I am an Escaped Lunatic" lay scattered across his writing desk, which may have inspired portions of his narration. Much like Keyser Söze from *The Usual Suspects*, in which the narrator explains a crime spree in a detective's office by inventing the story based on items within the office, the audience is forced to confront some legitimate questions. Everything Crane narrates becomes the subject of inquiry. He admits to telling the audience "more than you wanted to know" because he writes for money, and, as a passive, alienated man, his story needs enhancement in order to create the type of story Cain would envy. We're allowed no outside perspective, no newspaper accounts, or a venture outside of his mind; we can only judge based on what he narrates.

Crane's description of how he and Doris met provides a case in point for the audience. Crane, sitting bedside and watching a drunken Doris sleep, details their life together. He pauses the narration when a call comes from Big Dave. Crane leaves to meet him at the clothing store, stabs him in self-defense, and then returns home to pick up the narration of the mundane account as if nothing had ever occurred: "It was only a couple of weeks after we met that Doris suggested getting married." For Crane, the event of the murder, the catalyst of the entire story, carried little meaning for his audience compared to the miserable nature of his marriage and job. To him, murder is his one moment of action, and he allowed it to speak for itself.

That one lone moment of erupted violence allows the Coens to take their love for Cain and to reformat his domestic noir much as they re-crafted Dashiell Hammett for *Miller's Crossing* or Raymond Chandler for *The Big Lebowski*. Both *Postman* and *Double Indemnity* have proactive characters missing some component in their lives, and the characters commit murder in order to preserve it once found. Huff held a respectable position as an insurance salesman. Chambers, though an aimless drifter, seemed perfectly satisfied with his hand in life. Simple jobs and complacency were enough to satisfy until they met their femme fatales. Crane, on the other hand, has everything a man could desire: the steady job, the comfortable home, and, most importantly, the dame, his beautiful wife. The Coens, however, allow a role reversal; Crane becomes the husband without concern for an affair. Love drives the other characters, leaving opportunity to drive Crane. He embraces the chance for independence once an opportunity is presented in the form of a dry cleaning venture.

Crane knows nothing about this newfound industry, but in Tolliver he encounters someone who speaks with a point that Crane wants to hear. Tolliver explains that it's the biggest business opportunity since the invention of the car. Tolliver delivers his pitch in a fury, and Crane hangs on each word: "Dry cleaning. . . My first instinct was no, no, the whole idea was nuts. But maybe that was the instinct that kept me locked up in the barbershop, nose against the exit, afraid to try turning the knob." It's not until Doris asks him to shave her legs that he decides to transform. As she sits in the tub and asks him to perform his barber duties he realizes his inability to escape his occupation and he reaches his breaking point. Crane has everything other men desire, yet he cannot muster the urge to stay. If someone questions the definition of Chambers and Huff's manhood, they at least fall under more basic definitions. They can blame unbridled lust as a motivating factor. They would kill to have the love of a woman. But as for Crane, he only ponders dry cleaning. Like Chambers and Huff, Crane will stop at nothing to succeed in gaining freedom as he doesn't give a second thought to blackmailing Big Dave. Even in a catatonic state, the barber knows an opportunity. Also, by placing these three characters next to each other an interesting observation can be made: each allows someone else to stand accused of the murder he committed. Chambers allows charges for his lover. Huff sees his beloved Lola arrested. Crane lets his wife Doris stand trial, resulting in her tragic death.

In the end, moments before death, the men's magazine asks Crane about remorse. He vaguely admits to guilt in causing others pain, but he regrets nothing: "Not a thing. I used to. I used to regret being the barber." His summarization of the lives he ruined and the focus on his life as the barber suggests that, ultimately, Crane remains a selfish, passionless man. Seated on the electric chair, he still cannot betray the very thing that defined him, the very thing he regretted most of all: he inspects the haircuts of those who came to witness his death. Nonetheless, his final thoughts ponder his loveless marriage to Doris in perhaps his one true moment of self-reflection. He's unsure about the afterlife, but he's not afraid of what lies beyond this life: "Maybe the things I don't understand will be clearer there, like when a fog blows away. Maybe Doris will be there. And maybe there I can tell her all those things they don't have words for here."

DORIS CRANE:
"LIFE IS GODDAMN WONDERFUL"

In death, Ed Crane finally expressed a grain of passion for his deceased wife. Doris never had the opportunity to express such emotion, but it's obvious she regretted many aspects of her life. Whatever Doris initially saw in Ed had evaporated years ago. Whatever type of man Ed evolved to, Doris no longer wanted. She never asked much of her husband, using him for social gatherings three different times in the film only to uphold that perfect image of 1950s marital bliss. Clearly, Doris's role is the supposed femme fatale, but she doesn't serve in the same capacity as the standard noir woman, even as she exhibits fatale traits: a beautiful drinker with great sexual prowess. Nonetheless, she's already married to the protagonist, which disallows the usual love-for-murder plot. Not that it doesn't exist; it just plays out uniquely when compared to Cain's domestic reactionary violence.

If Crane is a modern man, then Doris is a modern woman. She defies what a 1950s woman should be, and her strength (present before she ever met Ed) is hinted at throughout the film. She is the one who plans. She lives a life independent of her husband, earns her own income, and only includes him to secure the expected married couple persona. Beyond disliking her husband, Doris loathes her family and her Italian heritage as much as Crane hates his life as the barber. At a family member's wedding with inhibitions down, she fully reveals herself and her discontent for life. Doris despises her own Italian blood. Her brother Frank embraces family life at the wedding, but Doris buries her discontent of family values when surrounded by them, igniting her need to drink. From that point, the real Doris emerges, warning her newlywed cousin about the pitfalls of marriage, about the false nature of love. Crane attempts to prevent any verbal outbursts, but she resists, once again asserting her independence.

As the femme fatale, Doris torments Crane to an extent with her reluctance to care about his unhappiness and utter depression. Doris oozes sexuality, but Crane remains numb. She first appears when Crane walks into the house as she's in a state of undress. He pretends not to notice, dreading her explanation to the audience: "Oh yeah. There was one other thing." He tells that she, unlike him, loves her work as an accountant, loves knowing where things stand. Crane notices her clothing and lustful scent, but finds only disdain, negativity. But Doris—with her clothing, job, and displayed sexuality—is an independent woman. Granted, her role serves as the noir woman, but she's a modern woman: intelligent, motivated, sexual, and successful.

Doris more or less flaunts her affair with Big Dave by having him and his wife over to dine. She laughs hysterically at Big Dave's false stories of military service while Crane and Ann sit like bystanders, as if missing the joke. Big Dave attempts to invite Crane into the conversation, but Doris belittles his military inability, offers no support, and only refers to him after Dave's attempt to connect on a military level—a man's connection. The scene demonstrates the duality of the loveless marriages in the film; the Cranes' relationship matches the loveless nature of Big Dave and Ann. And, though Crane and Ann share no bond beyond alienation, Doris finds a sexual draw to Big Dave, the absolute opposite of Crane. A massive man, a successful manager of his wife's store who strives to open his own store, Big Dave has it all. He's even a war veteran, leading Crane to believe Doris had an affinity for "all that he-man stuff." He further notes, "Sometimes I had the feeling that she and Big Dave were a lot closer than they let on."

Big Dave and Doris clearly use each other to achieve their own goals. Doris embezzled in order for Dave to open his own store (meaning she would manage her own store). Both would gain further independence. Once arrested for Big Dave's murder, all of her independence and desire vanishes; Doris puts up no defense, no cries of false detainment. She accepts her adulterous ways and the punishment seems fit. She never confides in Riedenschneider and only once reaches out to her husband. She admits to cooking the books, but stops before disclosing anything else, asking Crane if she should reveal everything to him. He, however, remains uninvolved. It's the last time she talks.

Doris, facing murder charges, seems most disappointed that her pride in her once-great accounting abilities had ended; she knew they'd be caught. Her final acceptance of fate stays in line with the plots of *Double Indemnity* and *Postman*, though with some differences. Doris displays guilt, (something the other women lacked) as she commits suicide after learning of her pregnancy with Big Dave's child. She is unable to cope with having a dead man's bastard child and believes she has nothing to live for. Her career and life died with Big Dave, as did her chance to manage a store of her own and become a modern, independent woman.

Perhaps the most telling sequence of the Cranes comes after Doris is dead and Crane lays unconscious after his car wreck with Birdy. In Crane's flashback, he sits on the porch one afternoon, enjoying a smoke. A man approaches asking about their gravel driveway, selling him on modernization. Crane listens to his pitch, showing neither interest nor disdain. However, the arrival of Doris shows who controls the home. She proceeds to question the salesman, rips his brochure in half, and tells him to get lost. She marches inside for a drink and Crane follows. They sit on opposite ends of the couch; she drinks, he smokes. They say nothing until he states her name, but she cuts him off, "Nah, don't say anything. I'm alright." The scene ends, not explaining their coded conversation but giving viewers insight into their daily lives. Neither was happy; neither knew a way out. Of all the flashback memories he could experience near death, Crane recalled an average day and an average argument between them, representing the mediocrity and dullness of the marriage.

BIRDY:
"YOU'RE AN ENTHUSIAST"

Crane lacks connection with any character until he encounters teenaged pianist Birdy at the Nirdlinger Christmas party. Others danced to modern music and drank themselves into oblivion while Crane wandered the store until hearing a piano and found Birdy playing with her back to him. They had a meaningless conversation until interrupted by Doris, but a connection was established. Crane maintains surface level relationships with various people, but the youthfulness of Birdy brings out a hint of emotion. She's planted as a sexual fishing lure, but Crane falls for something more desirable, beautiful, and peaceful: a piano. Birdy might have something to do with that, but the combination of her and the music of Beethoven equals something he never experienced. He offers no narration for their meeting, but actually engages in the conversation. He even offers an uninformed compliment by asking if she made up the song. Clearly, with their first encounter, Crane feels smitten with her, but not in the usual manner. It's not sexual; he sees youthfulness, potential, and opportunity. Everything he remains without. He attempts to mentor her in terms of a future career, and explains that it's never too early to plan ahead "before it all washes away." Crane, while talking to Birdy, reflects upon his own life. He can't watch her future be discarded like a lock of cut hair. He wants to manage her career, to witness something good, to have a single positive element in his life.

The Coens carefully use Birdy as a Lolita-like character—her first encounter with Crane suggests some sexual inclination. The Coens toy with her possibility as a love interest, as Crane, with Doris dead, begins to spend time with her, even visiting her home when her father is away. The notion of a grown man visiting an unaccompanied teen implies a sexual tension, and the Coens dangle opportunity as Crane visits her alone in her room. While he discusses her future, she sits on her bed, legs carefully exposed with sexual innocence. She's presented with the expected wholesomeness of the period, yet this purity leads to the most awkward scene in *The Man Who Wasn't There*. After Birdy's failed tryout with the French music instructor Jacques Carcanogues in San Francisco, they drive home and Birdy expresses her appreciation of Crane and recognizes his disappointment. Crane barely responds throughout the exchange; he concentrates on the road, loads another cigarette in his mouth, and ignores the failure. At this moment, all her innocence and his asexual nature surface; they misunderstand each other. Crane wanted her supposed musical skills, but Birdy makes a move. She slides her hand over his thigh: "I wanted to make you happy." She leans over his lap, and her head disappears below the steering wheel. Crane's obvious displeasure shows; he's shocked that she would even understand such ideas. She, like the dissolution of the family structure, erodes expectations of a pure period—neither possessed innocence. At least if Big Dave were able to ask, "What kind of man are you" again, we'd understand that Crane has certain lines he will dare not cross.

THE MEN WHO WERE THERE: *"I LOOK ALRIGHT?"*

When Freddy Riedenschneider informs the audience that "the more you look, the less you know," he's instructing the audience to closely examine everyone, and that if we do, we're bound to discover something unexpected. Beyond such words of wisdom, Riedenschneider is a hollow, showy character. He exists to demonstrate his skills in court, loving the power and himself. Likewise, Frank appears completely content until Crane finally acts on impulse, thus destroying his life as the only family man—despite not having a family to call his own. He is the barber and relishes the position. One character mirrors Crane, a man who wanted more, a man who also married into his work: Big Dave. They possess nothing of their own, and live double lives: Big Dave had the affair, Crane is an empty shell. Thankfully, Big Dave is a man of action, and represents the stock Cain character, someone who does not hesitate to act under a threat.

Noir movies typically have someone in the way, someone blocking the path of someone else's success. For *The Man Who Wasn't There,* that role falls to Big Dave, who represents Crane's means to an end to escape the barbershop world. He's a man of wealth and physical stature, someone capable of delivering expressive stories about a wild past. He questions Crane's character, but Riedenschneider questions the Big Dave persona and his fraudulent nature. He presented himself to the town of Santa Rosa as a war hero with tales of weary battles in WWII. Riedenschneider's private eye discovered he only served in a secretarial capacity and he uses his faulty stories to discredit the victim as a liar, along with discrediting audience expectations created by actor Gandolfini, whose alter ego, Tony Soprano, from *The Sopranos* looms large over Big Dave. His anger seems comparable to Soprano's; he's a tough guy instead of a false war hero. Although he lied about war heroics to impress those around him, Big Dave shows no hesitation in the attempted murder of Crane or the murder of Tolliver. The Coens insert no element of humor within his acts, especially with the altercation between himself and Crane, which amounts to a brutal attack of sheer aggression. And if Crane were able to ask to define Big Dave's manhood, he'd probably discover that both he and Big Dave shared a duality in where they stood in a world that never realized who they truly were.

* * *

The Man Who Wasn't There is more or less an old movie, but one that asks for a close examination of the characters to uncover what defines them. Critically, the Coens' ninth picture received the standard mixed reviews. Some critics rightfully understood: "Of all the Coen films, *The Man Who Wasn't There* is most purely beautiful. It's a bloodless *Blood Simple*, with a droll, slyly understated sense of humor."[8] But perhaps *Rolling Stone*'s Peter Travers summarizes the film best: "Think of Bogie in 1941's *The Maltese Falcon*, when he cradles that chunk of cold black stone and makes a point that goes to the not-so-stony heart of what film is to the Coens: 'Ah, the stuff that dreams are made of.'"[9] Unfortunately, *The Man Who Wasn't There* never found an audience. The film never received wide release and stands as their worst box office performance since *The Hudsucker Proxy*. Considering the movie plays as an art house experiment, there's little surprise that audiences didn't flock to theaters to see a black and white movie about a barber who dreams of being a dry cleaner and his reactionary violence.

10

Cruel Intentions

Intolerable Cruelty (2003)

"Only love is in mind if the Massey is signed."[1]

CAST: George Clooney (Miles Massey), Catherine Zeta-Jones (Marylin Rexroth), Geoffrey Rush (Donovan Donaly), Cedric the Entertainer (Gus Petch), Edward Herrmann (Rex Rexroth), Paul Adelstein (Wrigley), Richard Jenkins (Freddy Bender), and Billy Bob Thornton (Howard D. Doyle).

Intolerable Cruelty. Directed by Joel Coen. Universal City, CA: Universal Studios Home Entertainment, 2003.

All Coen brother features have objects to focus on such as *Miller's Crossing*'s hat, *Barton Fink*'s head, *Raising Arizona*'s baby, *The Big Lebowski*'s rug, or *The Man Who Wasn't There*'s hair. *Intolerable Cruelty* is no different, but its ideals are more apparent to satisfy mainstream audiences. Obvious elements of greed and deception appear, but its one unavoidable object comes via the Massey Prenup, a document so iron-clad it's taught at Harvard Law. The document's inner workings, though, remain an impenetrable mystery because the Coens avoid any actual legal-speak. Only what the prenuptial agreement does matters—driving, motivating, and terrorizing all characters as the entire plot revolves around Miles Massey's masterpiece.[2] This written document motivates characters in unseen ways as it "determines the subjects in their acts, in their destiny, in their refusals, in their blindness."[3] No matter the legality, the Massey Prenup steers the future of two heartless, devouring, deceptive people, and drives them together to commit preventive violence. They discover that, despite how they behave professionally, they can still learn that "love is good." Only a legal agreement can grant eternal love, and, if it fails, characters can always resort to preventive violence in order to solve their dilemma.

Talent always seems attracted to the Coen brothers, but actual mainstream, name brand stars have only peppered their films randomly with Paul Newman in *The Hudsucker Proxy* as the biggest. Without marquee names, a Coen Brothers Feature means avoiding the mainstream label and finding smaller, appreciative audiences. But in their second outing with George Clooney—and the addition of Catherine Zeta-Jones, Billy Bob Thornton, Cedric the Entertainer, and Geoffrey Rush—the Coens finally entered into the world megaplex cinema with their most accessible film to date. On the surface, *Intolerable Cruelty* follows the typical romantic comedy: it's a story of forbidden love and questionable ethics—man meets woman, he loses her, gets her, loses her, gets her, and everyone lives happily ever after. Nevertheless, it still contains many of the classical Coen trademarks, such as powerful men behind desks, men in hats, crime, and murder.

Intolerable Cruelty opens with an establishing shot of modern Los Angeles with the discovery of an affair between a woman and her producer husband, Donovan Donaly, which alludes to the infidelity, disillusion, and the social satirical tone to come. The state of marriage in America has become an industry all its own, which leads us to Miles Massey, a nationally known divorce lawyer due to the previously mentioned Massey Prenup. Unfortunately, life feels incomplete for Miles; he's run out of challenges, run out of things to buy, and he can only obsess so much over his perfect, glistening teeth. But another job soon arrives. Suspicious wife Marylin Rexroth, a serial divorcée who's prepared to milk her latest husband for every penny, hires a private eye Gus Petch, who bursts into the hotel room to record the exploits of her train-loving adulterer husband Rex Rexroth. Rex, in turn, hires Miles to defend him, and does so viciously. Marylin's lawyer Freddy Bender easily proves Rex's infidelity, but Miles and his assistant Wrigley outmaneuver him, proving Marylin's dishonest nature. Despite the victory, Miles falls in love with her, but unbeknownst to him, he's finally met his match. Marylin retreats to her friend's empty mansion to plot her revenge, and Marylin soon returns, asking for the Massey Prenup for a new prospective husband, oil tycoon Howard D. Doyle. A disappointed Miles assigns them his document, but at their wedding, Doyle eats the document with barbeque sauce. Newly divorced, Marylin and Miles rejoice with love and they wed. She signs his famous agreement, but on the eve of the wedding, she rips the document, leaving both exposed. The problem comes from Marylin being broke, as Doyle was nothing more than a cheap soap opera actor. Now Marylin has access to Miles's money. After meeting with his decrepit boss, Herb Myerson, Miles hires an asthmatic hit man to prevent further embarrassment. After that fails, the couple decides to finally split, and as they prepare to make it official, they fall in love once again. Afterward,

Donovan returns to produce Marylin's idea for a new show, Gus Petch's "America's Funniest Divorce Videos."

Regardless of the romantic comedy label, *Intolerable Cruelty*, being a Coen movie, manages to seep past ordinary comedy components, utilizing flashes of black comedy, film noir, and the classic screwball comedy format. Unfortunately, including so many elements creates a film that can't decide what it aspires to be. It's dark, cute, funny, dangerous, kinky, and distasteful with inspirations coming from the Coens' usual place: the golden era of Hollywood when rapid-fire dialogue, exaggerated performances, and ludicrous plots ran wild in films like George Cukor's *Adam's Rib* or Billy Wilder's *Major and the Minor*. It's an amusing exercise for the Coens, but when compared to their other films, it fails to match the wit or creativity. With that said, the most successful aspects of the film come from the acting (top-notch performances), the writing (with the Coens usual witty and memorable dialogue), and the unique characters (lacking ethics, having oddball quirks, and behaving unacceptably). In most of their films, they find a balance among these attributes, always inserting a grounded, straight-angled character to juggle the eccentrics of the leads. They tend to match polar opposites: H.I. McDunnough and Leonard Smalls, Barton Fink and Charlie Meadows, Jerry Lundegaard and Carl Showalter, Ed Crane and Big Dave, Tom Reagan and Bernie Bernbaum. Each pairing represents the duality of human nature. Each brings a sense of order.

Intolerable Cruelty ends up surprisingly void of the balancing act, as neither Miles nor Marylin are versed in violence. They're equals, not doppelgangers. They're morally corrupt, leaving the audience no one to root for or care for. Moments do emerge here and there in which the audience extends sympathy toward one character or another, but mostly this film marks the Coens' first and only soulless creation, one that lacks their usual flair for deeper meanings and literary motifs. Sure, characters randomly quote Shakespeare and other poetics, but it's a false exercise that never appears legitimate. The characters seem to have memorized a few lines; they don't embody a literary soul. Overall, the film lacks the Coens' trademarked biting edge. It lacks impending violence and becomes more slapstick than black comedy, more broad humor than ingenious jokes.

Despite the unethical characters, despite the negative tone toward marital bliss, the message "love is good" still bleeds through. It's as plain a theme as the Coens have ever created, but they don't reveal it until midway through the film. It's unlike *Miller's Crossing*'s revelation of friendship, character, and ethics. In fact, the characters of *Intolerable Cruelty* reject those ideals. It expects people to embrace love in an environment that has disowned the word, where characters scramble to earn no matter what or who interferes. Johnny Caspar from *Miller's Crossing* claimed that family made a man: "You're missin' out on a complete life. I know, kids, big deal, but still, I'm tellin' ya." Apparently, no one from *Intolerable Cruelty* received the message.

But how could they? *Intolerable Cruelty* takes place in plastic Los Angeles, a city many see as the downfall of man where sin, sex, a lack of ethics, a lack of character, selfishness, and violence all run rampant. It all serves as perfect fodder for commentary on modern society. Explanations aren't needed for the way people behave, as Miles and Marylin live among and represent the elite social class in L.A. They believe in material possessions, bank accounts, and perfect teeth. *Intolerable Cruelty* is the first Coen movie to decidedly focus on the haves instead of the have-nots. Marylin might be in search of money to elevate her status, but she will always live as if rich, even if she's not. Greed and selfishness overwhelm the characters, and they are unable to experience any sort of true happiness. It creates a conversation about the morality of the country, a discussion about the state of marriage, ethics, and true love. *The Man Who Wasn't There*, though set in 1949, gave subtle insights into the dissolving state of marriage with characters presenting the perfect family picture while home life eroded. *Intolerable Cruelty* shows the progression, or perhaps the erosion, of American martial bliss.

As the Coens first modern setting since *Raising Arizona*, it's obsessed with prenups, procedures, and gaining capital through marriage. Where *The Man Who Wasn't There* found marriage a dull yet important aspect of life, *Intolerable Cruelty* demonstrates that ending marriages is an important industry where divorce lawyers bleed the system and women search for a target to marry in order to gain financial independence. All characters remain completely fixated on their life's mission: Miles on the law; Marylin on money; Gus Petch on nailing people; Herb Myerson on the law; Wrigley on Miles. Echoing the life of the workaholic, each character has no time for love, is devoid of middle-class values, and has no grounding in a so-called normal life. All emerge vacant and fearful of love for various reasons: Miles because of his profession, Marylin because of her "carnivorous" marriage tendencies. And none, except Donovan, appears capable of violence. The only character with a seemingly normal lifestyle is Gus Petch, who not only loves his work, but also watches football games with his friends, and enjoys the standard domestic lifestyle—the type of existence all other characters run from.

Sometimes running only gets a person so far. When those characters' solutions dry up, they turn to an alternative solution to protect their livelihoods: violence. Of course, not even the Coens can enter into mainstream waters and not become a little deluded. It's Coen-lite as the violence remains relatively absent until the third act, where a death occurs not for love or money, but to preserve dignity. The initial act of assault with Donovan that begins the film introduces viewers to the tone expected, something in between realistic and comedic, which places it in line with *Raising Arizona, The Hudsucker Proxy,* and *O Brother, Where Art Thou?* as relatively bloodless and comedically violent films. When something of a murderous nature occurs, it mirrors the tone of the picture.

Violence actually bookends *Intolerable Cruelty*. The film opens with dual attempted murders. Donovan, after catching his wife cheating, pulls a pistol from the night stand and awkwardly aims the gun at her lover. Whether or not he would've executed the murder we'll never know, for his wife clubs and then stabs him with his Daytime Television Lifetime Achievement Award. The music and the tone suggest comedy, but Donovan's attempted murder by shooting from the balcony as they escape is the first indication of preventive violence. Donovan's fortitude in photographing his wounds explains his preemptive strike against her—he's ready to protect his wealth with evidence to protect whatever dignity remains.

Near the conclusion, the second eruption of brutality develops after Marylin humiliates Miles. A preeminent divorce attorney cannot lose his own divorce case, so his boss Myerson decides to bend the law in order to protect the firm's reputation, and hires hit man Wheezy Joe to end the problem. He's the classic comedy hit man: large enough to evoke carnage, but old and oafish enough to create comedic chaos. The angst produced by Wheezy is lackluster and lessened even further by his inability to distinguish the difference between a pistol and an inhaler when he shoots himself through the mouth. Wheezy is such a thin character and his death is so outlandish that the Coens use the moment to exploit a sight gag: the shattered glass from the passing bullet creates a perfectly shaped heart. Even if characters cross all lines of absurdity, most manage to retain some form of morals. Miles and Marylin, in their lone moment of preventive violence, fail in this regard. They both engage in potential murder, and both expect the death of the other to prevent further damage to their reputations. In the end, neither could commit the deed themselves. As members of the haves social class, they would never dirty their own manicured hands.

MILES MASSEY:
"JUST LOOKING FOR AN ASS TO MOUNT"

It speaks to Miles Massey's place in life that as a middle-aged, ultra-successful divorce attorney with everything one could desire, he only discovers that "love is good" after colliding with a heartless con artist. Before then, he lived a life of material desire; he tells Wrigley that he's bought so many cars he has a tab at the dealership. He's rebuilt his home twice, remodeled his home in Vail, and seems a regular at the dentist for obsessive teeth whitening. He's unafraid of a challenge, living for the test, and views compromise as death: "Struggle and challenge and ultimate destruction of your opponent. That's life." He admires men such as Ivan the Terrible, Attila the Hun, and Henry the VIII because of their ability to destroy their opposition. In court, he views the opposition as the enemy, and consistently uses war metaphors, describing his office to Rex Rexroth as a "war room for the duration of the campaign." He refers to gaining the net worth of a husband as obtaining a "map of enemy territory." Miles, when engaging in law, is utterly ruthless, incapable of losing the challenge.

Under this impenetrable skin, Miles demonstrates signs of erosion. His first scene in court shows two sides of him. He sits in a depressive state while the opposing lawyer questions his client about sexual practices. Miles acts oblivious to his client's agony over the revealed details and instead focuses on lecturing Wrigley about his mental state. Miles remains unsure of his life's direction and fulfillment. Something unknown is missing. He's purchased as many toys as possible to fulfill his emptiness, yet his tank remains empty. When Miles's chance for cross examination comes, Miles stands undisturbed by his social life and slaughters the competition, a sweet-looking, secretary-type woman. No matter where his personal life sits, his professional life always wins, as his depiction as a lawyer rarely strays.

In his first scene in his office, Miles attempts to bend, refold, and glue together a story that alters a jury's perception away from the fact that his client had engaged in adultery. Despite her disagreement over the ideas that range from her husband having an affair with a man, to his supposed abusive nature, Miles promises her that the truth appears so clearly to him, and he will "make it equally as transparent to any jury." No matter the situation, Miles willingly forges ahead, flexing the law in order to create the winning story needed to succeed. To him, fact or fiction never matters, only what people will believe. He only takes Rex Rexroth's case because, despite the video evidence of his infidelity, "It's a challenge." Beyond this rugged exterior is someone bored by the routine, someone unable to find satisfaction if not engaged in destroying an opponent. For all his experience and success, he has yet to discover that love is good.

Clooney embodies his best Cary Grant impression for Miles, personifying playboy charm and pencil-thin values. And, much like Tim Burton's seeming joy in mutilating Johnny Depp's pin-up status, the Coens equally revel in revoking Clooney's attributes, creating vain and empty roles that directly play off his bachelor persona. He's the perfect Coen foil with an ability to be simultaneously unethical, charismatic, revolting, disingenuous, and likeable. The Coens don't toy with his looks like Burton does Depp, but they carve Clooney hollow. In *O Brother*, his idiotic character, Everett, obsessed over perfect hair, and they give the same treatment to Miles in this film. As Ethan explains, "George decided that his character is a descendent of the guy Everett McGill he played in *O Brother, Where Art Thou?*. He's kind of glib and taken with himself."[4] Clooney apparently fell in love with mildly reprising the role: "Everett was all about hair. Miles—he's all about teeth. So he's always getting his teeth cleaned and checking his teeth."[5]

What the reprisal means is that Clooney has once again added another character to the Coen list of buffoonish leading men, regardless of the romantic comedy format. Miles falls in line with all Coen creations that remain suspended in life, in search of an answer to the enigma of happiness, and not as smart as they appear. Normally, the Coens' main roles feed from the bottom of whatever aspect of society they're a part of, but that isn't true for Miles. He's probably their only lead character who is not a complete loser, and who has everything a man could desire. He's built a career around his Massey Prenup and brags about it to an extent, evoking its name to strike fear in others.

Miles's greatest challenge doesn't arrive in court, however; it arrives in the form of Marylin Rexroth. She ignites a spark that permeates through his clichéd body as he states, "You fascinate me." The moment she walks into his conference room for an initial divorce negotiation against her husband, it is love at first sight—taken straight out of the romantic handbook. Miles has been devoid of love for a lifetime and, after the meeting, he immediately invites her to dine, despite the ethical problems. Given Miles's professional-life-first modus operandi, the dinner serves two purposes: one, he initially is "looking for an ass to mount," and two, he cannot escape his predatory lawyer ability, hiring Gus Petch to break into her home while they dine in search of evidence to use against her in court. Miles cannot change his nature. As he once told Mr. Rexroth: "The fault, dear Brutus, lies not in our stars, but in ourselves." But with Marylin on the witness stand, Miles displays signs of weakness. He passes in front of her, studying her as if deciding to proceed with her destruction or not. Nevertheless, Miles cannot change his court persona. The self-described destroyer does just that, introducing Heinz, the Baron Krauss von Espy with dramatic flair, a man Marylin hired to find her a fornicating husband (Mr. Rexroth), thus ending her chance to earn millions. All this leads to the introduction of the Massey Prenup, the document that drives the final half of the film. Miles and Marylin use the agreement to define love and trust as it is signed and destroyed multiple times. It's not until the conclusion that trust is defined, as both parties emerge financially secure with Marylin inheriting the late Rexroth's fortune.

Miles's lowest moment occurs after Marylin's marriage to oilman Howard Doyle, for his life remains vacant due to her request for his own attorney-proof agreement. As Wrigley effectively reminds him, "Only love is in mind if the Massey is signed." Distraught, Miles goes back and forth with Marylin, and as they again dine, the dinner signifies just how lonely and alienated they both are. But when he realizes she's gone forever from him, with Doyle, Miles envisions his future without her and dreams of his boss, Herb Myerson. Miles fears and respects Myerson because of the old man's dedication to the law. Myerson exists as the living, breathing attorney, muttering billing charges between gasps for air—all lawyers, especially Miles, strive to emulate him. When he thinks of Myerson—an 87-year-old with magazines such as "Living Without Intestines" decorating his waiting room—Miles fully understands the future: reclusive, lonely, soulless, and loveless. But Myerson's character is much more than fear and motivation for Miles;

Myerson provides *Intolerable Cruelty* with the mandatory dream sequence, the most obvious one since *Blood Simple* when Abby awakes in a cold sweat after seeing her dead husband. Myerson suddenly appears more devilish than usual, drooling facts and numbers as lightning strikes in the distance. It's a vision of a damning life that waits for Miles, and he awakes in a sweat, which only highlights his need for Marylin. He rushes into Marylin's room and they soon marry, leading to his keynote address to N.O.M.A.N., a divorce attorney's organization.

Here, Miles finally realizes what that unknown element in his life was all along. He disposes of his speech and speaks from the heart, telling the audience that he's "naked, vulnerable, and in love." He explains that what they practice destroys the most important human emotion, and everyone remains frightened by that emotion when they shouldn't. And, though the scene emphasizes the emotional element, Miles serves as the Coens' conduit to achieve the intended social commentary. Only moments before, in Caesar's Palace, Miles delivered a monologue about the state of ethics in America and the declining level of human nature. However, the Coens slide in an element of social class as Miles declares his resignation from his law firm and as president of N.O.M.A.N. at the conference: "I intend to devote myself to pro bono work in East Los Angeles, or one of those other [places]." Miles is aware that less fortunate people exist; he just isn't sure where they live.

MARYLIN REXROTH:
"PEOPLE DON'T GO ON SAFARIS BECAUSE THEY HATE ANIMALS"

Marylin Rexroth exists, much like Miles, as a vacant character without romantic interests, without ethics, and without any real personality. In a sense, she's a character fit for film noir: she lives without a heart and is only driven by greed. It's hard to imagine her uttering a line such as "love is good." She's a predator more than a flower for plucking.

The Coens, with all their previous experience creating femme fatales, do very little with her. It is as if the Coens fashioned a noir woman outline by withholding elements that would round out her character. As a professional divorcée, Marylin rivals Miles in terms of professionalism; she knows exactly what she needs and never allows moral quarrels or potential violence to disrupt the job. Her ability to focus on her work makes her a unique Coen character—she's an independent, dependent, successful criminal woman. Of the Coen women, she embodies the strength of Ed McDunnough, the independence of Doris Crane, and the brazenness of Amy Archer. She's their most sexual character, flirting and hinting with Miles with nearly every sentence uttered. For someone like her, a document like the Massey Prenup represents a career deathblow, her kind's kryptonite. Her beauty and femme fatale black widow abilities allow her to manipulate any man she desires, and, true to that cliché, Marylin never acts out violently—that's what her men are for. Unless that man hires Miles Massey.

Like Miles, Marylin's role reflects America's unrestricted greed. Both obsess over material possessions to an extreme. Marylin willingly forgoes any prospect of a so-called normal existence, and she will go to any length in order to secure a victory, even researching her husbands to find the proper prey. Her first appearance perhaps defines her character more than any other sequence. In private investigator Gus Petch's office, she watches the footage of her husband's affair. Marylin has no real reaction, and Petch takes notice that she takes the news well. Marylin does not put on an act. She lets him (and the audience) know her motives from the outset. She doesn't find the situation amusing, but it will be her "passport to wealth, independence and freedom." Petch, in his own poetic manner, sums up her mission best: "Sounds like to me that you gonna nail his ass."

Socially, on the other hand, Marylin can maintain life outside of her profession. Her heartlessness must withstand both roles in order to earn an income. She cannot afford to allow anyone near her heart. Her network of quasi-criminal friends consists of women compelled by bank accounts, not by domestic structures. They reject motherly instinct and instead embrace and yearn for wealthy independence. Yet, none of them seem happy. They move from man to man in search of earning another payday. Her friends, led by Sarah Sorkin, sit poolside dressed in matching white robes and discuss their conquests that they achieve through settlements. Marylin arrives late to the robe gathering and doesn't match, draped in red like a demon from her meeting with Petch. Marylin attempts to explain the hardships of the initial divorce proceedings, but it doesn't matter to them. It's always onto the next target; they already have another husband in line for her. This goes beyond even Marylin's capabilities: "Sarah, only one husband at a time."

Marylin personifies Miles's ultimate match. Like him, she's a professional; she's heartless and will do whatever is needed to claim victory. Her efficiency and her ability to destroy men creates a fascinating challenge for Miles—she represents the unattainable woman. Marylin keeps herself available until she has acquired the funds needed in order to embrace the life she feels owed, that is, one in which she is no longer dependent on men. No real background is needed for such a woman as she's the stereotypical gold digger with her own pathetic support group that shares a similar moral compass. She's an actress who enjoys her work, as is demonstrated by her on-cue crying at the Rexroth trial. She never hesitates when informing people of her career choice. During their first dinner where they shoot poetry and one-liners back and forth, she explains to Miles: "This divorce means money. Money means independence."

The Coens do, however, reveal hints that Marylin's heart isn't granite. She's concerned about turning into her friend Sarah, just as Miles dreads mutating into his soulless boss. After all, Sarah suffers the ultimate catch-22:

she has the freedom she desired, but now lives in fear that karma will revisit her. Though professionally beaten, Marylin reinvents her career to seek revenge on Miles, luring him into love only to shatter him. Her devious plot of deception and manipulation, which includes leading Miles to believe that "love is good," brings out Marylin's best femme fatale qualities. Nevertheless, she, unlike that stereotype, falls victim to the romantic comedy stereotype.

INTOLERABLE AND CRUEL CHARACTERS: *"I LOVE TRAINS!"*

The Coens continually demonstrate a flair for creating characters who make the word "quirky" seem tame. *Intolerable Cruelty* doesn't deviate from that tradition and boasts many oddball roles, even if all have minimal screen time. Rush, Thornton, and Cedric the Entertainer among others surface and vanish depending on where the story has turned. Like Marylin, these characters live as hollow entities, established for the simple task of further defining either Miles or Marylin, inflating the story, or delivering a few memorable, very strange one-liners. As the character that begins the film, Donovan Donaly sets the socially satirical and odd tone that underpins *Intolerable Cruelty*. He is the modern man of Hollywood: ponytail, convertible Jag, egotistic, and arrogant. His decision to immediately brandish a pistol after catching his wife involved in an affair is a direct reflection of the influence of American violence—even though Rush and his character are Australian. Regardless, the eccentric nature of Donovan equals the eccentric nature of Hollywood. But Donovan, like all the characters, lives in a self-absorbed world and willingly employs violence to protect his little piece of the world.

With Donovan representing the Hollywood elite, Gus Petch acts as the lone representative of the modern working class. With so many of the Coens' films based on the noir and detective genre, Petch portrays the modern Hollywood detective minus the skills and tact the public expects with the job—in Petch's words, "You want tact, call a tactician." His sleuthing abilities seem absent, and that fact is made into a joke as he stretches in spandex inside Marylin's home. Above all, he takes the notion of the sleazy P.I. to another level, employing a paparazzi approach to the voyeuristic work. A detective like Jake Gittes from *Chinatown* or Sam Spade from *The Maltese Falcon* captured compromising evidence from a distance or in the dark, but Petch's antics strike the audience like an episode of Candid Camera. In the case of Rexroth, Petch bursts into his motel room touting a massive camera with lights glaring and shouting, "I'm going to nail yo ass!" Also, unlike classic private investigators, such as Spade or Philip Marlowe, Petch demonstrates no inclination to cause violence. His world is one of surveillance, not action. And though he's the lowest on the economic ladder in the film, no other character possesses his egotistical confidence—outside of Miles. He means what he says, as if his name alone is an effective guarantee: "God damn it! I'm Gus Petch!" Miles's name might be synonymous with prenuptial agreements, but Gus throws his name around as if his techniques were also part of Harvard instruction.

While other characters appear to fit naturally in *Intolerable Cruelty*'s world, several appear for pure amusement. Heinz, the Baron Krauss Von Espy assumes the role of the very strange. His purpose is not only to be the surprise shock witness, but to showcase the absurdity the Coens love to personify. He has no depth beyond his exaggerated accent and his dog that needs little bones for his teeth. However, he does enhance Marylin's character, showing the depth she'll descend in order to locate a victim. Von Espy acts as a high-end pimp and searches for a victim. That victim is Rex Rexroth, the wealthy real estate man whose love for trains stands as one of the more bizarre addictions in a Coen film. He's nothing more than a patsy for Marylin, but so is her next husband: Howard D. Doyle (a character whom Thornton plays like an inside joke). In *The Man Who Wasn't There*, Thornton played a virtual ghost with no emotion and minimal dialogue. Thus, just as they did for Steve Buscemi in *Fargo* and in *The Big Lebowski*, the Coens reversed his character, making Doyle a chatting buffoon willing to reveal any trivial detail that comes to mind. Later, it's revealed as an act, but Thornton's performance stands as one of the best in the film.

Last out of all the minor characters, Miles's right hand man, Wrigley, possesses the most screen time. His character seems like it was taken from *The Simpson's* character Waylon Smithers, a man who lives and breathes for his boss yet seldom finds respect nor appreciation for his labors. Wrigley appears infatuated with Miles, and remains constantly irritated at Miles's affection for Marylin, always suggesting an alternative to her. Every other man falls under her spell when she appears except for Wrigley, who remains faithful to Miles no matter the situation. He resolves depression, arranges murder, or analyzes illegal material; he's willing and able if Miles just asks. Loyal to a fault, no matter the hour, Wrigley is always there for his master. But Wrigley has other attributes: he's decidedly naïve, unsure of all of Miles's tricks and maneuvers. His solutions often only feed Miles's need for material possessions, such as suggesting that Miles simply needs a new car to resolve his funk. Like Smithers, Wrigley also possesses potential homosexual overtones. For example, he never turns his head toward the irresistible Marylin, cries uncontrollably at the very mention of a wedding, and he chooses to present berry spoons as a wedding gift which Miles mocks. He's in such direct contrast to the overt sexuality of Miles that his character functions as the comic relief instead of allowing any sort of obvious sexual desire to interrupt the story. In an extreme oppositional way, he could allude to Ed Crane's asexual nature, though he truly seems to love his work and Crane could not stand his. Regardless, while Miles and Marylin represent the cruel upper class, the secondary characters of the film express that not everyone is driven exclusively by greed.

* * *

Intolerable Cruelty broke new ground for Joel and Ethan Coen when released. It not only became their first movie to emerge from a script not their own, but it was their first venture into the mainstream—a romantic comedy with top-notch stars. In the two years between *The Man Who Wasn't There* and *Intolerable Cruelty*, the Coens strayed into uncharted territory. They produced *Bad Santa* with Thornton, which was about a mean-spirited and unrelenting Santa Claus. Then came the quite public failing of their $60 million dollar Brad Pitt project *To the White Sea*, a virtual silent film that died due to budget concerns. After the black and white art-murder house *The Man Who Wasn't There*, which invoked many classical Coen elements, *Intolerable Cruelty* does a 180. They had originally done some script work on *Cruelty* years before, and the project floated around Hollywood for roughly eight years, passing through the hands of various directors and actors. The Coens teamed up with their second mega-producer, Brian Grazer, for the first time in a decade (the first being Joel Silver for *The Hudsucker Proxy*) and decided to take on the project with a star or two in hand. Critically, the film received typically mixed reviews with one critic declaring it was "not shudder-worthy."[6] Even with the complaints about the overall success of the work, they manage to take even a tame genre like romantic comedy and play against expectations. Expectedly, *Intolerable Cruelty* performed mildly at the box office. It represents one of three Coen films considered their least worthy cinema entries—the first being *The Hudsucker Proxy*, the second being this film, and the third being *The Ladykillers*.

The Killing Joke

The Ladykillers (2004)

"Behold there is a stranger in our midst, come to destroy us!"[1]

CAST: Tom Hanks (Prof. G. H. Dorr), Irma P. Hall (Marva Munson), Marlon Wayans (Gawain MacSam), Ryan Hurst (Lump), Tzi Ma (The General), George Wallace (Sheriff Wyner), Diane Delano (Mountain Girl), and J. K. Simmons (Garth Pancake).

The Ladykillers. Directed by Joel Coen and Ethan Coen. Burbank, CA: Walt Disney Video, 2004.

Most of the time, when a renaissance musical group rents a practice facility, the group appears capable of producing such music. However, when that band consists of an eccentric linguistics professor, an explosives expert, a Vietnamese general, a football player, and a loud-mouthed janitor, someone's eyebrow should have raised. But with the motivation of greed and the promise of a stolen reward, common sense dissipates. It emerges as the only concern, even if it means creating necessary and accidental violence in the wake of the crime. No one bothers to worry whether the band can actually pass as authentic.

Greed isn't exactly a novel concept. In a heist movie, it's easy to overlook considering it's such an obvious, apparent theme. Throughout their careers, the Coen brothers have incorporated greed in various films, ranging from *Fargo*'s lust of the big deal to *Raising Arizona*'s greed for a child. In the crime genre, using it as a motivating factor doesn't exactly forge new ground—economic gluttony is a constant thread. That thread usually remains relegated to a minor part of the story with the lead characters embarking on bigger, more encompassing problems. Nevertheless, *The*

Ladykillers (the Coens' second straight mainstream comedy) breaks that trend with a centralized story driven exclusively by greed. Wanting and obtaining, however, remain two distinct ideas, even as pyrotechnic expert Garth Pancake applies a mantra to any situation: "Easiest thing in the world." He often repeats the phrase as an answer to any situation; it's a belief that all the characters share. Each one risks everything with the faith that robbing a casino will be no problem and that their lives will change forever with newly acquired funds. All they need is a plan and the desire to accomplish it. This idea—that both greed and violence appear to be the easiest things in the world to utilize—becomes the mantra for *The Ladykillers*. And as they soon discover, nothing could be further from the truth.

The story of *The Ladykillers* begins with a passing trash barge beneath a bridge of the sleepy town of Saucier, Mississippi, as it heads toward a garbage island. In town, local law Sheriff Wyner sleeps in his office when elderly nuisance Marva Munson enters to deliver her usual complaints about a neighbor's modern music. They shrug her off, and when she returns home, the eccentric Professor Dorr wants to rent a vacant room in her home. On supposed sabbatical leave, Dorr desires to perfect his musical skills, claiming to have a band of Renaissance musicians who'll practice in her droll root cellar because it "improves the acoustics." In actuality, Dorr has gathered a motley batch of criminals: Pancake, inside man Gawain MacSam, tunnel expert General Nguyen Pham Doc, and hired muscle Lump Hudson. Their plan? Infiltrate Mrs. Munson's home to tunnel through her cellar into an underground casino vault to steal money with no one the wiser. Things progress with minor setbacks, but the job's a success. The moment she returns from church, Pancake's tunnel detonation explodes late and showers the root cellar with loot just as Mrs. Munson opens the basement door. They have a problem. Dorr attempts to fabricate a story for their way to freedom, but she won't bite; instead, she offers them a choice: return the money and attend church weekly with her, or take their chances with Sheriff Wyner. They decide to improvise at the last moment. Kill Mrs. Munson and keep the money. Unfortunately, she doesn't die easily, but they do. Each man somehow winds up dead through accidental violence due to his own idiotic nature. The next morning after she believes the men have all vanished, Mrs. Munson discovers the money and informs Sheriff Wyner of their crime, but he doesn't believe the tale. He leaves the money to her, which she donates to Bob Jones University.

In a way, the Coens have always made ensemble pictures. Leads always remain clear; but, in Coen films, complementary characters round out the story to add realism and depth, creating a distinctive, populated Coen world. Led by Goldthwait Higginson Dorr III, PhD (Tom Hanks in his first comedic role in over a decade), the men of *The Ladykillers* all have harder edges and appear less accessible. As the criminal mastermind, Dorr's anything but the standard issue villain, even if his one and only motivation comes through going money simple. Despite being a supposed mastermind of criminal enterprise, Dorr loathes modern civilization. He's unable to converse with the working class, and he's adverse to violence. He's the atypical Coen creation, even if the character and the film come from established material—the 1955 British export, *The Ladykillers*. Regardless, Dorr's inability to act out violently defines the film's violence as both necessary and accidental homicide.

The Ladykillers attempts to recapture the zaniness of *Raising Arizona* with offbeat characters and dark humor, leaving the romantics of *Intolerable Cruelty* behind. Much like that earlier effort, everything appears exaggerated. Not to the effect of something like *The Hudsucker Proxy*, but it's still a part of hyper-reality.

Nevertheless, the Coens' first full-fledged remake of an existing film isn't much of a remake. Ethan explains, "We really like the original movie. It's a strong story premise. It just has good bones. We ripped out the spine of it, kept that and threw out everything else."[2] The spine the Coens kept ended up being the passing trains (barges), the daylight heist (tunnel casino robbery), the ending, and the old lady and the professor, but the Coen additions give birth to an entire new movie body with an American slant.

Directed by Alexander Mackendrick and starring Alec Guinness and Peter Sellers, the renowned classic Ealing Studio film focused on another heist and another old lady, Miss Wilberforce (Katie Johnson), and remains one of the best British caper movies ever made. The criminals chose her home due to the proximity of the railroads, only to see their perfect crime thwarted by the sweet, elderly lady. She emerges as a warm center to enjoy, despite the chaos surrounding her, and the film evolves into a comedy of manners with the difficulty of dispatching the old woman. She's not so easy to kill.

The Ladykillers returns the Coens to Mississippi where characters relish the history of what was. Perhaps the Coens perform at their best when engrossed in Americana and avoiding major metropolitans. Only their third present-day movie, *The Ladykillers* works as a modern examination of America's past with ethnicity and race dominating much of the conversation. *O Brother, Where Art Thou?* only dipped its story's toes into the proverbial pool, but *The Ladykillers* employs race relations to define characters. No effort for serious discussion or analysis is made, yet each character reflects different aspects of American society. The Coens' decision to replace the original, frail, elderly woman with a strong Southern African-American woman provides a regional stamp. Her dominant religious beliefs and classical Southern principles amplifiy her revulsion of modern music and young African-American men. The opening sequence details her disgust for the new traditions in culture, and, referring to hip-hop music, she says, "It don't make me wanna go hippity-hop!"

At the same time, all characters beyond MacSam and Lump represent the past on two levels: clothing and mindset. On a clothing level, both Pancake and the General haven't updated their clothing since the 1970s. Mrs. Munson and her friends keep vintage Southern apparel alive. Dorr dresses like an early 20th century Southern Gentleman. Only MacSam and Lump bring *The Ladykillers* into the present. Beyond external appearances, the various mental states of the characters segregate them in terms of morals and generations. Pancake provides the bridge between Mrs. Munson and MacSam, explaining his arrival in Mississippi during the civil rights movement as a part of the Freedom Riders, who were concerned citizens willing to venture South to aid local black people in obtaining their civil rights. MacSam—whose character represents the plight of violence of modern society and everything Mrs. Munson despises— responds to Pancake with a modern sense on such historical events: "I don't vote, so fuck you. And the bus you rode in on!" Later, when MacSam fails to kill Mrs. Munson, Pancake revisits the civil rights theme but mixes greed with his 1960s ideals, telling him to accept his responsibilities: "Look, with equal rights come equal responsibilities." Both Pancake and Mrs. Munson still view and discuss race openly, but, for the younger generation like MacSam and Lump, that movement exists as nothing more than photos and footage in history. Meanwhile, the General, obviously not American, reflects the 1960s (for Vietnam forever remains connected with that period). He's the ultimate tunnel rat, the face of the former enemy now equalized by a universal desire.

Lastly, Professor Dorr appears like a character frozen during the production of *O Brother*, thawed, and thrust into modern society. Beyond his Mark Twain appearance, Dorr lives in the past by not only representing the poetic version of a Southern gentleman, but by studying dead tongues, loving classical music, and engrossing himself in literature from another era. He explains that he finds in literature "the accum'lated wisdom a mankind which succors me when the day is hard or the night lonely and long." Gathering and maintaining a group of varied and culturally different individuals must have originally seemed like the easiest thing in the world to Dorr, but the collection of characters creates a deep cultural facet to the story, elevating the film beyond pure popcorn fluff.

Thematically, the violence of *The Ladykillers* comes accidentally and out of necessity, which revives the usual Coen black humor in death. Every injury or homicide happens because of attempts to preserve something—only to have misfortune interfere. Those murdered find death by their own hand. The Coens allow chaos to unfold only when the money is stolen, allowing ravenous behavior to overtake the criminals, which blinds their common sense. The first act of necessary violence committed occurs early with the General's introduction: two thugs rob his Hi-Ho Donut only to meet the General, who dispenses swift justice to prevent harm to his family. The brutal, slapstick manner sets the tone for both assault and murder. Mrs. Munson's incessant slapping of MacSam for language happens because she cannot allow him, the only black man among the criminals, to continue his foul and disrespectful behavior. She inflicts the necessary assault while informing him of the lesson that it's the only way.

Death only arrives after the crime's completion when the group decides to kill Mrs. Munson—an act that defines the group, as no one wants the task. Not hardened thugs, they're just greedy and believe that murder, like the robbery, will be the easiest thing in the world. MacSam barks a barbaric, modern solution to walk up and shoot her in the head to make "everything simple again!" Dorr, on the other hand, shudders at the notion of death: "It is the active nature of the crime, though, that so horrifies—the squeezing of the trigger, the plunging of the knife." He looks toward Poe for a resolution: "We have the cellar. We have masonry and trowel. Perhaps we could simply. . . immure her." For each character, the murder momentarily overshadows the money until the General finally makes the choice for them, applying Buddhist metaphors to justify killing her. Once the verdict is reached, each man sets out to commit acts of necessary violence, which results in his own accidental homicide. The violence they attempt to inflict boomerangs, in a sense, to prevent an innocent death.

GOLDTHWAIT HIGGINSON DORR, III, PHD: "I LOVE, LOVE, LOVE THE WORKS OF MR. ED G'ALLEN POE"

Ripe with stereotypes that emulate every possible expected attribute, *The Ladykillers* has one character with no stereotype: Professor G.H. Dorr. As the misfit criminal ringleader, he appears effectively original: he is draped in a white overcoat, suit, bow-tie, and cane. Also, he resembles a demented Colonel Sanders with a skittish laugh, exaggerated front teeth, and a Mark Twain southern drawl. More than an optical joke, Dorr acquires the Coens' characters' passions: non-violence, skittishness, an outcast nature, and not being as intelligent as one lets on.

Dorr's alleged brilliance does nothing more than to alienate him from others. He happily informs anyone in audible distance about his various collegiate degrees and his depth of knowledge in literature, dead tongues, and Renaissance music. He's not of this time; nevertheless, he follows the universal and timeless motivation of monetary gluttony. This fact raises doubts about his authenticity. Is he a con artist or a desperate professor? No explanation is given in terms of his personal motives, and Hanks presents the character in such a manner that enhances the confusion. Dorr is an uncomfortable combination of likeability and seediness, he speaks in riddles fit for a PhD programs. Even with embellished attributes, he remains three-dimensional. He handles all components of the crime with a certain carefulness, as if he doesn't want to offend anyone, especially Mrs. Munson. Regrettably, the Coens don't allow Dorr space for development, but what they do allow rounds out his character—or at least makes him oval as he reveals small pieces about his life, notably information about his father. Dorr explains that his father was the librarian of the state nervous hospital in Meridian, and once told a young Dorr that he was unlike other boys. Not only did his father have mental problems, but perhaps he fueled the Professor's eccentricity by driving him to escape through literature. Clearly, Dorr embraced separation at an early age, and his father helped define the differences.

For Dorr, his alienation comes not just via his appearance or mental state, but from his love of literature. His explanation of this passion develops during one of the few bonding moments between him and Mrs. Munson. The two of them sit together one evening, reading with the windows cracked. Mrs. Munson pauses her own reading to observe his infatuation, leaving Dorr to confess that he often feels more comfortable "in these ancient volumes than I do in the hustle-bustle of our modern world. To me, paradoxically, the literature of the so-called 'dead tongues' has more currency than this mornin's newspaper." Perhaps he reveals a hint of what motivates him within this statement as he explains his loneliness and discontent with modernization. He yearns for the past and (conceivably) desires the casino money in order to disappear into a world where he can recite poetic passages and drift off to a mind filled with his love for Edgar Allen Poe. Perhaps, then, life will be the "easiest thing in the world." This admiration for Poe enhances his depth; it's a passion the rest of the characters lack. Dorr seems to be a manifestation of the Coens' own preoccupation with the past, echoing their own love for literature. After all, his existence seems derived from a literary character, pulled from the pages of some distant book, reflecting the mid-19th century he adores.

Even Dorr's recruiting methods echo old-fashionedness considering the fact that he gathers his ensemble of criminals through a simple newspaper ad in the Memphis Scimitar. The notion of placing such a classified ad adds to the absurd nature of the entire ordeal, but even Dorr's choice in papers is out of date—the Scimitar closed shop twenty years before.[3] Communication and dealing with outsiders isn't easy for Dorr, but he instructs Lump at the film's end to ponder the fortune, and says that, "The comedy must end." His desire, his utter greed brought him to design an elaborate scheme. As a man of intellect, he justifies his reasons to rob the casino to Mrs. Munson, explaining that it's "a painted harlot," pulling people in to commit sin by infusing the false promise of reward with greed. He understands that if he can convince Mrs. Munson to believe in her Good Book, that she'll see that they are working in the name of God. He even promises that whatever money they earn they will donate to charity.

Lastly, Dorr uses Mrs. Munson's beliefs against her, but he carries an extreme fear of the church and religion. As a professor who only studies and does not engage in the outside world, Dorr divides people academically by their beliefs. When the men reach the moral dilemma of whether or not to kill Mrs. Munson, he looks to the General for answers due to his supposed Buddhist beliefs. Dorr desires an easy answer to justify bloodshed, to justify, as he calls it, the "reasons of moral repugnance." When Dorr encounters the possibility of engaging in religious practice, the idea creates immediate apprehension: "I shudder. I quake." Mrs. Munson's very mentioning of church attendance draws panic: "And... engage in divine worship?" For him, the Bible contains worthy literary value, not religious value—it offers advice just the same as any other book. Dorr prizes the accumulated wealth of mankind more for its information than its religious message. He holds faith in his own mind and abilities, but he cannot share a belief in something he cannot visually witness.

In spite of his lack of faith in a higher being, Dorr rejects violence. This is best demonstrated near the end when he handles a silver pistol by pinching the stock with two fingers as if it were a foreign object (much like the violin he picks up at the start). As he informs Lump, "I am the professor, [. . .] the thinker, the 'brains of the operation,' trained in fact in the arts of cogitation." He exhibits no qualms in sentencing someone else to die, but cannot fathom committing the deed himself. He tells Lump he would murder Mrs. Munson if forced, but that act seems difficult to imagine.

The Coens do create a parallel to Poe with the ending. With Lump dead and the money left only to Dorr, a raven from Poe's masterpiece "The Raven" appears—much to Dorr's pleasure. He again recites "To Helen": "The agate lamp within thy hand... Ah, Psyche, from the regions which are Holy Land!" Poe's poetic raven breaks the neck of the bridge's gargoyle, which, in turn, sends Dorr to his doom.

MRS. MARVA MUNSON: "*YOU BEEN TRIED AND FOUND WANTIN'*"

Much like the Professor, Mrs. Munson is lonely, lost in an altered world with morals and ideals no longer in line with her Southern Christian roots. Dorr might find peace with Poe, but Mrs. Munson finds solace in the Bible—both study and memorize their respective works. It's her belief and faith in God that makes her the lone character with religious fortitude; she walks away from sermons having internalized the preacher's words. She recites verses as if they were handed down by God Himself. A strong African-American woman without fear, Mrs. Munson is an unstoppable force not only mentally, but physically as well, with her round physique and a bosom that begs to push someone out of her way.

The movie opens with Mrs. Munson airing her complaints about modern youth and their love for disrespectful "hippity-hop" music. She expresses shock at the use of harsh language, especially the self-reference of African Americans: "You know what they call colored folks in them songs? Have you got any idea? Niggaz! [. . .] Sweet lord a-mercy, izzat where we at?" Quickly, it becomes evident that she often offers similar complaints as the sheriff goes through the motions, dismissing her compliant and playing along with false concern. She is, after all, a widow with nothing better to do than complain about the actions of others. But there's more to her accusations and isolation: much like the original film's Miss Wilberforce, the outside world views her as someone at the end of her mental rope. She constantly brings up her late husband, Othar, as if he remained capable of expressing complaints. She tells the sheriff that he doesn't like the music either. They, like Dorr and his men, dismiss her and her ideals.

Throughout the film, Othar's portrait hangs above the fireplace mantel, serving as Mrs. Munson's watchful protector. The painting can't physically act, of course, but Othar's face alters moods according to the situation. When Dorr attempts to lead Mrs. Munson into temptation, Othar's glare turns into a scowl—one that only Mrs. Munson can see. Others might view her endless conversation with her deceased husband's painting as borderline-crazy, but the love she expresses is felt immediately. She doesn't ramble endlessly, but speaks to him in conversational terms, never pretending he'll respond.

Nevertheless, Mrs. Munson accurately predicts what's to come. Her parting shot with Sheriff Wyner lays the groundwork for Dorr's introduction: "The Apostle John said: Behold, there is a stranger in our midst come to destroy us!" The next scene has Dorr rapping at her door, and her prophecy comes to fruition. Her beliefs warn against the ease of greed and the violence it creates. Mrs. Munson lives a life free of such chaos and that stranger, a man dressed in white, enters into her home like Satan himself. After the introduction of Dorr's men in their outside lives, Mrs. Munson listens in church as her preacher preaches against worshipping false idols. The sermon serves as an effective prediction as he warns against the garbage island "where scavenger birds feast on the bones of the backslidin' damned!" If ever someone foreshadowed events to come, the preacher did so with his psychic-like abilities.

Like Mackendrick's version, Mrs. Munson personifies the moral center. In contrast to the original film, however, Mrs. Munson fails to capture the same adoration. Although Mrs. Munson is an enjoyable character filled with quotable lines and a handful of unique qualities, she emerges as expected. She's a churchgoing Southern woman who yearns to be respected. In the original, Miss Wilberforce seems unassuming, loveable, and fights the stereotypical grandmother persona. She seems sadly senile, and her frail figure adds to the comedic nature of the film considering the fact that such a small woman takes down a well-organized criminal plan. Mrs. Munson also disperses the criminals, but offers nothing wholly original—she is a failed Coen character, lacking distinction or the ability to redefine herself. Her imposing figure, the very opposite of Miss Wilberforce, removes the irony. The viewer expects this proud, very large, very vocal woman to take no grief, especially from criminals who attempt to bribe her into silence. No one can buy off her values, and Dorr has great difficulty attempting to erase them.

Lastly, Mrs. Munson's cat, Pickles, acts as another element of Poe brought to life, though nothing like what the audience might expect: "The Black

Cat." Pickles watches over her with utter devotion, observing the men's deeds, judging them at every turn. He appears at opportune times to interfere. Dorr's first appearance has Pickles scrambling up a tree after Mrs. Munson forces Dorr to climb to retrieve the cat. It not only distracts Dorr, but he plummets to the ground and knocks himself unconscious. At one point, Pickles even steals Pancake's finger and disappears after one of the tunneling setbacks during the panic of the explosion. Once Mrs. Munson is safe and the men are all dead, Pickles returns to the bridge with Pancake's severed finger and drops it onto a barge. He had stowed it away until all the men found their way to garbage island, and the birds feasted on their bones.

GARTH PANCAKE AND THE LADYKILLERS: "THERE'S NO 'I' IN TEAM"

Professor Dorr and Mrs. Munson might be the focal points of *The Ladykillers*, but the merry band of criminals deserve their own examination. Without them, Dorr would be unable to carry out his planned violent deeds. The Coens usually succeed at avoiding clichés; or, at the very least, the Coens bend the idea the cliché. In attempting to cast different criminals with different backgrounds, these four characters come across less believable, less fulfilled. They (minus Pancake) seem to be carbon copy criminals, offering little inventiveness or depth. Each simply represents the parts the crime needed for Dorr's casting call. Dorr even describes them by their generic roles: the tunnel expert, the jack-of-all-trades, the inside man, and the muscle. They each play into the expectations; they are not original or realistic characters, they are merely counterfeit recreations. That's not to say that the Coens lost their creative juices with the film. After all, this project was meant for mainstream audiences, where full-fledged comedic characters are few and far between.

The Ladykillers managed a few standouts, notably Simmons's effectively strange Garth Pancake. Much like Dorr, he's a man not of this modern world; he's like a lost African explorer stuck in the South, complete with hiking boots and a safari jacket. He lives by his catch phrase, even if nothing he encounters ends up being the easiest thing in the world. He applies his trademark phrase in all sorts of situations, such as working with stage dogs and setting detonations. However, an affliction that enhances his character, a struggle with irritable bowel syndrome, grants awkward moments of discomfort for the criminals and the audience. Noticeably, something odd happens to him throughout the film: he pauses during conversation with a distant, disembodied stare. But when it reoccurs later in the middle of the robbery, Pancake takes the opportunity to teach MacSam about the struggles of his condition. While comedic, it also provides further insight into Pancake. He seems neither embarrassed nor boastful, and he appears grateful for MacSam's supposed understanding of his needs.

Besides Mrs. Munson, Pancake appears as the only character with a personal life. He freely admits his dependence on the love of his life, Mountain Girl. He thinks nothing about revealing all information to her, thus breaking the number one rule of the group. Unfortunately, Pancake cannot comprehend the notion: "I don't keep secrets from Mountain. That's not how you maintain a loving, caring relationship." During a meeting at The Waffle House, Mountain freely approaches the group as if a part of them. He cannot fathom when the other members, notably MacSam, balk at her sudden appearance and insult her by calling her his bitch. Pancake will not allow anyone to disrespect his love, and, manhood challenged, he prepares to battle, even when MacSam brandishes a gun. When the incident cools, Pancake's true worries emerge, making him seem less heroic: "Little punk. Oh, look at this. I got blueberry syrup on my safari jacket!"

As Pancake's nemesis, Gawain MacSam is as inept as Pancake. Regardless of his simplistic role as the inside man in the casino, his actions are neither effective nor professional. He's unable to exhibit self-control and harasses customers when they have "an ass that could pull a bus." As a prideful and stubborn man, when MacSam is fired he must recommit himself to offer a bribe to his casino boss, complete with a card, candy, and a $100 bill. The card and candy only help to explain the complex and unbalanced nature of the group. The very decision of how to reinsert MacSam back into his position initiated a near collapse of the gang. He's quick to violence, pulling a gun on Pancake in the argument over Mountain Girl, and it's his erratic behavior that ultimately kills him.

With the movie based in the South, MacSam personifies the stereotypical, modern African-American male: loud, obnoxious, gun-carrying, and disrespectful toward others. MacSam receives one opportunity for development during his necessary attempted murder of Mrs. Munson after he draws the short straw. He marches up the stairs and cocks his gun, but while approaching her with a pillow in hand to muffle the sound, the Coens insert their mandatory flashback, one to his childhood where a young MacSam approaches his mother with a puppy. She threatens a beating and further punishment once his father arrives home. This small scene implies a damaged childhood that would prevent him from killing Mrs. Munson. He snaps out of the dream when Mrs. Munson catches him sobbing behind her, clutching the pillow. Like his own mother, she thoroughly lashes him while informing him of her displeasure that he is involved with such criminal trash. When he returns to the basement and announces he cannot perform the task, even though he claimed, only moments before, how simple murder could be. Knowing murder isn't the easiest thing leads to yet another argument with Pancake. It's their last fight, and when MacSam pulls his pistol it goes off during the skirmish, killing him to create the first accidental death.

The General receives another short straw in terms of character development. A Vietnamese immigrant, the General says little and does little beyond smoking cigarettes. His role is, as Dorr explains, that of the tunnel expert because of his experience with the "soil of his native French-Indochina." Much like American film stereotypes of Vietnamese soldiers, the General never smiles, remains stiffly posed, and sports a Hitler-style mustache. The General agrees that Mrs. Munson must die, but he does not offer his services—even though he clearly possesses the experience. He kills Pancake and Mountain Girl without hesitation after they attempt to rob the loot while the gang is disposing of MacSam's body. When the time comes for the death of Mrs. Munson, Dorr declares, "I believe, at last, we have the right man for the job." Despite his ability to strike silently (as demonstrated by the murder of Pancake), the General is undone by his own love for cigarettes. Throughout, Mrs. Munson scorns him for his constant smoking in her home, and, when he makes his approach for murder, his ego about his abilities clouds his judgment. He hides the cigarette inside his mouth, but he chokes and falls down the stairs and accidentally breaks his neck.

Lastly, Lump exists as a basic, stereotypical Neanderthal, with his mouth constantly agape and a slow, near-mentally-challenged type of speech. The other criminals conceivably could be involved in the crime, but Lump seems less likely—he's nothing more than a brawny football player. Dorr, during his criminal introductions, summarizes his role as "a goon, an ape, a physical brute." Lump, despite his limited capabilities, offers both ideas and ethics to the gang. When MacSam is fired, Lump suggests bribery as the best option. At the end, when all the Ladykillers are dead (minus himself and the Professor), Lump develops a conscience after sending so many bodies over the side of the bridge. Dorr explains that the deed of the murder now falls to Lump, but Lump suddenly indicates sympathy for Mrs Munson. He explains that he cannot murder "a nice old lady like that"—even if it means forfeiting the money. After Dorr belittles him and reduces him to the cliché he is, Lump decides that he cannot allow the death of Mrs. Munson, and follows the path of necessary violence by pointing the gun at Dorr: "Who looks stupid now?" He pulls the trigger. Silence. Lump, confused, stares down the barrel and accidentally shoots himself in the head, looking very stupid in the act.

* * *

Moments before Lump's unintentional death, he repeats a line from *Blood Simple* when the private investigator shoots the bar owner and says, "Who looks stupid now?" The private eye indeed ends up looking stupid. The Coens, however, stole that line, in turn, from the original *The Ladykillers*, which connects their work together. Ethan states, "It's kind of a classic bonehead gag. It all kind of fit somehow and comes full circle."[4] The line links the start of their career to their latest work, but the film failed to garner the same respect that *Blood Simple* did. After all, it earned just over $39 million at the box office with a production budget of $35 million.[5] It left a stale taste among critics, despite the presence of Tom Hanks. As *Rolling Stones*'s Peter Travers summarized: "Sadly, *The Ladykillers* never lives up to its promise. [. . .] The Coens turn the film into an academic exercise."[6] It's the exercise notion of remaking an existing film that removes the luster from their eleventh feature. The Coens appear to simply go through the motions, enjoying the creation of mayhem through lighthearted violence. However, the Coens would return to solidify their place as masters of the crime story in their next film.

12

The Unrelenting Country

No Country for Old Men (2007)

"I don't have some way to put it. That's the way it is."[1]

CAST: Tommy Lee Jones (Sheriff Bell), Josh Brolin (Llewelyn Moss), Javier Bardem (Anton Chigurh), Woody Harrelson (Carson Wells), Kelly Macdonald (Carla Jean Moss), Deputy Wendell (Garret Dillahunt), Tess Harper (Loretta Bell), Barry Corbin (Ellis), and Stephen Root (Man behind the desk).

No Country for Old Men. Directed by Joel Coen and Ethan Coen. Burbank, CA: Walt Disney Video, 2007.

A violent contract killer, a blue-collar welder, and a world-weary sheriff are all players in the ensemble *No Country for Old Men*, Joel and Ethan Coen's adaptation of Cormac McCarthy's grim crime novel about man's strength of will, of word, and of dedication. It's about death and fate, about American violence, about how the Old West's carnage never ended; it just erupts in cycles. Set in 1980, the film depicts monstrously evolving chaos when men kill without purpose—without ethics. Every Coen brother movie has utilized violence as a way to enhance realism, entertainment, and narrative. Each film employs bloodshed in various ways, but *No Country for Old Men* effectively encapsulates all those elements to formulate the nature of American violence: dirty, bloody, unforgiving, gruesome, and unrelenting.

No Country for Old Men kills for more. It personifies the way the Coens use violence for social commentary—that America's lust for blood isn't a modern occurrence, but a part of American history. As one character states, "What you got ain't nothing new. This country is hard on people." Judging from the title, it's easy to decipher the social commentary with its constant references to the elevation of the murderous drug trade along the Mexican border. The film never masks the problem as a modern occurrence. Unrelenting violence always surfaces; it's just that old men can't play that game. Death remains every person's fate, it just becomes a matter of when and how. Characters can attempt to run from the violence, but there's no need because no one has a say in death. As the film's villain explains, "That's the way it is." Regardless, the hero sheriff cannot comprehend modern chaos and claims, "I don't want to push my chips forward and go out and meet something I don't understand." The movie becomes defined by this notion of understanding the evolution of violence, understanding what makes it, and how one battles it.

Until *No Country for Old Men,* the Coen brothers' only other adaptation came from Homer's *The Odyssey* for *O Brother Where Art Thou?*. Calling it an adaptation seems a stretch, though, considering they claim never to have read it. The inspiration for the majority of their works comes from literary influences, but none that are officially adapted. Their choice of *No Country for Old Men* represents a complete adaptation, embodying McCarthy's novel with minimal tampering or alterations and with much of the dialogue coming straight from the text. The occasional scene or incident differs, but the novel remains complete—something rarely accomplished in Hollywood. Vaguely, Joel explains their choice: "We read it and thought, 'Yeah, this would make an interesting movie.'"[2] The Coens insert their pitch-black humor to enhance McCarthy's bleakness, but the comedy occurs naturally. The Coens curb their usual love for exaggeration, creating their most understated work to date. Some critics commented that the movie represents a maturation for the brothers because they finally stopped combining genres; however, *No Country for Old Men* remains a mash-up, combining neo-western, crime, road, horror, chase, and gangster movies. And while none of the characters recite Shakespeare or Poe (for nearly all Coen films derive from literary sources), the Coens allow the greatness of McCarthy to speak for itself, as the Coens barely alter his novel. And why would they, considering critics have stated that McCarthy "must be acknowledged as a talent equal to William Faulkner."[3]

No Country for Old Men opens like all Coen films, with an establishing shot of the landscape with barb-wire fences, wide-open emptiness, and the vast west Texas plains. A narration breaks the silence by informing the viewer about the way things used to be. He speaks of how things have changed and how he no longer has the ability to understand that change. The narration drops out when a deputy arrests a man in black and escorts him back to the station. While the deputy explains his control of the situation over the phone, the man sneaks up behind the deputy, strangles him, and then calmly escapes by stealing a police cruiser. He's Anton Chigurh, a

Mexican bounty hunter/professional killer, and he murders again moments later when he pulls over a man in order to switch cars. Elsewhere in the plains, hunter/welder Llewelyn Moss stumbles across an extinct drug-trade shootout, finding bodies, dead dogs, drugs, and one dying man begging for water. Moss leaves a truckload of heroin undisturbed and discovers a bagged two million dollars. He returns home, but the image of the dying man devours his conscience, so he revisits the scene with water just as another pickup arrives. Moss is shot, but he survives, and he informs his wife, Carla Jean, that she must leave and he must disappear. Meanwhile, narrator and rugged local Sheriff, Ed Tom Bell, and Deputy Wendell investigate the scene on horseback and decipher Moss's involvement. Before they can reach him, Chigurh is already on his trail with a tracking device hidden in the money.

What follows consists of three different men in three separate, interwoven tales engaging in a cat and mouse game through anonymous motels near the Mexican border. Bullets fly and two of the men wound each other and escape to tend to their wounds while the third man picks up the evidential pieces. Concurrently, another bounty hunter, Carson Wells, is called in to stop Chigurh and find the money. He manages to locate Moss, but Chigurh kills Wells for inconveniencing him. Chigurh, in turn, offers Moss a deal to spare his wife in return for the money. Moss refuses, and is killed offscreen while waiting for his wife in El Paso. Later, after Carla Jean buries her mother, she receives a visit from Chigurh to make due on the broken deal. He kills her (though never shown), and leaves only to be side-swiped causing a car wreck. He survives, and he disappears in broad daylight. The film ends with Bell retired and retelling two dreams about his father, and then it cuts to black.

The unresolved conclusion caused many moviegoers to balk at its ambiguous nature and its lack of the classic Hollywood, here's-what-happened-and-why finale. But ambiguity is the point. Where *Fargo* followed strands of predictable storytelling with a hero who saves the day and characters audiences can root for, *No Country for Old Men* plays as a conventional/unconventional movie. The film is conventional with its generic crime thriller plot of a cop, a criminal, an unlucky working stiff, and a bag of money. It's unconventional because it has little resolution, a potential protagonist who dies at the three-quarter mark, a hero who never acts, and a killer without motivation. Ethan explains, "It is unconventional. The good guy never meets the bad guy." Adds Joel, "Nor did it strike us that even if it was unconventional it would lead to an unsatisfying thing for movie audiences."[4] On the surface, it's all an archetypal cat-and-mouse chase. Moss is the mouse that took the unintended bait, caught in a maze without an exit. He's intelligent and skillful, but unprepared for a stalker of Chigurh's caliber as the psychotic cat. Bell emerges as the old hound dog on both their tails.

Throughout the Coens brothers' careers, they recraft clichéd tales and reintroduce them to the public without a recycle sticker attached. Crime and murder occur, but, with *No Country for Old Men,* the trivial aspects matter: air vents, screws, tent poles, locks, phone records, socks, and boots. The small things help to create an effective character study without any explanation of motive. Characters can only react and deal with whatever consequences come their way because, "That's the way it is."

The result is a film that doesn't fill in the gaps, forcing audiences to judge characters solely on their characteristics. Moss, as the common man, possesses the persona of the American working stiff. Sheriff Bell portrays the potential hero, but always remains two steps behind and never catches his big break by happening upon the occurrence of a crime. Chigurh embodies a killer with a personality like few villains before him. A figure of fate and death. Some could view Moss as greedy or as someone who can't pass up a good opportunity. Bell is past his prime to deal with modern crime, hence the title of the film. Chigurh equals chaos, an entity without reason or a normal mode of operation. The rest of society fails to exist to them, which, in many ways, summarizes the movie. American values only exist in old men. The younger generation holds a nihilistic viewpoint. No one, beyond Bell, believes in anything. If they once did, that day has passed. The money, as in *Fargo,* doesn't matter because the plot becomes an exercise in "a narrative superstructure to communicate the ultimate fatalistic meaninglessness of violence."[5] The $2 million becomes a MacGuffin, a popularized Alfred Hitchcock term that denotes an unimportant object that drives the film, because what matters comes from Bell's perspective on the situation. He sees the changing world. After reading a newspaper account about people with dog collars escaping from killers, Bell summarizes the state of American civilization: "Who are these people?" He no longer understands his world.

While Bell's narration offers a simplistic viewpoint of America, it only fits that *No Country for Old Men* lacks a definable musical score, allowing the elements that produce a neo-Western to create the drama: the land, the soaring bullets, and the tension. The film also brings the Coens' careers full circle; their twelfth film owes more to their first film, *Blood Simple,* than just the Texas landscape. It's a straightforward story with the starkness of the land, the dark comedy, and the action. Also, it's arguably their meanest since *Miller's Crossing* and *Blood Simple* in terms of unsympathetic characters and brutality. If *Blood Simple* is a modernistic film noir, then *No Country for Old Men* is the modern Western with the grizzled cowboy sheriff, the outlaw hero in the white hat, and the villain in black. Shootouts erupt in the middle of town without citizen outcry. The men take bullets and barely grimace. They dress their own wounds, saw off shotguns, and create tools on the fly. In other words, the men are survivors: rugged cowboys, both good and bad, set loose in 1980 to do their worst. Texas itself brings forth the automatic cowboy mindset, something both Bell and Moss capture perfectly. Moss exudes not just the image of the lone hunter, but his very actions define the setting. The characters, as in all Coen works, become extensions of their surroundings. Moss isn't just tough, but he's Texas tough. The first personal items he purchases with the $2 million are boots and a hat.

In contrast, the women of *No Country for Old Men* serve no purpose other than to offer support. They do not influence the story in regards to action or the decisions that the men make. It's as if the setting were indeed in the Old West, as if the women lacked the right to vote. Tough minded and independent they might be, but both Carla Jean and Loretta Bell (Tess Harper) mainly just complement their husbands and care for them. They exist outside the mens' world and cannot understand the unrelenting violence the men face until faced with it themselves.

The savagery of American violence begins with Chigurh's introduction: a quick one-two punch of strangulation and a bloody cattle gun. The strangulation in particular demonstrates the level of the Coens' capability to create realistic carnage—to allow the audience to understand the horror that violence delivers. It's not enough that people die or that blood flows, but once again, it's about the trivial details in deaths. When Chigurh struggles to choke the deputy, a barrage of boot marks tattoo the floor with hundreds of black streaks pointing to the desperation for life when death approaches. Afterward, Chigurh calmly gets up, removes his cuffs, washes the blood from his wounds, and disappears. Chigurh's second murder (the man with the car) illustrates two points. One is the trusting nature of people if someone appears official. Why else would a man allow someone to place a cattle gun against his forehead and tell him to hold still, only to have a rod shot through his brain? Second, Chigurh's weapon of choice matters as it explains a viewpoint on society. We are cattle waiting for the slaughter, and Chigurh is the butcher, killing as if it's just another day on the job.

Over the duration of *No Country for Old Men*, Chigurh kills a total of 12 (possibly more) people, and, curiously enough, the violence devolves as the film progresses. During the first half of the film, the Coens never shy from unleashing Chigurh. When he strikes, he kills without mercy. The imaged violence from his shotgun and cattle gun resonates. The unrelenting nature of his acts not only disturbs, but also appears completely realistic, demonstrating the ugliness of violence. The devolution of violence starts with Chigurh's shootout with Moss in the hotel. Aside from the truck owner who is shot in the head after Moss flags him down, both the hotel clerk and Wells's deaths occur offscreen. Wells's death in particular demonstrates that murder means nothing. Calm beyond comfort, the camera pans away when Chigurh shoots Wells with a silenced shotgun as the phone rings. He answers. It's Moss, and while they talk, blood oozes across the room toward Chigurh's feet. Not moving, he places his feet up on the bed and continues the conversation as the blood continues to spread across the floor. By the time he keeps his promise of visiting Carla Jean, the resolution and the violence appear incomplete. Though we're not shown Carla Jean's death, when Chigurh exits and checks the bottom of his socks for blood, it's a clear indication that his brand of violence has struck again.

LLEWELYN MOSS:
"I'M FIXIN' TO DO SOMETHIN' DUMBER'N HELL, BUT I'M GOIN' ANYWAYS"

The Coens know how to make characters underwhelming and average, usually lacking effective social skills, normalcy, and steady jobs as they sit a few rungs down on the social status ladder. They live on the outskirts of the norm, fighting their way to achieve their own definition of success. For Moss, life is no different. A welder living in a trailer home, he's another chump living a meager existence content with deer hunting in the middle of the wide-open Texas plains and watching TV with his wife. Whatever ambition he holds, the Coens never grant him the opportunity to express it. Moments after the audience meets the man, he discovers the bag of money, thus altering his life before defining it. The audience is left with only his behavior to evaluate. He's a tracker, capable of following wounded animals and humans, and he's no stranger in the face of carnage, exemplified by his discovery of the shoot-out. With rotted bodies, decaying dogs, bullet casings, and riddled pick-ups, Moss marches into the scene like a soldier. Without reacting, keeping his rifle drawn, and never stuttering in the wake of the violence, his Vietnam background becomes evident. He inspects the dried bloodbath with curiosity, not disgust.

Ethically, however, Moss shows no sympathy for the death in the desert. He discovers one Mexican, begging for water. Demonstrating no compassion, Moss removes the dying man's weapon and clip and plainly tells him, "I ain't got no water." He immediately thinks of the last man standing, about the possibility of money. Nevertheless, Moss is not heartless. His moral choices reflect the difference between himself and Chigurh. As much as Moss believes he can match a heartless killer, that he can match chaos with chaos, he cannot. A conscience controls him. Carla Jean explains that Moss can take care of himself, that he won't quit, and that he's never backed away from a challenge. But she, along with all characters, fails to understand what they face. Moss has an idea of the danger and understands people will look for the money, but he cannot sleep. He lies in bed with his mind swirling about the dying man begging for water, and he knows he's about to embark on something he'll regret.

Doing so unleashes a vacuum of loneliness and despair. Moss runs from his wife. He runs from Chigurh. He attempts to keep ahead of him, but never can. The money creates an empty world that Moss never complains about, but he's not someone who would. He's willing to disrupt their lives and risk death, as *Fargo's* Marge Gunderson states so eloquently: "And for what? For a little bit of money." Whereas Marge's prisoner, Gaear Grimsrud, fails to respond, Moss's answer would echo the one he gives to Carla Jean: "Things happen. You can't take 'em back." His ideals lead him down his own path. The moral implication of keeping blood-stained money never bothers him. He's a Texan, willing to handle problems without help from others. With his military background and mechanical attributes, he believes he can "take all comers." Unfortunately, unlike his opposition Chigurh, Moss has roots and lives with common morals—elements he cannot afford to have in the face of unrelenting violence.

Socially, Moss falls in line with all Coen leads, living in basic solitude with his wife Carla Jean. Sheriff Bell interviews no one beyond her—no family or friends. There is only one mention about his family before he returns to the scene of the slaughter, and it is when he tells Carla Jean to tell his dead mother that he loves her. The Coens seldom provide detailed backgrounds of their characters; people simply exist in their day-to-day worlds. Moss reveals relatively nothing about his past, his desires, his loves, or his motivation. Most directors feel compelled to reveal some element of personality through conversations, narrations, family pictures, or snapshots from newspapers, but few allow action to dictate the information. What the viewer does realize comes from his dry sense of humor, and his prideful skills as a welder and hunter. But he's no criminal; he just understands opportunity.

Moss exhibits no fear or intimidation when faced with an enemy. He is willing to battle anyone because even he would agree with Chigurh that, "That's the way it is." He's cool under fire during the heart-stopping perusal when he returns to give the dying man water. After a pickup truck attempts to run him down, a pit bull stalks him through a river. The faster Moss swims, the closer the animal comes. Moss emerges from the water first and has the fortitude to eject a bullet, remove the clip, blow the chamber dry, thrust the clip back into place, and shoot just as the dog leaps for his throat. In another scene, after Moss discovers the transmitter hidden in the money and starts to have an idea of what he's facing, he sits on a bed in another hotel room with a shotgun at his side. He expects someone to kick in the door, so Moss flips off the lamp to prepare. The killer's feet approach the door, and he moves away to turn off the hallway light. What Moss doesn't expect is the lock to shoot across the room at him, but he doesn't falter. Moss stands his ground, fires the shotgun, and escapes out the window. He's the only man willing to attack Chigurh. And when they battle on the street, Moss unloads the shotgun and wounds him. Moss, unlike Bell, is willing to understand his enemy. He has "put his soul at hazard" and decided to be part of this violent world. A modern 1980s man, Moss can fight fire with fire as long as he has the right boots and hat.

ANTON CHIGURH: *"WHAT'S THE MOST YOU EVER LOST ON A COIN TOSS?"*

A killer sporting a Prince Valiant hair style and lugging around a cattle gun and an oxygen tank sounds more fit for a slasher sequel to something like *Slumber Party* than one of the most memorable characters of the last 20 years. Cold-blooded psychos are nothing new in cinema, and, if done right, their impact can bewilder and instill fear. *Psycho*'s Norman Bates, *Night of the Hunter*'s Harry Powell, *Silence of the Lambs*'s Hannibal Lecter, *Seven*'s John Doe, or *The Dark Knight*'s Joker all murder for various reasons, but their demeanor, their actions elevate them above the common murderer. Some, like Bates and Lecter, go to great lengths to explain backgrounds and motivation. Others—like Doe, Joker, and Chigurh—provide no explanations, allowing the mystery of motivation to enhance their characters; they are individuals nearly impossible to understand. Bell claims he doesn't want to "go out and meet something I don't understand." But how could he understand someone who kills without purpose, without pleasure. Chigurh portrays the embodiment of evil living outside societal rules. Only he knows whatever code by which he lives. The outside world views him as fellow bounty hunter, Carson Wells, does when he asks Chigurh:

"Do you have any idea how goddamn crazy you are?"

"You mean the nature of this conversation?"

"I mean the nature of you."

Simultaneously, Coen villains always live by their own sense of ethics. From *Blood Simple*'s Loren Visser, to *Raising Arizona*'s Leonard Smalls, to *Miller's Crossing*'s The Dane, to *Barton Fink*'s Charlie Meadows, to *Fargo*'s Gaear Grimsrud, they exist on a separate plain with a disgust of civilized life, of normalcy. Only their values and beliefs matter because they are destroyers without conscience. The characters invoke violence for reasons ranging from insanity, to professionalism, to greed, but all share the commonality of alienation, unable to function among average people. Someone like Gaear kills without warning, evoking terror in Middle America; however, the separation between him and Chigurh comes from Gaear's motivation. All of his murders are motivated by his greed, something Chigurh cares nothing for. However, when Wells describes Chigurh, saying that he's without "a sense of humor," the description fits both Chigurh and Gaear. Both men exist without a vocal personality and immediately become agitated if they feel disrespected.

Nevertheless, Chigurh represents the Coens' natural progression of violence, a frightening representation of contemporary society. He acts as death, fate, and destiny, slaughtering people like livestock. The other characters might be remorseless, but none kills with the freehand that Chigurh wields, executing without greed, without purpose. Whatever motivation drives him lies within. As a person, Chigurh stands alone with a sense of principles and ethics known only to him.

The film begins with Chigurh's non-violent arrest, but why would a man of his capabilities allow himself to be captured? The drug-transaction-gone-bad had yet to occur, so he could have challenged himself to a game of fate. Perhaps he allowed the arrest in order to practice Houdini-like maneuvers. He waits patiently for the perfect chance to strangle the deputy with his own cuffs. The man's death is brutal and painful to watch, and Chigurh exhales not in pleasure, not in excitement, but as if he had completed an effective workout. The murder and escape all unfold with such precision that it cannot be chance. If Houdini said, "I do tricks nobody can explain," [6] perhaps Chigurh defies his own fate. A bored Chigurh murders in his spare time as if it is a hobby.

If Chigurh toyed with defying his own destiny, he brought destiny to others. In one of the most celebrated scenes, one that exemplifies Chigurh as the decider of fate, he forces people to gamble their lives on a coin toss much like the Batman villain, Two-Face, does. The scene equates to more than a demonstration of Chigurh's intimidation; it's the first glance into what makes him tick. With individualistic ethics comes bewildering actions. Chigurh purchases gas, and when the proprietor inquires about the weather where Chigurh came from, the simple comment cannot pass: "What business is it of yours where I'm from, friendo?" The man's small talk results in a near death because Chigurh cannot engage in common pleasantries. He does not understand, nor does he intend to assimilate among normal people. Their conversation becomes a myriad of Chigurh enigmas, starting with his disbelief that the man could have married into his line of work. For a man who doesn't believe in God's rules, Chigurh has his own. Chigurh, as the embodiment of Death, has an option if he chooses to exercise it: a simple coin flip to decide the proprietor's fate. Chigurh explains that the quarter traveled 28 years to arrive here, that it was the coin's destiny to find him. And when the man chooses heads and his life is spared, Chigurh wants the man to recognize the importance of the quarter. He cannot lose the coin, and keeps it somewhere safe because if he loses track of it, it will "become just a coin. Which it is." This scene is a perplexing episode that exemplifies a mystifying character.

Considering the Coens leave Chigurh an enigma, perhaps the best description of him comes from fellow bounty hunter Wells, the man hired to track down both the money and the man. He's the only living man with intimate knowledge of Chigurh and he offers a puzzling background of information. When the unnamed man who hires Wells attempts to pry out information, Wells remains vague. He only admits to knowing Chigurh on sight and to understanding his methods. The man desires to understand the level of danger that Chigurh poses, to which Wells answers, "Compared to what? The bubonic plague? He's bad enough that you called me. He's a psychopathic killer but so what? There's plenty of them around." Wells exists contrary to Chigurh, another professional with his own code of conduct. It's not until Wells visits Moss in the Mexican hospital that he reveals more intimate knowledge of Chigurh. Moss, being an independent survivalist, refuses to admit he's encountered something he cannot comprehend, that he's met something new. Wells attempts to set him straight by explaining that Moss does not understand that he's facing someone with whom no one can make a deal: "He's a peculiar man. You could even say that he has principles.

Principles that transcend money or drugs or anything like that. He's not like you. He's not even like me." The cocksure Wells believes in his abilities, in his own strength; however, he falters when facing death. He knows Chigurh cares nothing for money, but he offers it all the same, and begs like all the others. Despite his credentials, Wells cannot match something that he actually understands.

Chigurh's final sequence implies more than it answers when he visits Carla Jean. He grants her the same chance to remain alive with a flip of a coin: "This is the best I can do." Chigurh, for his unconventional rational and ethics, gives Carla Jean a conventional answer for why he must kill her: "I gave my word." His word, his bond is part of what makes him uniquely deadly. Earlier, he killed the unnamed executive because he had hired Wells and the Mexicans to do his job. The man broke his word, a crime for which Chigurh can justify murder because they had already "picked the one right tool." But for Carla Jean, she, unlike the gas station proprietor, unlike Wells, will not play his game. She refuses to beg, she refuses to choose heads or tails, which produces one of the few moments in which Chigurh loses his temper, demanding she call it. But Carla Jean refuses to break. She understands him and knows what her destiny holds. The Coens avoid showing her slaughter, but her death is clear.

In the end, Chigurh must escape as "you can't stop what's coming." Despite the seriousness of the car wreck when he's sideswiped (his bone rips through the flesh of his arm), he cannot face capture at the hands of Bell. Chigurh does not panic, and, just as Moss purchased clothing from onlookers to aide his escape, Chigurh does as well. He pays a kid for his shirt, creates a sling, and wanders off into the sunset. As the unholy trilogy of death, faith, and destiny, his wrath must continue as the representation of chaos. His kind will always live on, whether the law understands him or not.

SHERIFF ED TOM BELL: *"I FEEL OVERMATCHED"*

The story of the retiring cop on his final case is about as a novel a concept as casting Tommy Lee Jones as a weary officer of the law. In *The Fugitive*, Jones played US Marshal Samuel Gerard, a role that netted him an Oscar and transformed him from effective supporting player to star. It's the type of role Jones isn't against revisiting. He plays the same mold—whether as sheriff, detective, or military man—in seemingly every other movie. Nonetheless, his role of Sheriff Ed Tom Bell adds depth to his clichéd image. No longer stressed, demanding, or intimidating, Bell's a tired man who is short on answers. The world has changed, but he isn't sure when it did, and doesn't know if he still wants to be part of it.

Leftover from 1950s, Bell comes from a place where a man's word meant something and a firearm never seemed necessary. Despite the hailstorm of violence that engulfs him, Bell only pulls out his gun on a single occasion. Before then, he'd send his deputy into a situation first and tell him he's using him for cover. Jones as Sam Gerard never expressed emotion when he chased his fugitive. He famously told Harrison Ford, "I don't care," when Ford's character claimed innocence. On the other hand, Bell contemplates and reflects, creating the lone introspective character in *No Country for Old Men*. He serves as narrator and voice of reason bringing a conscience to the story, because, as the outsider examining the carnage left behind, he's unable to comprehend the weight of all the death. He observes not only as a sheriff, but as a man watching his world change. As an aging sheriff, Bell depicts the difference of age and social class—age, not in years, but in a belief in outworn American values. These values included simple respect for your fellow neighbor and courtesies like using sir and madam to address others.

Moss and Chigurh act and react without explanation, accepting whatever lies before them. For Bell, acceptance doesn't come as easily. He's a professional, never flinching at danger or at the sight of rotting bodies, but at his advanced age, he's become passive, desiring time to understand the man he chases. He attempts to place himself in the criminal's world. Inside Moss's trailer, Bell doesn't panic when he notices Chigurh's still-sweating bottle of milk sitting on the coffee table. Instead, he grabs a glass, pours his own milk, and sits on the same couch where Moss and Chigurh sat, drinking and staring at the same blank television. When Deputy Wendell asks if Moss understands his level of trouble, Bell responds, "I don't know. He ought to. He seen the same things I've seen and it's certainly made an impression on me." For Bell, the "it" he's referring to is Chigurh, a man of unrelenting violence the likes of which no one has seen. Wells claimed Chigurh was "a psychopathic killer but so what? There's plenty of them around." Perhaps that's true in his world, but Bell's world isn't the same. Bell's America shouldn't have this nature of unrelenting violence. In his world, murders have a motive. Killers have a reason to kill. But not Chigurh.

The three main characters never have definitive scenes together. Moss and Chigurh briefly engage, but never face-to-face, as they battle from a distance. In contrast, Bell has his own near encounter with Chigurh. After the death of Moss, Bell returns to the scene of the crime. At the door of room 114, the lock's been blown out. Chigurh has been there. Bell stands there and stares at the hole. The film cuts to Chigurh hidden in the dark behind the door, eyeing the same blown out lock. For the first time, Bell removes his Colt pistol and enters the room. It's empty, and the lock on the bathroom window remains latched. He walks back into the bedroom, and sits on the bed only to notice the removed air vent. A coin lies next to it, heads up.

Questions emerge at this point. Does the coin signify Bell's fate? If it does, then Bell did not call sides as required by Chigurh. In addition, would someone of Chigurh's nature hide? Throughout the film, he's a careful, calculating man, but he never hides. He either confronts someone outright or attacks him at a safe distance. That leaves a final question. Was the image of a concealed Chigurh a figment of Bell's imagination? Bell has no idea as to the man's appearance, but an image of Chigurh in the shadows with only a hint of light invokes devilish qualities like that of an imagination attempting to comprehend what lies on the other side of a door, trying to picture the image of death. Regardless, once inside, Bell noticeably crashes the door against the wall, closing any possible gap for a man to stand. By the time Bell searches the room and sits on the edge of the bed in total relaxation, he's back in his own world until he notices the dropped coin and the removed air duct. Bell never expresses genuine fear, but in that sequence, he appears hesitant for the first time.

After the death of Moss, the story adds a new wrinkle when Bell travels to visit his crusty, wheelchair-bound Uncle Ellis. The man lives in filth, making a fresh pot a coffee a week and allowing cats to rule the home. But it's more than a social call. It's a scene in which many of the themes of the film come full circle. Bell talks about revenge with his paralyzed uncle, a former officer who was wounded by a criminal recently put to death. Ellis, however, would not take revenge, understanding that the time spent focusing on the past only means "more is going out the door." Ellis offers the outsider's perspective. Already altered by violence, what Bell has encountered is nothing new. Ellis knows of Bell's plan to retire and when he asks him why, Bell can only respond with: "I don't know. I feel overmatched." The notion of not understanding modern violence resurfaces as Ellis recounts a story of how Ellis and Bell's uncle died. He explains that this unrelenting violence Bell faces isn't unique: "This country is hard on people. You can't stop what's comin'. It ain't all waitin' on you. That's vanity." Violence has and will always be a part of American history, whether anyone likes it or not. Bell can no more prevent Chigurh's fury than he can stop aging.

Much like Marge Gunderson in *Fargo*, Bell doesn't appear until after the crime has occurred and Moss's troubles have doubled. But, while Marge's husband supports her and remains a partner in her life, Bell's wife, Loretta, conveys the impression of a kindly woman keeping the home warm until Bell's arrival. That's not to say she doesn't carry weight as he expresses fear in hurting her horse while using it on duty. The film concludes with Loretta glaring at a retired Bell as if he had invaded her world. He sits dumbfounded at the kitchen table without any idea on how to proceed in life. Nevertheless, Bell confides in his wife, explaining two dreams in perhaps his most introspective scene from some time after the significant events earlier in the film. One dream he barely recalls, but it involves him losing money, an allusion to Moss's death. The second explores his own mortality, perhaps a display of his acceptance that death eventually comes for all. He sees a younger version of his father riding a horse in mountains back in the olden days. His father passed him carrying a horn with fire. Bell knows his father waits for him with a fire prepared at the top of the mountain: "I knew that whenever I got there he would be there. Out there up ahead." It's comforting to Bell not only in death, but as reassurance that his and his father's laws will continue to battle a force like Chigurh.[7] But then his dream ends with Bell's final line, "And then I woke up." The dream stops just as abruptly as *No Country for Old Men*, as the film snaps to black.

Throughout, Bell measures himself against his father and his generation. He attempts to live up to their standards and understand the things they told him. His dream implies approval from his father as Bell lived his life the best he could. He never became Moss. He never stepped over the edge. He explained in the opening narration that he, his father, and grandfather were all law men. Bell even had the chance to serve at the same time as his father, for they were sheriffs at the same time: "I think he was pretty proud of that. I know I was." At the start of the film, Bell muses about the way his America had changed: "The crime you see now, it's hard to even take its measure." And though things had changed, Bell and all the men of *No Country for Old Men* realized that it is "the way it is." Nothing can be done to alter the events, but Bell recognizes it's nothing he can be a part of.

* * *

No Country for Old Men stands as the Coens' biggest success to date, both critically and financially, earning $75 million at the box office.[8] *Fargo* identified Joel and Ethan Coen as skillful filmmakers, but *No Country for Old Men* solidified them as masters of their craft. Earning four Oscars including Best Picture, Best Director, Best Adapted Screenplay, and Best Supporting Actor for Javier Bardem, the moment meant a full realization of a career spent on the sidelines. The occasional negative review appeared, but *No Country for Old Men* stands as the Coens' best reviewed entry since *Fargo*. Todd McCarthy of *Variety* declared it "a scorching blast of tense genre filmmaking shot through with rich veins of melancholy, down-home philosophy and dark, dark humor." He continues, claiming it as "one of their very best films, a bloody classic of its type destined for acclaim."[9] Overall, this stands as the Coens' movie that broke down mainstream barriers despite its unconventional nature. Yes, *Fargo* received seven nominations and earned two Oscars, but, for all its praise, it did not exhibit the level of maturity found within *No Country for Old Men*, which, for all intents and purposes, is a stark, mean, unforgiving film. The Coens toned down the routinely eccentric behavior of their characters in favor of a more direct, minimalist approach. Humor still exists, but it appears in smaller doses, to play naturally—not for laughs. And considering that music always defines their films, it seems only fitting that *No Country* plays virtually silently beyond the echoes of gun shots and the whispering of the plains.

13

Burning Paranoia

Burn After Reading (2008)

"Appearances can be . . . deceptive."[1]

CAST: George Clooney (Harry Pfarrer), Frances McDormand (Linda Litzke), John Malkovich (Osbourne Cox), Tilda Swinton (Katie Cox), Richard Jenkins (Ted), David Rasche (CIA officer), J.K. Simmons (CIA Superior), and Brad Pitt (Chad Feldheimer).

Burn After Reading. Directed by Joel Coen and Ethan Coen. Universal City, CA: Universal Studios Home Entertainment, 2008.

Whenever an exchange of government secrets takes place, the moment plays out in a tense, teeth-rattling episode. *Burn After Reading* contains such a scene with the exchange unfolding on a busy Washington D.C. street. One man enters a parked car and delivers an unconvincing menacing glare at the driver, leaving the driver unimpressed and annoyed. A problem quickly becomes apparent. The driver has no idea what secrets he's purchasing, and the other man has no idea what he's doing. That other man, Brad Pitt's character Chad, stupidly states, "Appearances can be deceptive." In doing so, he refers to more than his own moronic blackmail scheme. Throughout Joel and Ethan Coen's twelve feature films, the brothers continually toy with deceiving audiences by altering stereotypes, clichéd plots, stock characters, and genres. For their thirteenth film *Burn After Reading,* the Coens again play with deception—this time elevating it to another level with a tale of paranoia amid a group of midlife-crisis-Washingtonians. Their middle-aged dread comes not just from the ticking clock of life, but as a reaction to the unknown, to the fear of possibility.

The Coens effectively fuse the spy genre within a movie that contains no actual espionage; they engage with the notion of Big Brother, despite the fact that no passing of secret information transpires. Needless to say, people spy, lie, and blackmail; their own actions bring forth the government's eye. Their dread, their fear of the unknown, produces a rising level of paranoia that causes characters to react violently without reason. Each begins to suspect the other as they all learn that, "Appearances can be deceptive." As *Burn After Reading* progresses and the suspicion increases, characters lash out with paranoid violence as if faced with no alternative.

Burn After Reading encompasses six lead characters all living in a state of flux. They've all reached a moment of crisis. The story begins with the demotion of Osbourne Cox, an analyst with the CIA. Osbourne's superior suggests his skills have eroded, that he's developed a drinking problem. Osbourne balks at the notion, quits, and makes a drink as soon as he arrives home. He doesn't have the chance to inform his wife, Katie, of his decision, because they soon host a dinner party where Katie's lover, U.S. Marshal Harry Pfarrer, and his wife join them for mundane conversation and expensive snacks. When Osbourne finally informs Katie of his job loss, she expedites divorce proceedings to be with Harry, and obtains Osbourne's financial records, placing them on a disc. Elsewhere at a doctor's office, Linda Litzke explores the possibility of plastic surgery to recapture her youth. She works at Hardbodies, a fitness center with an idiotic personal trainer, Chad, and her boss, Ted. There, she talks openly about the procedures and her new venture into Internet dating. Meanwhile, Katie doesn't realize that Harry has been Internet dating. He meets Linda just as the Osbourne disc falls into Linda and Chad's hands. They believe the disc contains high-level government secrets, so they blackmail Osbourne. After he refuses to pay, they take it to the Russians and promise more information. Chad breaks into the Cox home to snoop, but is shot by Harry who believes he's a government spook. The equally suspicious Osbourne, after being locked out of his home, returns with a hatchet for more liquor and discovers Ted in the basement in search of more government secrets for Linda. In a paranoid state, Osbourne savagely hacks him to death. At the same time, the government watches everything unfold and has no idea what just transpired.

The notion of men behaving stupidly, reacting without thought, isn't an uncommon thread in the world of the Coen brothers. *No Country for Old Men* focused on Texas men and their ability to react to any violent situation. Those characters had strength and a code of conduct even if that code wasn't exactly moralistically normal. *Burn After Reading* plays as *No Country for Old Men's* antonym: suburbanized people without any ability to react. Isolated in multi-storied homes, neutered by marriage, or alone and single, each person has an obsession to make life tolerable: Harry runs, Osbourne drinks, Linda thinks about plastic surgery, and Chad strives to stay hydrated. They represent America's obsession with fitness, with retaining a youthful appearance. Harry's exercise habits have become part of his psyche. If he fails to run, he falls into a depression. Linda, on the other hand, works at an establishment that alludes to the perfect body. No one in the gym, however, displays the body of perfection they all seek (save Chad), which creates an endless, repetitious cycle of trying to obtain something that few ever will.

In addition, *Burn After Reading* comments on modernization, how people pick and choose what advancements they accept. Linda, despite repetitively commenting on her lack of computer aptitude, engages in Internet dating to find the man of her dreams. Ted warns against people who cruise the Internet, even as Linda freely admits that she and Harry cruise the Net. Nevertheless, everyone has been relegated to a state of mental mistrust, reacting to their own warped viewpoint, not to any actual threat. Fear drives and motivates the characters, even if no one understands what frightened them to begin with. Characters all obsess over something, and no one appears grounded in basic societal values. Everyone lives independently, as if their actions have no consequences, as if no one will notice when they fight back against veiled threats.

Burn After Reading unfolds like a reaction to the success of the *Bourne Identity* franchise, where anxiety dominates the lives of anyone who realizes someone could be watching. These Coen characters all remain in a state of crisis, as all parties involved attempt to find some unknown happiness after realizing that their current situation isn't good enough—a common Coen theme. There's a mystery component, an X-factor out there. It's just a matter of whether they can live long enough to find it.

As much as *The Big Lebowski* incorporated mistaken identity to define its violence, all deaths that occur in *Burn After Reading* happen as a result of mistaken paranoia. Everyone believes someone is someone else, and no one can decipher exactly what transpired. The CIA chief effectively summarizes the situation by asking, "What did we learn?" In the end, only the audience learns that paranoia kills while the characters remain too stupid to understand.

That idea, the cluelessness, the unresolved plot, echoes the spy genre, where the act of spying and the agent involved emerges as more important than the target. After all, the disc, "the raw intelligence," echoes the money in both *Fargo* and *No Country for Old Men*—the disc is nothing more than a MacGuffin. Here, the characters live in the world of Washington politics and believe pertinent information could be found lying on a gym floor; it could happen in a city like D.C. The Coens never reveal what the disc actually contains—not that it matters. What does matter is how that object changes those who encounter it, the supposed power it creates. Chad becomes a gluttonous "Good Samaritan" as a result of the object; Linda envisions the object as a means to complete her surgeries. They transform from mere gym employees to blackmail artists, stopping at nothing to retrieve a financial reward that they supposedly deserve. For Osbourne and Harry, their lives dissolve the moment the disc surfaces. Osbourne's suspicion of CIA backstabbing grows.

Harry suspects that agents hide around every street corner, yet he never stops to question why. Then again, none of the characters ponder such a sensible question.

Seemingly, *Burn After Reading* doesn't begin with the Coens' traditional establishing landscape shot of the surroundings; instead, it's a Google Earth view of America that quickly zooms down to focus on Washington. Much like Will Smith's *Enemy of the State,* the unseen satellite eye suggests paranoia before a single event occurs. By the time the camera transitions inside CIA headquarters, the setting of the nation's capital automatically brings forth an expected state of panic—regardless of profession, regardless of social status, anyone could stumble upon "raw intelligence" at any time. Spies follow citizens in unmarked government vehicles wearing matching suits and sunglasses. That's what Washington does. It implies a new age Big Brother. The Coens enhance this state of paranoia through suspenseful music and lurking, hidden camera angles that suggest someone is watching at all times. By the film's end, we realize that the government indeed spied, but only did so because of the characters' actions, not because they were targets initially. If D.C.'s heritage comes with an expected past, so do the characters: everyone in *Burn After Reading* mentally exists in a different time period as each lives in the past to some extent. Chad looks as if he still embraces the early 1990s. Harry cannot accept his age. But it's Linda's decision to take the disc to the Russians that solidifies the film's stance of not fully embracing the present. Much like *The Big Lebowski,* characters in *Burn After Reading* relish history, connecting current day with the espionage of the Cold War. In light of this, the audience can answer Osbourne's quandary: "Why the fuck would they go to the Russians?!" For Linda and Chad, it's obvious: they've learned through high-profile cases and films such as *Breach* that big money exists in selling secrets to the Russians.

As *Burn After Reading* embraces the spy film genre, the inclusion of the CIA comes with a satirical look at espionage. The scenes within CIA headquarters all incorporate the same clichés: men walking, long hallways, pristine offices, neatly-dressed officials. Big Brother really does observe all, but in the Coen world, the men in charge remain just as clueless as Chad. The CIA men do their jobs accordingly, just a part of the stereotype, forced onto a job without knowledge of what they're doing. They know the players; they know their violent paranoid actions. The motivation, however, remains a mystery. The film doesn't begin with governmental morons. Instead, it dismisses Osbourne, the weak link in the CIA chain, which leads the audience to believe that they understand their actions. The government isn't completely inept. As an agent reports to his CIA superior who asks what they've learned, it's evident that they are as clueless as anyone is. When neither knows, he states, "I don't fucking know either. I guess we learned not to do it again. Although I'm fucked if I know what we did."

After the unrelenting, unpredictable violence of *No Country for Old Men*, *Burn After Reading* contains some remnants of that savagery—perhaps the Coens hadn't gotten the brutality out of their systems. With only two on-screen deaths, it pales in comparison to *No Country for Old Men*, *Fargo*, or *The Ladykillers* in body count or carnage, but the violence echoes its gritty spy genre influence: the deaths are brutal, bloody, and realistic. Paranoid violence is contagious. In spite of the comedy label, *Burn After Reading* never lightens its physical assault. The very concept of espionage action produces levels of panic and intimidation, inducing natural responses. The film acts as a summation of those feelings and the reaction to them. Even the most docile individual, the most passive-aggressive character, could act violently if in danger, if unjustly pursued.

The first half of the film remains void of violence with no character having a plausible reason (or the gall) to act. As tension mounts, it's clear someone will strike. It just becomes a matter of whose distrustful nature swells first. For Harry, the swelling finally explodes in his shocking shooting of Chad, a scene that not only serves as an entry into chaotic violence, but adds an additional layer to the film's sexual overtone considering Chad's uncertain sexuality. Like *The Man Who Wasn't There*'s Ed Crane, Chad expresses no sexual inclination and emerges asexual. Chad helps Linda choose dates with the general interest of a friend helping out, yet never makes mention of any dates for him. Apparently, he lives for Hardbodies.

Just before Chad's death, an allusion could be drawn as the scene echoes Hitchcock's *Psycho* as Norman Bates watches Marion Crane undress through a hole in the wall. Chad, hidden in the closet, witnesses Harry's disrobing and subsequent shower. Opportunity existed to escape, but Chad remained, uncertain how to flee. Chad expresses no sexual lust for Harry, but it's an obvious parallel.

Harry's eventual gun discharge into Chad's face was effectively foreshadowed as he redundantly mentions that he's packing heat: "It's no big deal [. . .] I don't think about it—'course, you're not supposed to think about it." That lack of action mirrors Sheriff Bell from *No Country for Old Men* who never pulled his pistol despite the job. Regardless, just as Bell finally did, Harry ultimately removed his gun from its holster. Prior to that moment, his anxiety level had reached a peak with the mysterious cars tailing him and countless affairs. When Harry opens the closet doors, his instincts remain and he blows a hole through Chad's grinning face. The moment enhances Harry's cowardly nature, and he runs from the episode, tumbling down the stairs and darting to the kitchen for a knife. He calls out to the intruder as if the man survived a gunshot to the forehead. He goes back to the corpse, and kicks it despite the overwhelming evidence that it's already past tense.

Likewise, another violent strike comes via Harry's nemesis, Osbourne. As the only former spy, Osbourne's already suspicious of his wife, career, and the world in general. His paranoid violence occurs when he returns to his former home to reclaim what he deems he is owed. He discovers Ted in the basement. Osbourne, though, does not react because of the break in or his wife's betrayal, but because, for once, he holds the upper hand: "Guess what. Today I win." All frustrations erupt as he shoots Ted, yet somehow, he's foiled by a deadly three-hole punch, causing him to drop the gun and chase him up the stairs. Considering Osbourne had already regressed as a man, he fittingly enough grabs the primitive hatchet to dispense with Ted, savagely and repeatedly chopping at his skull. Offscreen, we learn that an ever-present agent shot Osbourne, but the effect of Harry and Osbourne's paranoid violence had already been felt throughout the world of *Burn After Reading*.

HARRY PFARRER:
"I TOLD MYSELF I WAS GONNA STOP BEING PARANOID"

If George Clooney is listed in a Coen brothers feature, his character comes with expectations: he will no doubt be cowardly, idiotic, vain, hollow, and prideful more so than other characteristics. In previous films, Everett *(O Brother, Where Art Thou?)* had been prideful about his hair, and Miles *(Intolerable Cruelty)* obsessed about his teeth. For *Burn After Reading*, Harry's vanity is his physique; he always feels his midsection, as if he might gain weight on a moment's notice. Of course, he doesn't need the extra exercise. Harry's a sex addicted, adulterous, exercise fanatic deep into a midlife crisis. Where Clooney's previous characters, Everett and Miles, searched for missing components in life, Harry yearns for something he cannot reclaim: his youth. While in bed with Katie, Harry remarks that he married too young and now he felt his mortality: "You start to think, well, there's no more time for dishonesty." As a married man, he uses his midlife crisis as an excuse to engage in wild, youthful behavior, sleeping with one woman after another. He comes clean with Linda, giving her "full disclosure" that he's married, even if he lies about being separated. He uses his career as a Marshall to attract his women. He unbuttons his collar to show off his gold necklace, and he exudes sexuality upon meeting women by telling them about the big gun he carries—a fact he disingenuously dismisses: "It's no big deal." Regardless, he's an aging ladies man wearing a gun to impress dates; whatever front he puts up, Harry's a lonely, insecure man. He expresses his love for each woman, and claims his solidarity: "You and me are rock solid." When an affair falters, he calls his wife and expresses his sudden need. When that fails, he turns to a new flame, Linda, in a depressive state. At the start of the film, Harry mocks Osbourne's notion of having a psychiatrist, but if any character needs psychological help, it's Harry. His dishonesty and inability to express a truthful emotion describes the first of many unsympathetic characters in *Burn After Reading*.

Perhaps no character embodies paranoia like Harry. He feels eyes upon him, and each time he attempts to intercept the potential spies, they disappear and leave Harry glaring menacingly in the street. As a U.S. Marshal,

Harry, unlike Osbourne, has no real reason to suspect foul play. Nothing suggests that Harry's work is dangerous or that any personal threats exist. A serial adulterer, he could fear reaction from an angry husband or lover, but the Coens never reveal such distress. Instead, Harry is naturally observant, inquiring about flooring ("What is that, forbo?") and able to detect potential intelligence work because he himself is practiced in the art of deceit. He lies to his wife, to Katie, to his Internet women, to himself.

Nonetheless, beneath that suave exterior, Harry reflects the working-class Coen man with greatly exaggerated intelligence—a fact that doesn't prevent him from believing he's an authority on all subjects. He completes his wife's sentences and dominates any discussion he enters. If Clooney's previous characters were potentially related (as Clooney suggests they are), then Harry is their sleazy cousin discovering his sexual prime. He sweats lustfulness, for it's his only focus in life. He dedicates time and endless energy to create a special sex chair for his wife. It is, in his mind, a work of art, and he reveals it like a proud inventor to Linda, who responds, "It's fantastic." As his life crumbles, only sex remains for Harry. When he leaves Katie soon after Chad's death, the only object he storms out of the house with is his carnal wedge cushion. By the time he receives divorce papers, he destroys his wife's present, the sex chair— the summation of his erotic nature. At the film's end, Harry's lifestyle had finally eroded, leaving him a paranoid wreck who attempts to flee to Venezuela to escape a nonexistent scheme to capture him.

OSBOURNE COX:
"YOU REPRESENT THE IDIOCY OF TODAY"

Nearly all characters in *Burn After Reading* experience some form of midlife crisis. With Osbourne, it's unknown to what extent he loathed his existence before unceremoniously leaving the CIA; however, it's clear that he viewed the bottle as a source of relief. And the moment he leaves the agency, his life erodes, falling into utter disarray. He fails to gain consulting work; he fails at his memoir when his writing stalls as he's distracted by *Family Feud* and booze. He fails to care. Osbourne has reached the cliché crossroad, unsure how to progress. Obviously intelligent, his pride in his own brilliance created a distance from others. The world is out to get him, and he views the rest of civilization as inferior, all belonging to "a league of morons." During his confrontation with Ted, Osbourne reveals his disgust for his surrounding world: "You're one of the morons I've been fighting all my life." Several scenes illustrate this behavior. His very reaction to his CIA demotion ("This is a crucifixion!") results in not only paranoid thought, but his belief in his elevated societal status—as if he is owed the position.

Osbourne's first encounter with Harry shows the differences between their characters. As a member of the working class, Harry can converse in communal situations, feeling at home with all levels of society. Osbourne, on the other hand, speaks with negativity and in a condescending tone, correcting minor speaking faults and assuming everyone has a shrink. Even his tone alludes to a distinct difference between his Ivy League status and everyone else. However, if "a league of morons" surrounds Osbourne, then he willingly includes himself as an honorary member. After all, Osbourne deals with his blackmailers himself instead of contacting the authorities. He calls in a favor to an old CIA friend for background information and surveillance, but Osbourne appears more curious about who they are than interested in rectifying the situation. He's bored with life, and this dumbed-down mystery, whether intended or not, makes him paranoid. He must know the truth, even if no truth exists.

In remaining true to the characters of *Burn After Reading,* Osbourne cannot accept the modern age. He yearns for the Cold War and seeks approval from his comatose father. The world has changed around Osbourne, yet he still yearns to please his father—even as he creates excuses for failure. He believes government service no longer remains the same as when he served: "Things are different now. I don't know, maybe it's the Cold War ending. Now it seems like it's all bureaucracy and no mission." In many respects, Osbourne acts as a perverse reflection of Sheriff Bell from *No Country for Old Men:* both men followed their fathers, both remain proud to have worked alongside their fathers, and both seek their father's approval in their actions and decisions. Yet neither man can receive that approval as Bell's father had long been dead and Osbourne's father remains just as distant. Their fathers are a reminder of the way things used to be. Likewise, Bell and Osbourne offer moral commentary on the state of the nation. Though they demonstrate radically different ideals, both have grown tired of a system they no longer understand: "Independent thought is not only not valued there. They resist it. They fight it." Whatever skills Osbourne obtained from the CIA, he lost in alcohol and the monotony of the job. Besides, how could he not observe the warning signs of Katie's affair and the looming divorce? If he remained indifferent to the infidelity like *The Man Who Wasn't There*'s Ed Crane, he would have failed to react with violence upon finding Ted in his basement. Osbourne kills not just for the supposed affair, but Ted becomes a summation of Osbourne's hatred for the modern world.

With Osbourne and all other characters infected by paranoia and stupidity, only Katie remains unaffected. She—the stereotypical, stiff British woman—never suspects, never bothers to care for any other character. She divorces Osbourne at his lowest moment, wanting to prevent any possibility of him taking advantage of her, living off of her wealth. Her lawyer states, "Here is a man practiced in deceit," as he refers to Osbourne's CIA career, but in truth, Osbourne hides very little. He drinks so much that his employers have taken notice, and empty glasses populate the Cox home. Still, Osbourne does not carry on an affair. On the other hand, it is Katie who is "practiced in deceit," engaging with a married man at length. Regardless, only she remains status quo, and she acts as if she's in a different film altogether. Everyone around her loses sanity while she continues on, business as usual. She's proud, ruthless, and vocally clear that she never sets out to "hammer" anyone. She doesn't seek to ruin Osbourne. She's simply over him.

It's hard not to agree with Katie. Though the Coens withhold any background information about their marriage, it's clear Katie had long since moved on. Osbourne is unemployed, pudgy, and newly single. The Coens show his midlife crisis through visual disintegration: a slow devolution, leading to his physical and emotional erosion. Physically, Osbourne starts the film with a suit and bow tie, the very image of his Princeton roots. By the time he murders Ted, he has completely unraveled. The expensive wardrobe is now replaced with slippers, a robe, and boxer shorts. Whatever pride he once had for the exterior world vanishes once his mental world breaks down, because, emotionally, his state of mind reflects his state of undress. In short, bureaucracy no longer motivates Osbourne: "I just got so tired. [. . .] Of swimming against the current." He withdrew from the only thing he ever knew, effectively resigning himself to the bottle.

LINDA LITZKE AND HARDBODIES: *"I HAVE GONE JUST AS FAR AS I CAN GO WITH THIS BODY!"*

Linda's first appearance is perhaps as unflattering a scene as any character's introduction into a film. She sits in a doctor's office in a hospital gown and is poked, probed, and marked on all her unsightly places. She desires to turn back the clock on her body that she deems no longer fit for someone her age. As an employee of Hardbodies, Linda feels her appearance can no longer deceive those around her. She desires the image flaunted by the media—to be a woman she never was to begin with. The Coens carefully avoid surrounding her with attractive women. Even those who frequent Hardbodies are far from pinup status. The result is to demonstrate that Linda has succumbed to a pessimistic viewpoint of herself; she feels she is no longer attractive, no longer able to deceive others about her age. She obsesses over the surgeries to the point that she never materializes as a three-dimensional character. She's vain and bare, unable to capture sympathy—even if she never asks for it. In fact, no character captures the audience's sympathy; everyone in *Burn After Reading* descends and emotionally erodes, leaving no one to root for. There's no Marge Gunderson, no Dude, no one character who offers a commonalities with which the audience can connect. Linda embodies this idea: as her friends disappear and die, as the federal government arrests her, she still only cares about her surgeries. She willingly accepts all charges they place against her if they'll just pay to make her beautiful. It's a flaw in the film, similar to the mistake made in *The Hudsucker Proxy*: puppet-characters simply waiting for their strings to be pulled.

Comparing Linda to McDormand's iconic character, Marge, invokes certain undeniable similarities: positive energy and the usage of humble phrases. As an officer, Marge never exhibits negative thinking, but she never has to explain herself. She projects warmth and common humanistic caring, able to appreciate a beautiful day regardless of the mass murderer in her back seat. For Linda, no matter the situation, she believes in the power of positive energy. With persistence and hard work, she can accomplish anything. When people produce negative energy (which Chad, Harry, and Ted do), Linda abolishes such thoughts: "I don't like the snideness, nor the negativity." It's as if she attended an empowerment lecture, took notes, and integrated the ideas into her own life. Yet, Linda never sees the irony in her pessimistic body image. She expects the people around her to express optimism, but it's only to better insulate her own fragile psyche.

Similarly, Marge speaks with the manners of an elementary school teacher in spite of her position as the police chief. Linda, however, takes it a step further, spewing out one peculiar comment after another: "I have very limited breasts, a ginormous ass and I have this gut that swings back and forth in front of me like a shopping cart with a bent wheel." Her doctor eloquently describes her, telling her she has a way with words. Linda has allowed her obsession about the perfect body to block what's right in front of her in Ted. She dates distasteful, uninteresting men even though Ted, a markedly less distasteful man, obviously fawns over her. She's either too dense or too self-absorbed to realize that the very person she seeks has an office only a few feet away from hers.

Linda's partner in crime, Chad, emerges as *Burn After Reading's* standout. The Coens had long expressed interest in working with Pitt, and they didn't hesitate making him perhaps their most moronic creation: the ultimate 1990s "mimbo." Layered in spandex and drinking from water bottles like a nursing child, Chad's an airhead with a streaked pompadour hairdo. He looks like an extra from *Bill and Ted's Excellent Adventure.* Upon discovering the disc, Chad reacts like someone who has seen one too many movies of intrigue. He leaps to the conclusion that a regular burned disc with "signals and shit" contains intelligence: "I think that's the shit, man. The raw intelligence." Try as he might, Chad barely formulates ideas, possessing only a few key words. He appears incapable of deviating from his limited train of thought. In a sense, Chad resembles an idiotic version of Pitt's character, Tom Bishop, from *Spy Game*, who was a captive CIA operative facing death. It seems Chad owned that film and summoned Bishop's attributes for his own spy game.

Beyond helping his friend Linda and igniting the paranoid violence, Chad has little to do. He never states an amount for his cut of the reward and willingly follows along once Linda states that the money will "put a big dent in my surgeries." Nevertheless, as Linda ponders the idea of the reward, she expresses social commentary on America's sense of entitlement. She compares extorting money from Osbourne with that of frivolous lawsuits, equating it with the notion of slipping on the ice at a fancy restaurant: "This is our opportunity, like, you don't get many of these." Not fully comprehending, Chad goes along with whatever Linda recommends. The "raw intelligence" is their patch of ice, and, to them, it's worth $50,000 in return for what Osbourne never lost.

From the beginning, Chad works as Linda's idiotic pawn. Two scenes describe this reality best. The first comes through Chad's meeting with Osbourne, where he attempts to mimic whatever spy film he draws upon. On Linda's recommendation, he arrives at the meeting in an ill-fitting suit to present professionalism, but he rides his bicycle, listening to his iPod. The fact that Chad carries his helmet into Osbourne's car epitomizes his amateur approach, as does his speaking in low, hushed tones and sticking to a minimal script. He repeats ideas: "Appearances can be deceptive. I am a mere Good Samaritan." Osbourne lectures him on the legality of blackmailing classified information, and Chad can only squint and stare until Osbourne finally punches him, leaving Chad fleeing the car like a wounded child. He's someone completely averse to violence, and when Osbourne presents the unexpected and painful assault, Chad can only curse—"You fuck!"—and run. The second scene occurs once Chad breaks into Osbourne's home for additional information. There, he again attempts to play a man of intrigue, even down to removing all identifying marks for "deniability" at Linda's request. As Chad observes Harry and Katie walking into the house from his car, he has the perceptiveness to notice not one, but two cars surveying the house. Regardless, once the couple departs, Chad breaks into their home—despite people clearly watching. Once inside, Chad plays sleuth, sneaking through the home to avoid detection until he mistakenly remains in the closet a little too long. And, considering Chad broke into the basement and negated Osbourne's computer there, it speaks to his investigative skills.

If Chad portrays the child of Hardbodies, then Ted portrays the father. His comforting, humble nature indicates his care for his employees. He's the most normal, most believable character. If anyone elicits sympathy, perhaps Ted does. His love for Linda and her utter blindness to him helps provide the film with much needed heart. He's the only character given a past, revealing the fact that he spent 14 years as a Greek Orthodox priest. Naturally, the Coens give no explanation for his departure from the profession because Ted quickly changes the conversation, explaining to Linda that her desire to reverse time is unnecessary; no one can prevent life. Unfortunately, Ted is given minimal screen time, and by the time he breaks into Osbourne's home for information, his fate has been sealed. He falls into the femme fatale trap of noir women without a femme fatale or the noir genre present. Regardless of his initial disapproval of the discovery of the disc ("I am not comfortable with this."), Ted commits several crimes for Linda because of his hidden, loving desire.

Ted first attempts to steer her down the correct path, recommending the police once Chad has disappeared, but Linda's words scar him as she berates him because of his negativity toward the situation. In his mind, a brief crime venture will be worth it if it brings Linda closer. Caught in Osbourne's basement, Osbourne pulls a gun on him and recognizes him from the gym. Ted attempts to explain, "I'm not here representing Hardbodies," but Osbourne insults Linda, which causes him to defend her honor. Despite the stupidity of entering someone's home to steal supposed classified information, Ted, like Chad, never falls victim to paranoia. He never succumbs to violence. Chad said, "Appearances can be deceptive," but no one could have foreseen that the sudden appearance of a harmless burned disc could ruin not just the lives of those who handled it, but eliminate the entire staff of Hardbodies.

* * *

Following up a four-time Oscar-winning film, *No Country for Old Men*, with a goofy spy comedy shouldn't come as a surprise. Only twice have the Coens made similarly toned movies back-to-back. First *Miller's Crossing* and *Barton Fink*, then *Intolerable Cruelty* and *The Ladykillers*. Like the latter Coen comedies, *Burn After Reading* boasted extreme star power and followed in the tradition of stupid people making even dumber decisions. However, one consistent element remains in all Coen films. They split the critical vote. There's the negative: "Chilly, heartless, condescending: all the usual adjectives that the Coen brothers' detractors habitually fling can be flung in spades at *Burn After Reading*."[2] Another critic summarized the film, stating that the Coens have made a career "with impeccable technique and an exaggerated visual style, [. . .] but it's a wonder they keep making films about a subject for which they often evince so little regard, namely other people."[3] Nevertheless, mostly positive reactions triumphed, as Roger Ebert plainly explained, "This is not a great Coen brothers' film. Nor is it one of their bewildering excursions off the deep end. It's funny, sometimes delightful, sometimes a little sad, with dialogue that sounds perfectly logical until you listen a little more carefully and realize all of these people are mad."[4]

In spite of the usual critical uncertainty, the combination of post-Oscar buzz and the reunion of Clooney and Pitt allowed *Burn After Reading* to become their second highest grossing film to date (over $60 million domestically from a $37 million budget[5]), and continued the Coens' unconventional, unique path to mainstream success.

Notes

INTRODUCTION

1. Kent Jones, "Airtight," *Film Comment* 36, no. 6 (Nov.–Dec. 2000), 49.
2. Karen Jaehne, "Ethan Coen, Joel Coen, and *The Big Lebowski*," Film Scouts, 1998, http://www.filmscouts.com/scripts/interview.cfm?File=coens.
3. Raymond Chandler, *The Simple Art of Murder* (1934; New York: Vintage Crime, 1998), 15.
4. David Edelstein, "Invasion of the Baby Snatchers," in *The Coen Brothers: Interviews*, ed. William Rodney Allen (Jackson: University of Mississippi, 2006), 24.
5. Andy Lowe, "The Brothers Grim," in *The Coen Brothers: Interviews*, 97.
6. Jonathan Romney, "Double Vision," in *The Coen Brothers: Interviews*, 129.
7. Kristine McKenna, "Joel and Ethan Coen," in *The Coen Brothers: Interviews*, 176.
8. Chandler, 3.
9. McKenna, 181.
10. Chandler, 15.

CHAPTER 1

1. *Blood Simple*, DVD, directed by Joel Coen (1985; Universal City, CA: Universal Studios Home Entertainment).
2. Roger Ebert, 15th-anniversary review of *Blood Simple*, directed by Joel Coen, *Chicago Sun-Times*, March 1, 1985, http://rogerebert.suntimes.com/apps/pbcs.dll/article?AID=/19850301/REVIEWS/503010302/1023.
3. Dashiell Hammett, *Red Harvest, The Novels of Dashiell Hammett* (1929; New York: Knopf, 1979), 102.
4. Peter Körte and Georg Seesslen, *Joel and Ethan Coen* (New York: Limelight, 2001), 52.
5. Owen Gleiberman, "First Blood," *Entertainment Weekly*, July 28, 2000, 153.
6. James M. Cain, *Double Indemnity* (1926; New York: Vintage Crime, 1992), 101.
7. Dashiell Hammett, *The Maltese Falcon* (1930; New York: Vintage Crime, 1992), 1.
8. Körte and Seesslen, 60.
9. Ebert.
10. Stephen Harvey, "Pretty but Dumb," *Film Comment* 20, no. 6 (Dec. 1984), 66.

CHAPTER 2

1. *Raising Arizona,* DVD, directed by Joel Coen (1987; Beverly Hills, CA: 20th Century Fox Entertainment).
2. Michael Ciment and Hubert Niogret, "Interview with Joel and Ethan Coen," in *The Coen Brothers: Interviews,* ed. William Rodney Allen (Jackson: University of Mississippi, 2006), 27.
3. Ciment and Niogret, 27.
4. Erica Rowell, *The Brothers Grim: The Films of Ethan and Joel Coen* (Lanham, MD: Scarecrow Press, 2007), 41.
5. Rowell, 43.
6. Robert Louis Stevenson, *The Strange Case of Dr. Jekyll and Mr. Hyde,* Enriched Classic (New York: Washington Square Press, 1995), 76, 83, 88.
7. Box Office Mojo, http://boxofficemojo.com/movies/?id=raisingarizona.htm.

CHAPTER 3

1. *Miller's Crossing,* DVD, directed by Joel Coen (Beverly Hills, CA: 20th Century Fox Entertainment, 1990).
2. Box Office Mojo, http://boxofficemojo.com/movies/?id=goodfellas.htm.
3. Box Office Mojo, http://boxofficemojo.com/movies/?id=millerscrossing.htm.
4. Carolyn R. Russell, *The Films of Joel and Ethan Coen* (Jefferson, NC: McFarland and Company, 2001), 45.
5. Richard Corliss, review of *Miller's Crossing, Time,* September 24, 1990.
6. Sinda Gregory, *Private Investigations: The Novels of Dashiell Hammett* (Carbondale: Southern Illinois University, 1985), 116.
7. Dashiell Hammett, *The Glass Key* (1931; New York: Vintage Crime, 1989).
8. George Grella, "The Hard-Boiled Detective Novel," in *Detective Fiction: A Collection of Critical Essays* (Englewood Cliffs, NJ: Prentice Hall, 1980), 110.
9. Dashiell Hammett, *Red Harvest,* The Novels of Dashiell Hammett (1929; New York: Knopf, 1979), 112.
10. Steven J. Lenzner, "A Cinematic Call for Self-Knowledge: An Interpretation of *Miller's Crossing,*" *Perspectives on Political Science,* Spring 2001, 89.
11. Jean-Pierre Coursodon, "A Hat Blown by the Wind," in *The Coen Brothers: Interviews,* ed. William Rodney Allen (Jackson: University of Mississippi, 2006), 44.
12. Coursodon, 44
13. Lenzner, 6.
14. Roger Ebert, review of *Miller's Crossing,* directed by Joel Coen, *Chicago Sun-Times,* Oct. 5, 1990, http://rogerebert.suntimes.com/apps/pbcs.dll/article?AID=/19901005/REVIEWS/10050306/1023.

CHAPTER 4

1. *Barton Fink,* DVD, directed by Joel Coen (1991; Beverly Hills, CA: 20th Century Fox Entertainment).
2. Richard Schickel, "A Three-Espresso Hallucination," *Time,* August 26, 1991, 58.
3. Brigitte Desalm, "*Barton Fink,*" in *Joel and Ethan Coen,* eds. Peter Korte and Georg Seesslen (New York: Limelight, 2001), 122.

4. Erica Rowell, *The Brothers Grim: The Films of Ethan and Joel Coen* (Lanham, MD: Scarecrow Press, 2007), 116.
5. Jim Emerson, "That *Barton Fink* Feeling: An Interview with the Brothers Coen," Cinepad, http://cinepad.com/coens.htm.
6. Michael Ciment and Hubert Niogret, "A Rock on the Beach," in *The Coen Brothers: Interviews*, ed. William Rodney Allen (Jackson: University of Mississippi, 2006), 49.
7. Ciment and Niogret, 49.
8. Ciment and Niogret, 52.
9. Ciment and Niogret, 49.
10. Desalm, 132.
11. Carolyn R. Russell, *The Films of Joel and Ethan Coen* (Jefferson, NC: McFarland and Company, 2001), 89.

CHAPTER 5

1. *The Hudsucker Proxy*, DVD, directed by Joel Coen (1994; Burbank, CA: Warner Home Video).
2. Elisabeth Hickey, "Making a Killing by Proxy: The Coen Brothers Keep Filmmaking Quirky as They Go Commercial," *Washington Times*, March 13, 1994.
3. John Harkness, "The Sphinx without a Riddle," *Sight and Sound*, August 1994, 7–9.
4. Erica Rowell, *The Brothers Grim: The Films of Ethan and Joel Coen* (Lanham, MD: Scarecrow Press, 2007), 143.
5. Richard Alleva, review of *The Hudsucker Proxy*, directed by Joel Coen, *Commonwealth* 121, no. 10 (May 20, 1994), 24.
6. Desson Howe, review of *The Hudsucker Proxy*, directed by Joel Coen, *Washington Post*, March 25, 1994, http://www.washingtonpost.com/wp-srv/style/longterm/movies/videos/ thehudsuckerproxypghowe_a0b041.htm.
7. Alex McGregor, "Strangers in Hollywood," *The Age*, (Melbourne) June 30, 1994, 17.
8. Hal Lipper, "Another Fiery Tale from the Brothers Coen," *St. Petersburg Times*, March 14, 1993, 1F.
9. Box Office Mojo, http://boxofficemojo.com/movies/?id=hudsuckerproxy.htm.

CHAPTER 6

1. *Fargo*, DVD, directed by Joel Coen (1996; Santa Monica, CA: MGM).
2. Eddie Robson, "From *The Hudsucker Proxy* to *Fargo*: A Different Concept, a Different Kind of Film," *Post Script*, Winter/Spring 2008, 2.
3. Michel Ciment and Hubert Niogret, "Closer to Life Than the Conventions of Cinema," in *The Coen Brothers: Interviews*, ed. William Rodney Allen (Jackson: University of Mississippi, 2006), 72–73.
4. Noah Adams, "An Interview with Ethan and Joel Coen," NPR, *All Things Considered*, transcript, March 8, 1996.
5. William McDonald, "Brothers in a Movie World of Their Own, *New York Times*, March 3, 1996.
6. George Toles, "Obvious Mysterious in *Fargo*," *Michigan Quarterly Review* 38, no. 4 (Fall 1999): 13.
7. Ciment and Niogret, 76.

8. Toles, 17.
9. Toles, 13.
10. Ciment, 77.
11. Roger Ebert, review of *Fargo*, directed by Joel Coen, *Chicago Sun-Times*, March 8, 1996, http://rogerebert.suntimes.com/apps/pbcs.dll/article?AID=/19960308/REVIEWS/603080302/1023.

CHAPTER 7

1. *The Big Lebowski*, DVD, directed by Joel Coen (1998; Universal City, CA: Universal Studios Home Entertainment).
2. Chris Collis, "The Dude and I," *Entertainment Weekly*, March 21, 2008, http://www.ew.com/ew/article/0,,20184264,00.html.
3. Andy Greene, "The Decade of the Dude," *Rolling Stone*, Sept. 4, 2008, http://www.rollingstone.com/news/story/22694342/the_decade_of_the_dude.
4. In Louisville, Kentucky, there is an annual festival called the Lebowski Fest.
5. Andy Lowe, "The Brothers Grim," in *The Coen Brothers: Interviews*, ed. William Rodney Allen (Jackson: University of Mississippi, 2006), 97.
6. Jim Craddock, ed. *VideoHound's Golden Movie Retriever* (New York: Thompson-Gale, 2003), 460.
7. Richard Alleva, "Real Actors v. Real Slobs," *Commonwealth* 125, no. 7 (April 10, 1998): 23.
8. William Preston Robertson, The Big Lebowski: *The Making of a Coen Brothers Film* (New York: Norton, 1998), 42.
9. Jerry Speir, *Raymond Chandler* (New York: Frederick Ungar, 1981), 106.
10. Raymond Chandler, *The Big Sleep* (1939; New York: Vintage Crime, 1992), 1.
11. Greene.
12. Michel Ciment and Hubert Niogret, "The Logic of Soft Drugs," in *The Coen Brothers: Interviews*, ed. William Rodney Allen (Jackson: University of Mississippi, 2006), 101.
13. "You Know, for Kids!" http://www.youknow-forkids.com/biglebowski.htm.
14. Chris Peachment, review of *The Big Lebowski*, directed by Joel Coen, *New Statesman*, April 24, 1998, 45.
15. Alleva, 23.
16. Roger Ebert, review of *The Big Lebowski*, directed by Joel Coen, *Chicago-Sun Times*, March 6, 1998, http://rogerebert.suntimes.com/apps/pbcs.dll/article?AID=/19980306/REVIEWS/ 803060301/1023.

CHAPTER 8

1. *O Brother, Where Art Thou?*, DVD, directed by Joel Coen (2000; Burbank, CA: Walt Disney Video).
2. Jane Clayson, "Joel and Ethan Coen Discuss Their New Film," *The Early Show*, CBS, January 5, 2001, transcript.
3. Clayson.
4. Faulkner's short novel *Old Man* has another convict on an Odyssey journey that is set in Mississippi.

Notes   179

5. Jim Ridley, "Brothers in Arms," in *The Coen Brothers: Interviews*, ed. William Rodney Allen (Jackson: University of Mississippi, 2006), 136.
6. Rob Content, Tim Kreider, and Boyd White, "*O Brother, Where Art Thou?*" *Film Quarterly*, Fall 2001, 41.
7. Sean Chadwell, "Inventing That 'Old-Timey' Style: Southern Authenticity in *O Brother, Where Art Thou?*" *Journal of Popular Film and Television* 32, no. 1 (Spring 2004): 7.
8. Behind-the-scenes featurette for *O Brother, Where Art Thou?*
9. A. O. Scott, "Hail Ulysses, Escaped Convict," *New York Times*, Dec. 22, 2000, http://movies.nytimes.com/movie/review?_r=2&res=9C03E1D91F39F931A15751C1A9669C8B63.
10. Jonathan Romney, "Double Vision," in *The Coen Brothers: Interviews*, ed. William Rodney Allen (Jackson: University of Mississippi, 2006), 130.
11. Chadwell, 7.
12. Behind-the-scenes featurette.
13. Box Office Mojo, http://boxofficemojo.com/movies/?id=obrotherwhereartthou.htm.
14. Kent Jones, "Airtight," *Film Comment* 36, no. 6 (Nov.–Dec. 2000), 46.
15. Roger Ebert, review of *O Brother, Where Art Thou?*, directed by Joel Coen, *Chicago Sun-Times*, Dec. 29, 2000, http://rogerebert.suntimes.com/apps/pbcs.dll/article?AID=/20001229/REVIEWS/12290301/1023.

CHAPTER 9

1. *The Man Who Wasn't There*, DVD, directed by Joel Coen (2001; Universal City, CA: Universal Studios Home Entertainment).
2. Joel and Ethan Coen, *The Making of* The Man Who Wasn't There, DVD.
3. Andrew Pulver, "Pictures That Do the Talking," *The Guardian* (London), Oct. 12, 2001.
4. Pulver.
5. Eddie Robson, *Coen Brothers* (London: Virgin Film, 2003), 241.
6. Billy Bob Thornton, Joel Coen, and Ethan Coen, commentary to *The Man Who Wasn't There*.
7. Kristine McKenna, "Joel and Ethan Coen," in *The Coen Brothers: Interviews*, ed. William Rodney Allen (Jackson: University of Mississippi, 2006), 180.
8. Brian D. Johnson, "A Knack for Noir," *Maclean's*, Nov. 12, 2001, 54.
9. Peter Travers, review of *The Man Who Wasn't There*, directed by Joel Coen, *Rolling Stone*, no. 882 (Nov. 22, 2001): 96.

CHAPTER 10

1. *Intolerable Cruelty*, DVD, directed by Joel Coen (2003; Universal City, CA: Universal Studios Home Entertainment).
2. Pedro Lange, "The *Purloined Letter* and the Massey Prenup: Of Ethics, the Lacanian Real, and Nuptial Bliss in *Intolerable Cruelty*," *Post Script*, Winter–Spring 2008, 117.
3. Lange.

4. Production notes, *Intolerable Cruelty*, http://www.intolerablecruelty.com/index.php.
5. Production notes.
6. Elvis Mitchell, "A Lawyer's Good Teeth Help in Court and Love," *New York Times*, Oct. 10, 2003, http://movies.nytimes.com/movie/review?_r=1&res=9400E5DC173FF933A25753C1A9659C8B63.

CHAPTER 11

1. *The Ladykillers*, DVD, directed by Joel Coen and Ethan Coen (2004; Burbank, CA: Walt Disney Video).
2. Production notes, *The Ladykillers*, http://video.movies.go.com/ladykillers/main.html.
3. Ed Frank, "Memphis Press-Scimitar," *The Tennessee Encyclopedia of History and Culture*, 1998, http://tennesseeencyclopedia.net/imagegallery.php?EntryID=M078.
4. Production notes.
5. Box Office Mojo, http://boxofficemojo.com/movies/?id=ladykillers.htm.
6. Peter Travers, review of *The Ladykillers*, directed by Joel Coen and Ethan Coen, *Rolling Stone*, Feb. 6, 2004, http://www.rollingstone.com/reviews/movie/5949541/review/5949542/the_ladykillers.

CHAPTER 12

1. *No Country for Old Men*, DVD, directed by Joel Coen and Ethan Coen (2007; Burbank, CA: Walt Disney Video).
2. Ian Nathan, "The Complete Coens," *Empire*, January 2008, 172.
3. Madison Smartt Bell, "The Man Who Understood Horses," *New York Times*, May 17, 1992, http://www.nytimes.com/books/98/05/17/specials/mccarthy-horses.html.
4. Nathan, 172.
5. Royal Brown, "No Exit in Texas," *Cineaste* 33, no. 3 (2008): 8–13.
6. Transcript for *Houdini*, PBS.org, http://www.pbs.org/wgbh/amex/houdini/filmmore/transcript/index.html.
7. Brown, 8–13.
8. Box Office Mojo, http://boxofficemojo.com/movies/?id=nocountryforoldmen.htm.
9. Todd McCarthy, review of *No Country for Old Men*, directed by Joel Coen and Ethan Coen, *Variety*, May 28–June 3, 2007, 19.

CHAPTER 13

1. *Burn After Reading*, DVD, directed by Joel Coen and Ethan Coen (2008; Universal City, CA: Universal Studios Home Entertainment).
2. David Ansen, "The Coens' Funny Bones: *Burn After Reading* Is No *No Country*. In Fact, It's Downright Giddy," *Newsweek*, Sept. 15, 2008.

3. Manohla Dargis, "Coens Ask the C.I.A. for a License to Laugh," *New York Times*, Sept. 12, 2008, http://movies.nytimes.com/2008/09/12/movies/12burn.html.
4. Roger Ebert, review of *Burn After Reading*, directed by Joel Coen and Ethan Coen, *Chicago Sun-Times*, Sept. 11, 2008, http://rogerebert.suntimes.com/apps/pbcs.dll/article?AID=/20080911/REVIEWS/809119995/1023.
5. Box Office Mojo, http://boxofficemojo.com/movies/?id=burnafterreading.htm.

Filmography

FULL-LENGTH MOTION PICTURES

Blood Simple (1985)
Raising Arizona (1987)
Miller's Crossing (1990)
Barton Fink (1991)
The Hudsucker Proxy (1994)
Fargo (1996)
The Big Lebowski (1998)
O Brother, Where Art Thou? (2000)
The Man Who Wasn't There (2001)
Intolerable Cruelty (2003)
The Ladykillers (2004)
No Country for Old Men (2007)
Burn After Reading (2008)

OTHER WORKS (DIRECTED SEGMENTS)

Paris, I Love You (2006)
World Cinema (2007)

FUTURE PROJECTS ANNOUNCED

A Serious Man (2009)
Hail Caesar (2009)
The Yiddish Policemen's Union (2010)

Academy Awards and Nominations

AWARDS

No Country for Old Men
Best Directing
Best Picture
Best Adapted Screenplay
Best Supporting Actor (Javier Bardem)

Fargo
Best Screenplay
Best Actress (Frances McDormand)

NOMINATIONS

No Country for Old Men
Best Editing
Best Cinematography
Best Sound
Best Sound Editing

The Man Who Wasn't There
Best Cinematography

O Brother, Where Art Thou?
Best Adapted Screenplay
Best Cinematography

Fargo
Best Directing
Best Film
Best Editing

Best Cinematography
Best Supporting Actor (William H. Macy)

Barton Fink
Best Supporting Actor (Michael Lerner)
Best Art
Best Costume

Bibliography

BLOOD SIMPLE (1985)

Blood Simple. DVD. Directed by Joel Coen. Universal City, CA: Universal Studios Home Entertainment, 2001.
Cain, James M. *Double Indemnity.* 1926. Reprint, New York: Vintage Crime, 1992.
Ebert, Roger. Review of *Blood Simple,* directed by Joel Coen. *Chicago Sun-Times,* March 1, 1985, http://rogerebert.suntimes.com/apps/pbcs.dll/article?AID=/20000714/REVIEWS/7140301/1023.
Gleiberman, Owen. "First Blood." *Entertainment Weekly,* July 28, 2000, p. 153.
Hammett, Dashiell. *Red Harvest. The Novels of Dashiell Hammett.* 1929. Reprint, New York: Knopf, 1979.
Hammett, Dashiell. *The Maltese Falcon.* 1930. Reprint, New York: Vintage Crime, 1992.
Harvey, Stephen. "Pretty but Dumb." *Film Comment,* 20, no. 6 (Dec. 1984).
Seesslen, Georg. *Joel and Ethan Coen.* New York: Limelight, 2001.

RAISING ARIZONA (1987)

Box Office Mojo, http://boxofficemojo.com/movies/?id=raisingarizona.htm.
Ciment, Michael, and Hubert Niogret. "Interview with Joel and Ethan Coen." In *The Coen Brothers: Interviews,* edited by William Rodney Allen. Jackson: University of Mississippi, 2006.
Raising Arizona. DVD. Directed by Joel Coen. Beverly Hills, CA: 20th Century Fox Entertainment, 1999.
Rowell, Erica. *The Brothers Grim: The Films of Ethan and Joel Coen.* Lanham, MD: Scarecrow Press, 2007.
Stevenson, Robert Louis. *The Strange Case of Dr. Jekyll and Mr. Hyde.* Enriched Classic. New York: Washington Square Press, 1995.

MILLER'S CROSSING (1990)

Box Office Mojo, http://boxofficemojo.com/movies/?id=goodfellas.htm.
Box Office Mojo, http://boxofficemojo.com/movies/?id=millerscrossing.htm.

Corliss, Richard. Review of *Miller's Crossing. Time,* September 24, 1990.
Coursodon, Jean-Pierre. "A Hat Blown by the Wind." In *The Coen Brothers: Interviews,* edited by William Rodney Allen. Jackson: University of Mississippi, 2006.
Ebert, Roger. Review of *Miller's Crossing,* directed by Joel Coen. *Chicago Sun-Times,* Oct. 5, 1990, http://rogerebert.suntimes.com/apps/pbcs.dll/article?AID=/19901005/REVIEWS/10050306/1023.
Gregory, Sinda. *Private Investigations: The Novels of Dashiell Hammett.* Carbondale: Southern Illinois University, 1985.
Grella, George. "The Hard-Boiled Detective Novel," in *Detective Fiction: A Collection of Critical Essays.* Englewood Cliffs, NJ: Prentice Hall, 1980.
Hammett, Dashiell. Red Harvest. The Novels of Dashiell Hammett. 1929. Reprint, New York: Knopf, 1979.
Hammett, Dashiell. *The Glass Key.* 1931. Reprint, New York: Vintage Crime, 1989.
Lenzner, Steven J. "A Cinematic Call for Self-Knowledge: An Interpretation of *Miller's Crossing.*" *Perspectives on Political Science* (Spring 2001), 89.
Miller's Crossing. DVD. Directed by Joel Coen. Beverly Hills, CA: 20th Century Fox Entertainment, 2003.
Russell, Carolyn R. *The Films of Joel and Ethan Coen.* Jefferson, NC: McFarland and Company, 2001.

BARTON FINK (1991)

Barton Fink. DVD. Directed by Joel Coen. Beverly Hills, CA: 20th Century Fox Entertainment, 2003.
Ciment, Michael, and Hubert Niogret. "A Rock on the Beach." In *The Coen Brothers: Interviews,* edited by William Rodney Allen. Jackson: University of Mississippi, 2006.
Desalm, Brigitte. *"Barton Fink."* In *Joel and Ethan Coen,* edited by Peter Körte and Georg Seesslen. New York: Limelight, 2001.
Emerson, Jim. "That Barton Fink Feeling: An Interview with the Brothers Coen." Cinepad, http://cinepad.com/coens.htm.
Rowell, Erica. *The Brothers Grim: The Films of Ethan and Joel Coen.* Lanham, MD: Scarecrow Press, 2007.
Russell, Carolyn R. *The Films of Joel and Ethan Coen.* Jefferson, NC: McFarland and Company, 2001.
Schickel, Richard. "A Three-Espresso Hallucination." *Time,* August 26, 1991, p. 58.

THE HUDSUCKER PROXY (1994)

Alleva, Richard. Review of *The Hudsucker Proxy,* directed by Joel Coen. *Commonwealth,* 121, no. 10 (May 20, 1994).
Harkness, John. "The Sphinx without a Riddle." *Sight and Sound,* August 1994, pp. 7–9.
Hickey, Elisabeth. "Making a Killing by Proxy: The Coen Brothers Keep Filmmaking Quirky as They Go Commercial." *Washington Times,* March 13, 1994.

Howe, Desson. Review of *The Hudsucker Proxy,* directed by Joel Coen. *Washington Post,* March 25, 1994, http://www.washingtonpost.com/wp-srv/style/longterm/movies/videos/thehudsuckerproxypghowe_a0b041.htm.
The Hudsucker Proxy. DVD. Directed by Joel Coen. Burbank, CA: Warner Home Video, 1999.
Lipper, Hal. "Another Fiery Tale from the Brothers Coen." *St. Petersburg Times,* March 14, 1993. Box Office Mojo, http://boxofficemojo.com/movies/?id=hudsuckerproxy.htm.
McGregor, Alex. "Strangers in Hollywood." *The Age,* June 30, 1994.
Rowell, Erica. *The Brothers Grim: The Films of Ethan and Joel Coen.* Lanham, MD: Scarecrow Press, Maryland, 2007.

FARGO (1996)

Adams, Noah. "An Interview with Ethan and Joel Coen." *NPR: All Things Considered,* transcript, March 8, 1996.
Ciment, Michel, and Hubert Niogret. "Closer to Life than the Conventions of Cinema." In *The Coen Brothers: Interviews,* edited by William Rodney Allen. Jackson: University of Mississippi, 2006.
Ebert, Roger. Review of *Fargo,* directed by Joel Coen. *Chicago Sun-Times,* March 8, 1996, http://rogerebert.suntimes.com/apps/pbcs.dll/article?AID=/19960308/REVIEWS/603080302/1023.
Fargo. DVD. Directed by Joel Coen. Santa Monica, CA: MGM, 2003.
McDonald, William. "Brothers in a Movie World of Their Own," *New York Times,* March 3, 1996.
Robson, Eddie. "From *The Hudsucker Proxy* to *Fargo:* A Different Concept, a Different Kind of Film." *Post Script,* Winter/Spring 2008 p. 2.
Toles, George. "Obvious Mysterious in Fargo." *Michigan Quarterly Review* 38, no. 4 (Fall 1999): 13.

THE BIG LEBOWSKI (1998)

Alleva, Richard. "Real Actors v. Real Slobs." *Commonwealth* 125, no. 7 (April 10, 1998): 23.
The Big Lebowski. DVD. Directed by Joel Coen. Universal City, CA: Universal Studios Home Entertainment, 1998.
Chandler, Raymond. *The Big Sleep.* 1939. Reprint, New York: Vintage Crime, 1992.
Ciment, Michel, and Hubert Niogret. "The Logic of Soft Drugs." In *The Coen Brothers: Interviews,* edited by William Rodney Allen. Jackson: University of Mississippi, 2006.
Collis, Chris. "The Dude and I." *Entertainment Weekly,* March 21, 2008, http://www.ew.com/ew/article/0,,20184264,00.html.
Craddock, Jim ed. *VideoHound's Golden Movie Retriever.* New York: Thompson-Gale, 2003.
Ebert, Roger. Review of *The Big Lebowski,* directed by Joel Coen. *The Chicago Sun-Times,* March 6, 1998, http://rogerebert.suntimes.com/apps/pbcs.dll/article?AID=/19980306/REVIEWS/803060301/1023.

Greene, Andy. "The Decade of the Dude." *Rolling Stone*, Sept. 4, 2008, http://www.rollingstone.com/news/story/22694342/the_decade_of_the_dude.
Lowe, Andy. "The Brothers Grim." In *The Coen Brothers: Interviews*, edited by William Rodney Allen. Jackson: University of Mississippi, 2006.
Peachment, Chris. Review of *The Big Lebowski*, directed by Joel Coen. *New Statesman*, April 24, 1998, p. 45.
Robertson, William Preston. The Big Lebowski: *The Making of a Coen Brothers Film*. New York: Norton, 1998.
Speir, Jerry. *Raymond Chandler*. New York: Frederick Ungar, 1981.
"You Know, for Kids!" http://www.youknow-forkids.com/biglebowski.htm.

O BROTHER, WHERE ART THOU? (2000)

Behind-the-Scenes Featurette, *O Brother, Where Art Thou?*, DVD.
Box Office Mojo, http://boxofficemojo.com/movies/?id=obrotherwhereartthou.htm.
Chadwell, Sean. "Inventing that 'Old-Timey' Style: Southern Authenticity in *O Brother, Where Art Thou?*" *Journal of Popular Film and Television* 32, no. 1 (Spring 2004): 7.
Clayson, Jane. "Joel and Ethan Coen Discuss Their New Film," *The Early Show*, CBS, January 5, 2001, transcript.
Content, Rob, Tim Kreider, and Boyd White. "*O Brother, Where Art Thou?*" *Film Quarterly*, Fall 2001, p. 41.
Ebert, Roger. Review of *O Brother, Where Art Thou?*, directed by Joel Coen. *Chicago Sun-Times*, Dec. 29, 2000, http://rogerebert.suntimes.com/apps/pbcs.dll/article?AID=/20001229/REVIEWS/12290301/1023.
Jones, Kent. "Airtight." *Film Comment* 36, no. 6 (Nov–Dec 2000): 46.
O Brother, Where Art Thou? DVD. Directed by Joel Coen. Burbank, CA: Walt Disney Video, 2001.
Ridley, Jim. "Brothers in Arms." In *The Coen Brothers: Interviews*, edited by William Rodney Allen. Jackson: University of Mississippi, 2006.
Romney, Jonathan. "Double Vision." In *The Coen Brothers: Interviews*, edited by William Rodney Allen. Jackson: University of Mississippi, 2006.
Scott, A. O. "Hail Ulysses, Escaped Convict." *New York Times*, Dec. 22, 2000, http://movies.nytimes.com/movie/review?_r=2&res=9C03E1D91F39F931A15751C1A9669C8B63.

THE MAN WHO WASN'T THERE (2001)

Johnson, Brian D. "A Knack for Noir." *Maclean's*, Nov. 12, 2001, p. 54.
The Making of *The Man Who Wasn't There*, DVD.
The Man Who Wasn't There. DVD. Directed by Joel Coen. Universal City, CA: Universal Studios Home Entertainment, 2002.
McKenna, Kristine. "Joel and Ethan Coen Playboy Interview." In *The Coen Brothers: Interviews*, edited by William Rodney Allen. Jackson: University of Mississippi, 2006.

Pulver, Andrew. "Pictures That Do the Talking." *The Guardian* (London), October 12, 2001.
Robson, Eddie. *Coen Brothers*. London: Virgin Film, 2003.
Thornton, Billy Bob, Joel Coen, and Ethan Coen commentary to *The Man Who Wasn't There*, DVD.
Travers, Peter. Review of *The Man Who Wasn't There*, directed by Joel Coen. *Rolling Stone*, Nov. 22, 2001, p. 96.

INTOLERABLE CRUELTY (2003)

Intolerable Cruelty. DVD. Directed by Joel Coen. Universal City, CA: Universal Studios Home Entertainment, 2004.
Lange, Pedro. "The *Purloined Letter* and the Massey Prenup: Of Ethics, the Lacanian Real, and Nuptial Bliss in *Intolerable Cruelty*." *Post Script* (Winter–Spring 2008).
Mitchell, Elvis. "A Lawyer's Good Teeth Help in Court and Love." *New York Times*, Oct. 10, 2003, http://movies.nytimes.com/movie/review?_r=1&res=9400E5DC173FF933A25753C1A9659C8B63.
Production notes for *Intolerable Cruelty*, http://www.intolerablecruelty.com/index.php.

THE LADYKILLERS (2004)

Box Office Mojo, http://boxofficemojo.com/movies/?id=ladykillers.htm.
Frank, Ed. "Memphis Press-Scimitar." *The Tennessee Encyclopedia of History and Culture*, http://tennesseeencyclopedia.net/imagegallery.php?EntryID=M078.
The Ladykillers. DVD. Directed by Joel Coen and Ethan Coen. Burbank, CA: Walt Disney Video, 2004.
Production notes for *The Ladykillers*, http://video.movies.go.com/ladykillers/main.html.
Travers, Peter. Review of *The Ladykillers*, directed by Joel Coen and Ethan Coen. *Rolling Stone*, Feb. 6, 2004, http://www.rollingstone.com/reviews/movie/5949541/review/5949542/the_ladykillers.

NO COUNTRY FOR OLD MEN (2007)

Box Office Mojo, http://boxofficemojo.com/movies/?id=nocountryforoldmen.htm.
Brown, Royal. "No Exit in Texas." *Cineaste* 33, no. 3 (Summer 2008): 8–13.
McCarthy, Todd. Review of *No Country for Old Men*, directed by Joel Coen and Ethan Coen. *Variety*, May 28–June 3, 2007, p. 19.
Nathan, Ian. "The Complete Coens." *Empire*, January 2008, p. 172.
No Country for Old Men. DVD. Directed by Joel Coen and Ethan Coen. Burbank, CA: Walt Disney Video, 2008.
Smartt Bell, Madison. The Man Who Understood Horses." *New York Times*, May 17, 1992: http://www.nytimes.com/books/98/05/17/specials/mccarthy-horses.html.

Transcript for *Houdini*. PBS, http://www.pbs.org/wgbh/amex/houdini/filmmore/transcript/index.html.

BURN AFTER READING (2008)

Ansen, David. "The Coens' Funny Bones: Burn After Reading Is No No Country. In Fact, It's Downright Giddy." *Newsweek,* Sept. 15, 2008.

Box Office Mojo, http://boxofficemojo.com/movies/?id=burnafterreading.htm.

Burn After Reading. DVD. Directed by Joel Coen and Ethan Coen. Universal City, CA: Universal Studios Home Entertainment, 2008.

Dargis, Manohla. "Coens Ask the C.I.A. for a License to Laugh." *New York Times,* Sept. 12, 2008, http://movies.nytimes.com/2008/09/12/movies/12burn.html.

Ebert, Roger. Review of *Burn After Reading,* directed by Joel Coen and Ethan Coen. *Chicago Sun-Times,* Sept. 11, 2008, http://rogerebert.suntimes.com/apps/pbcs.dll/article?AID=/20080911/REVIEWS/809119995/1023.

Index

Note: Characters are listed alphabetically by first name.

Abby *(Blood Simple)*, 2–9
Action
  Blood Simple and, 3, 6, 8
  Burn After Reading and, 167
  Fargo and, 74
  Intolerable Cruelty and, 129, 134
  The Ladykillers and, 141, 143
  The Man Who Wasn't There and, 114–115, 122
  No Country for Old Men and, 155
  See also Motivation
Adam's Rib (Cukor), 127
Adelstein, Paul, 125
Affairs. *See* Love triangles
African Americans. *See* Race
Alice in Wonderland, 63
Aliens, 117
All the President's Men, 58
Allen, Woody, 25, 48
Alter egos, 36, 85, 86, 91, 127. *See also* Doppelgangers; Opposites
Altman, Robert, 84
Ambiguity, 47, 49, 60, 151
Ambition, 9, 86, 88, 94, 105, 113, 154
American Dream, 15, 16, 17, 23, 56, 59, 114
Amy Archer, 62–64
"Angles," 30

Anton Chigurh *(No Country for Old Men)*, 81, 150–151, 152, 153, 155–158, 157–158, 159–160
Appearances
  Blood Simple and, 8, 11
  Burn After Reading and, 163–164, 165, 171, 173
  Fargo and, 71, 72, 76
  The Hudsucker Proxy and, 63
  Intolerable Cruelty and, 130
  The Man Who Wasn't There and, 122–123
  Miller's Crossing and, 30
  O Brother, Where Art Thou? and, 103, 105
  Raising Arizona and, 25
  See also Clothing; Hair; Social standards; Teeth
Archer, Amy *(The Hudsucker Proxy)*, 62–64
Art films, 54
Arthur, Jean, 62
Audiences
  Barton Fink and, 50
  Blood Simple and, 10, 12, 13
  Burn After Reading and, 171
  Fargo and, 78
  The Hudsucker Proxy and, 56, 66
  Miller's Crossing and, 28, 33, 40

Authenticity (legitimacy), 99
    Fargo and, 70
    The Ladykillers and, 137, 141
    O Brother, Where Art Thou? and, 101, 102, 103, 105, 108, 109
    See also Realism

"Baby Face" Nelson *(O Brother, Where Art Thou?)*, 98, 100, 101
Backstories, 8, 74. *See also* History; The Past; *specific events*
Bad Santa (Coen Brothers), 136
Badalucco, Michael, 97, 111
Bardem, Javier, 149, 161
Von Bargen, Daniel, 97
Barton Fink *(Barton Fink)*, 47–50
Barton Fink (Coen Brothers), 43–54, 156
Batman (Burton), 157
Beauty, 171
Bernie Bernbaum *(Miller's Crossing)*, 35–38
The Bible, 47, 52, 66, 101, 142, 143. *See also* Faith; Religion
Big Dan *(O Brother, Where Art Thou?)*, 98, 101
Big Dave *(The Man Who Wasn't There)*, 112, 113, 114–115, 120, 122–123
The Big Lebowski (Coen Brothers), 3, 83–95, 98
The Big Sleep (Chandler), 28, 84, 88, 93
Bikers, 22
Bill and Ted's Excellent Adventure, 172
Birdy *(The Man Who Wasn't There)*, 112, 114, 121
Black and white, 98, 115, 123
"The Black Cat" (Poe), 144–145
Black comedy, *Blood Simple* and, 1
Blackmail, 112
    Burn After Reading and, 165–166
    The Man Who Wasn't There and, 114–115, 118
Blacks. *See* Race
Blaxploitation films, 67
Blood Simple (Coen Brothers), 1–14, 47, 100, 147, 152, 156

Bogart, Humphrey, 88, 114
Boots, 153, 155
Borowitz, Katherine, 111
Boundaries, 90
Bounty hunters, 16
The Bourne Identity, 165
Bowling alleys, 85
Box office
    Barton Fink, 54
    The Big Lebowski, 94
    Burn After Reading, 174
    Fargo, 81
    Goodfellas, 28
    The Hudsucker Proxy, 66
    Intolerable Cruelty, 136
    The Ladykillers, 147
    The Man Who Wasn't There, 123
    Miller's Crossing, 28
    No Country for Old Men, 161
    O Brother, Where Art Thou?, 109
    Raising Arizona, 26
Brains
    Burn After Reading and, 166, 169
    The Ladykillers and, 141, 143
    O Brother, Where Art Thou? and, 102, 103, 105
    See also Rationality
Breach, 166
Bridges, Jeff, 83, 94
Broslin, Josh, 149
Buddhism, 141, 142–143
Bunny *(The Big Lebowski)*, 92
Bunyan, Paul, 79
Bureaucracy, 170–171
Buried Ruined Choirs, 45
Burn After Reading (Coen Brothers), 163–174
Burnett, T-Bone, 109
Burton, Tim, 130
Buscemi, Steve, 27, 43, 69, 83, 91, 94
Business
    Barton Fink and, 50, 53
    Fargo and, 72
    Miller's Crossing and, 27, 31, 32–33, 34, 35, 36, 40, 41
    See *also The Hudsucker Proxy* (Coen Brothers)
Byrne, Gabriel, 27

Cage, Nicholas, 15
Cain, James M., 3, 8, 9, 111, 118, 119, 122
Campbell, Bruce, 55
Cannes Film Festival, 54
Capra, Frank, 56, 58, 60, 62–63
Carl Showalter *(Fargo)*, 79–81
Carla Jean *(No Country for Old Men)*, 151, 153
Carpenter, John, 25
Carson Wells *(No Country for Old Men)*, 151, 157–158, 159
Cartoons, 16, 56, 59, 64, 100. See also *specific characters and shows*
Cedric the Entertainer, 125
Chad Feldheimer *(Burn After Reading)*, 163, 165, 166, 167, 172–173
Chandler, Raymond
  Barton Fink and, 52, 53
  The Big Lebowski and, 84, 85, 88, 92
  The Man Who Wasn't There and, 111–112
  Miller's Crossing and, 29
  See also *specific characters; specific stories*
Chaplin, Charlie, 88
Character
  Intolerable Cruelty and, 133, 134–135
  The Man Who Wasn't There and, 111, 112–113
  Miller's Crossing and, 27, 29, 31, 33, 36, 40
  No Country for Old Men and, 152
  O Brother, Where Art Thou? and, 103, 106
Characterizations
  The Big Lebowski and, 84
  Blood Simple and, 13
  Fargo and, 74
  The Hudsucker Proxy and, 56
  Miller's Crossing and, 29–30
  O Brother, Where Art Thou? and, 99, 104–105
  overviews, 8
  See also Motivation

Charlie Meadows *(Barton Fink)*, 50–51, 156
Children. See Family
Chinatown, 93, 134
CIA, 166
Citizen Kane, 58
Classes, economic/social
  Barton Fink and, 45, 48, 50
  The Big Lebowski and, 85
  Burn After Reading and, 169
  The Hudsucker Proxy and, 56, 57, 58, 61, 64, 65
  Intolerable Cruelty and, 128, 132
  The Ladykillers and, 139
  No Country for Old Men and, 159
  Raising Arizona and, 18
  See also Common man
Clichés
  Barton Fink and, 44
  The Big Lebowski and, 85
  Blood Simple and, 3, 7, 14
  Burn After Reading and, 163, 166, 169
  Cruel Intentions and, 131, 133
  Fargo and, 71, 72, 74, 78, 79
  The Hudsucker Proxy and, 56, 57, 58, 60, 64, 65–66
  The Ladykillers and, 145, 147
  Miller's Crossing and, 28, 41
  No Country for Old Men and, 152, 158
  See also Stereotypes
Clooney, George, 97, 101–104, 125, 130, 163, 168
Clothing
  The Big Lebowski and, 87, 89
  Blood Simple and, 4
  Burn After Reading and, 171, 173
  Fargo and, 71, 72
  The Ladykillers and, 139–140
  Miller's Crossing and, 30
  No Country for Old Men and, 158
  See also *specific articles of clothing*
Cobb, Tex, 15
Cobbs, Bill, 55

Coen, Ethan
    Barton Fink, on, 50
    Fargo, on, 74, 81
    Intolerable Cruelty and, 130
    The Ladykillers and, 147
    No Country for Old Men and, 151
    O Brother, Where Art Thou? and, 97
    Raising Arizona and, 16
Coen, Joel
    Barton Fink, on, 51, 52
    The Big Lebowski, on, 84
    The Big Lebowski and, 92
    Fargo and, 71
    The Hudsucker Proxy, on, 57
    The Man Who Wasn't There and, 113
    No Country for Old Men and, 150, 151
    O Brother, Where Art Thou? and, 97, 100, 109
    Raising Arizona, on, 17
Cohn, Harry, 53
Cold War, 113, 166, 170
Columbo, 76
Comedy
    Barton Fink and, 44, 48
    The Big Lebowski and, 85
    Burn After Reading and, 167
    Fargo and, 76
    The Hudsucker Proxy and, 55
    Intolerable Cruelty and, 127, 128, 129, 135
    The Ladykillers and, 144
    Miller's Crossing and, 30–31
    No Country for Old Men and, 161
    O Brother, Where Art Thou? and, 100, 101
    Raising Arizona and, 16, 18, 24
    violence and, 26
Common man
    Barton Fink and, 45, 48, 50
    The Big Lebowski and, 85
    Fargo and, 70–71, 73, 76
    The Hudsucker Proxy and, 66, 113
    The Man Who Wasn't There and, 116
    No Country for Old Men and, 152
    O Brother, Where Art Thou? and, 100

Communication
    Barton Fink and, 45, 51
    Blood Simple and, 2, 3, 4, 5–6, 9
    Burn After Reading and, 169–170
    The Ladykillers and, 144, 146
    The Man Who Wasn't There and, 117
    O Brother, Where Art Thou? and, 103, 108
    See also Miscommunication
Complainers, 13, 138, 143
Continental Op *(Red Harvest)*, 3, 29, 86
Control
    Barton Fink and, 49
    Blood Simple and, 8
    Fargo and, 73, 74, 76
    Miller's Crossing and, 28, 36, 38, 39, 40, 41
    See also Independence; Power
Cool Hand Luke, 100
Corbin, Barry, 149
Corpses, 1, 5, 10, 46, 167
Corruption, 3, 29, 30, 44, 60, 64, 108, 127
Cowboys, 12–13, 93. *See also* Westerns
Credits, 30, 34
Creighton Tolliver *(The Man Who Wasn't There)*, 111, 118
Crimewave, 16
Critics. See individual critics
Cukor, George, 127
Cult classics, 84
Cyclops, Polyphemus, 107

The Dane *(Miller's Crossing)*, 156
The Dark Knight, 156
Dassin, Jules, 71
Davis, Judy, 43
Death
    complexity of, 10
    The Ladykillers and, 140–141
    The Man Who Wasn't There and, 114
    Miller's Crossing and, 30
    No Country for Old Men and, 150, 158, 160

O Brother, Where Art Thou? and, 104
See also Murders
Death of a Salesman, 75
Deception. *See* Appearances
Delano, Diane, 137
Delmar O'Donnell *(O Brother, Where Art Thou?)*, 106
Depp, Johnny, 130
Deputy Wendell, 149
Desires
   The Big Lebowski and, 88
   The Man Who Wasn't There and, 114
   Miller's Crossing and, 32, 38
   Raising Arizona and, 23
Destiny/fate, 16, 20, 46, 60, 157, 158
Detectives. *See* Private investigators
Die Hard, 76
Dignity, 128, 129
Dirty Harry, 76
Dishonesty, 102, 126, 168. *See also* Honesty
Divorce, 11, 90, 126, 164, 169, 170. See also *Intolerable Cruelty* (Coen Brothers)
Docu-noir films, 71, 73, 74, 77
Domestic noir, 3, 6, 8, 111, 114, 118
Donny *(The Big Lebowski)*, 93–94
Donovan Donaly *(Intolerable Cruelty)*, 134
Doppelgangers, 21. *See also* Alter egos
Doris Crane *(The Man Who Wasn't There)*, 112, 119–121
Dorr *(The Ladykillers)*, 138, 140, 141–143
Double Indemnity (Cain), 3, 9, 113, 114, 116, 117, 118, 120
Double-crosses
   Blood Simple and, 12
   Miller's Crossing and, 29, 41
Dr. Jekyll and Mr. Hyde (Stevenson), 17, 21
Dr. Spock's Baby and Child Care (Spock), 18, 23
Dreams
   Barton Fink and, 45, 47, 52
   The Big Lebowski and, 86
   Blood Simple and, 4
   The Hudsucker Proxy and, 56, 61

Intolerable Cruelty and, 132
Miller's Crossing and, 34
No Country for Old Men and, 160–161
Raising Arizona and, 21–22
Drifters, 3, 9. *See also specific characters*
Drugs, 74, 84, 88, 150, 151, 156, 158
"The Dude" *(The Big Lebowski)*, 84, 85, 86–92
Durning, Charles, 55, 97
Duvall, Wayne, 97

Ebert, Roger, 174
   The Big Lebowski and, 94
   Blood Simple, on, 1, 13
   Fargo, on, 81
   Miller's Crossing, on, 42
   O Brother, Where Art Thou? and, 109
Economic violence, 15
   Raising Arizona and, 17, 18–19, 26
   See also Money
Ed Crane *(The Man Who Wasn't There)*, 88, 112, 113, 114, 115–119, 121, 135
Ed McDunnough *(Raising Arizona)*, 22–24
Egos, 41–42
   The Big Lebowski and, 90
   Fargo and, 78
   The Hudsucker Proxy and, 61
Elliot, Sam, 83, 93
Ellis *(No Country for Old Men)*, 160
Emotion
   The Big Lebowski and, 87, 91–92
   Fargo and, 70–71, 72, 73, 74, 76, 79, 81
   Intolerable Cruelty and, 132
   The Ladykillers and, 142
   male or *Blood Simple* and, 9
   The Man Who Wasn't There and, 114, 115, 121–122
   Miller's Crossing and, 35, 36, 39, 41
   No Country for Old Men and, 159
   Raising Arizona and, 22
   See also Heart

Enemy of the State (Smith), 166
Ethics. *See* Morality
Evelle (*Raising Arizona*), 23–24
Everett (*O Brother, Where Art Thou?*), 98, 101
Evil, 19, 21, 24, 40, 59, 64, 104, 156
Evil Dead, 5
Expectations
   Blood Simple and, 7
   The Hudsucker Proxy and, 60
   overviews, 4

Faith
   The Ladykillers and, 138, 143
   No Country for Old Men and, 158
   O Brother, Where Art Thou? and, 101, 103, 105, 106, 109
   See also *The Bible;* God; Religion
Falk, Peter, 76
Family
   The Big Lebowski and, 92, 94
   Fargo and, 70–71, 73, 75, 76, 79
   Intolerable Cruelty and, 127, 128
   The Ladykillers and, 142
   The Man Who Wasn't There and, 113, 116, 119
   Miller's Crossing and, 35, 39, 41
   No Country for Old Men and, 155
   O Brother, Where Art Thou? and, 102, 103, 105, 107
   Raising Arizona and, 15, 17–18, 19, 20, 23, 24
   See also American Dream; Marriage; *specific family members*
Family films, *Raising Arizona* and, 22
Fantasy, 160
   Barton Fink and, 43–44, 47, 50–51, 52
   The Hudsucker Proxy and, 58, 65
   See *also* Dreams
Fargo (Coen Brothers), 156
   Blood Simple and, 10
   expectations and, 4
   opening shot, 98
   realism and, 99
   See *also specific characters*
Fatal flaws, *Miller's Crossing* and, 38
Fate/destiny, 16, 20, 46, 60, 157, 158

Fathers
   Burn After Reading and, 170, 173
   Fargo and, 73, 74
   The Ladykillers and, 142
   No Country for Old Men and, 151, 160, 161
   Raising Arizona and, 17, 20
   See also Family
Faulkner, William, 17, 49, 53, 100
Femme fatales
   Blood Simple and, 3
   Burn After Reading and, 173
   Intolerable Cruelty and, 132–133
   The Man Who Wasn't There and, 114, 118, 119
   Miller's Crossing and, 38
   See also specific characters
Film noir
   Barton Fink and, 44, 49
   The Big Lebowski and, 84, 85
   Blood Simple and, 1, 2, 3, 4, 10, 14
   Burn After Reading and, 173
   Fargo and, 79
   Intolerable Cruelty and, 132, 134
   love triangles and, 8
   The Man Who Wasn't There and, 111, 114, 116, 118, 119, 120, 122
   Miller's Crossing and, 29, 30, 36
   narration and, 13
   See also Docu-noir; Domestic noir; Femme fatales; Neo-noir; Private investigators; Slob noir; *individual writers*
Finney, Albert, 27
Fistful of Dollars (Eastwood), 29
Fitzgerald, F. Scott, 53
Flaherty, Lanny, 27
Flashbacks, 65
Flops, 54–55, 66
Forrest Gump, 100
Forsythe, William, 15
Frank *(The Man Who Wasn't There)*, 113, 116
Frank Chambers *(The Postman Always Rings Twice)*, 114
Frankenstein, 62

Freddy Bender *(Intolerable Cruelty)*, 126
Freddy Riedenschneider *(The Man Who Wasn't There)*, 111, 112, 113, 122
Freedom
  The Big Lebowski and, 86
  Intolerable Cruelty and, 134
  The Man Who Wasn't There and, 118
  O Brother, Where Art Thou? and, 100
  Raising Arizona and, 19, 25
  See also Independence
Freeman, J.E., 27
The French Connection, 76
Friendship
  The Big Lebowski and, 87, 90, 91
  Miller's Crossing and, 27, 32, 35, 36, 38, 39
The Fugitive, 158, 159
The Future
  Barton Fink and, 48
  Blood Simple and, 17
  Fargo and, 73
  The Hudsucker Proxy and, 56, 60, 63, 64, 65
  Intolerable Cruelty and, 121, 131
  The Man Who Wasn't There and, 121
  Miller's Crossing and, 33
  No Country for Old Men and, 161
  O Brother, Where Art Thou? and, 108
  Raising Arizona and, 20, 21, 22, 24

Gable, Clark, 101
Gaear Grimsrud *(Fargo)*, 79–81, 156
Gale *(Raising Arizona)*, 23, 24–26
Gandolfini, James, 111, 123
Gangsters, 98, 150. See also *The Godfather* movies; *Miller's Crossing* (Coen Brothers)
Garth Pancake *(The Ladykillers)*, 138, 140, 145–146
Gawain MacSam *(The Ladykillers)*, 140, 146

The General *(The Ladykillers)*, 146–147
George "Baby Face" Nelson *(O Brother, Where Art Thou?)*, 98, 100, 101
Getz, John, 1
The Glass Key (Hammett), 3, 29, 40
God, 65, 66, 98, 104. See also *The Bible*; Faith; Religion
The Godfather movies, 27, 40
Goldthwait Higginson Dorr III, PhD *(The Ladykillers)*, 138, 140, 141–143
Good and evil, 22, 25, 47, 59, 76, 108–109. See also Evil
Goodfellas, 27–28
Goodman, John, 15, 43, 83, 97, 107
Gould, Elliot, 84
Government, 166
Grant, Cary, 101, 130
Grazer, Brian, 136
Great Depression, 100, 105
Greed
  The Big Lebowski and, 92
  Blood Simple and, 12
  Fargo and, 72, 73, 79, 80
  The Hudsucker Proxy and, 58
  Intolerable Cruelty and, 128, 133, 135
  The Ladykillers and, 137, 142
  Raising Arizona and, 17, 18–19
  See also Money
Greek influences, 101
Guinness, Alec, 139
Gunderson, Marge, 75–79
Guns, *Raising Arizona* and, 19
Gus Petch *(Intolerable Cruelty)*, 126, 128, 134–135

H.I. McDunnough *(Raising Arizona)*, 15, 19–22, 33, 34
Hair, 103, 112, 117
Hall, Irma P., 137
Hammer, Mike, 86
Hammett, Dashielle, 3, 11, 28, 29, 52
Hanks, Tom, 137, 138
Hannibal Lecter *(Silence of the Lambs)*, 156

Happiness
  Barton Fink and, 49
  The Big Lebowski and, 86, 94
  Blood Simple and, 2, 8
  Burn After Reading and, 165
  The Hudsucker Proxy and, 63
  Intolerable Cruelty and, 128, 130, 133
  Raising Arizona and, 22
Harden, Marcia Gay, 27
Harper, Tess, 149, 153
Harrelson, Woody, 149
Harry Pfarrer *(Burn After Reading)*, 164, 165, 166, 167, 168–169, 169–170
Harry Powell *(Night of the Hunter)*, 156
Harvey, Stephen, 13–14
Hats
  Blood Simple and, 11
  Fargo and, 76
  Intolerable Cruelty and, 126
  Miller's Crossing and, 29, 30, 33, 34, 37, 38, 41
  No Country for Old Men and, 153, 155
Heads, 46, 49–50
Heart, 6, 34, 35, 48, 53, 114, 132, 173. *See also* Emotion
Heat, 76
Hedaya, Dan, 1
Heinz, the Baron Krauss Von Espy *(Intolerable Cruelty)*, 135
Hell, 6, 13, 20, 25, 47, 50, 51, 52, 79
Hemingway, Ernest, 37
Hepburn, Katherine, 62
Herb Meyerson *(Intolerable Cruelty)*, 128, 129, 131, 132
Heroes, 19, 88. *See also specific characters*
Herrmann, Edward, 125
"Hills Like White Elephants" (Hemingway), 37
Hippies, 86–87
His Girl Friday (Hawks), 58, 63
History, 100, 140, 149, 160, 166. *See also* Backstories; The Past; *specific events*

Hitchcock, Alfred, 4, 10, 111, 115, 156, 167
Hoffman, Philip Seymour, 83, 84
Hollywood, 44, 45, 48, 52–54, 134
Holmes, Sherlock, 87, 88, 89
Homer, 97
Homer Stokes *(O Brother, Where Art Thou?)*, 98, 108
Homosexuality, 35, 36–37, 114, 135
Honesty, 20, 29, 40, 80
  See *also* Dishonesty; Truth
Horror films, 1, 4, 12, 44, 46, 150
Howard, Moe, 101
Howard D. Doyle *(Intolerable Cruelty)*, 135
Huddleston, David, 83
Hudsucker, Waring *(The Hudsucker Proxy)*, 75
The Hudsucker Proxy (Coen Brothers), 55–67, 104, 112, 136
Humanity, 35, 63, 109, 172
Humor, *Blood Simple* and, 13
Hunchback of Notre Dame, 62
Hunter, Holly, 15, 97, 102
  O Brother, Where Art Thou? and, 107
Hurst, Ryan, 137

I Am a Fugitive from the Chain Gang (LeRoy), 100
Ideals, 125
  No Country for Old Men and, 154
Identity
  Barton Fink and, 44, 45, 46
  The Big Lebowski and, 83–84, 86
  Blood Simple and, 1, 2, 5–6, 12
  Burn After Reading and, 165
  The Man Who Wasn't There and, 118
  Raising Arizona and, 22
Illegal activity. *See* Law; Outlaws
In the Heat of the Night, 76
Independence
  Blood Simple and, 8–9, 13
  Burn After Reading and, 165
  Fargo and, 73–74, 75
  The Hudsucker Proxy and, 56
  Intolerable Cruelty and, 133
  The Man Who Wasn't There and, 118–119, 120, 121

Miller's Crossing and, 39, 41–42
  See also Freedom
Individualism, 13, 31, 140, 157. *See also* Identity
Innocence, 56, 60, 106–107, 122
Intolerable Cruelty (Coen Brothers), 5, 125–136
It's a Wonderful Life (Capra), 62

Jackie Treehorn *(The Big Lebowski)*, 93
Jake Gittes *(Chinatown)*, 134
James Allen *(I am a Fugitive from the Chain Gang)*, 100
Jealousy, 75
Jenkins, Richard, 111, 125, 163
Jerry Lundegaard *(Fargo)*, 72, 73–75, 76
Jersey Girl, 25
Jesus Quintana *(The Big Lebowski)*, 93
Jobs. *See* Employment
Joe Gillis *(Sunset Boulevard)*, 117
Johansson, Scarlett, 111
John Doe *(Seven)*, 156
Johnny Caspar *(Miller's Crossing)*, 27, 40–42, 127
Johnson, Katie, 139
Johnson, Robert, 100
Joker *(The Dark Knight)*, 156
Jones, Tommy Lee, 149, 158
Justice, *O Brother, Where Art Thou?* and, 109

Kafka, Franz, 46
Kasdan, Lawrence, 14
Katie Cox *(Burn After Reading)*, 164, 170–171
Key Largo, 52
Keyser Söze *(The Usual Suspects)*, 117
The Killers, narration and, 13
The Killing (Kubrick), 71
King, Christ Thomas, 97
King of New York, 27, 28
KKK (Ku Klux Klan), 97, 100–101
Krupa, Olek, 27
Ku Klux Klan (KKK), 97, 100–101
Kubrick, Stanley, 46, 71

The Ladykillers (Coen Brothers), 136, 137–148
The Ladykillers (Mackendrick), 139, 144, 147
Lang, Fritz, 58
Last Man Standing, 29
Law, 11, 109, 125–126, 130, 161
Lebowski, Jeffrey ("The Big Lebowski"), 87, 92
Lebowski, Jeffrey ("The Dude"), 86–89
Legitimacy. *See* Authenticity
Leigh, Jennifer Jason, 55, 62
Leo (Liam) O'Bannon *(Miller's Crossing)*, 40–42
Leonard Smalls *(Raising Arizona)*, 156
Lerner, Michael, 43
Leroy, Mervin, 100
Lethal Weapon (Martin Riggs), 76
Lies. *See* Dishonesty; Truth
Linda Litzke *(Burn After Reading)*, 164, 165, 166, 171–174
Little Caesar, 28
Llewelyn Moss *(No Country for Old Men)*, 151, 152–153, 154–155, 157, 159
Lolita (Nabokov), 114, 121
Loman, Willy, 75
Loneliness, 116
  The Ladykillers and, 142, 143
Loners, 20
  Raising Arizona and, 24
The Long Goodbye (Altman), 84
Loren Visser, P.I. *(Blood Simple)*, 11–14, 156
Loretta Bell *(No Country for Old Men)*, 153, 160
Los Angeles, 45, 85, 86, 87, 88, 92, 93, 98, 126, 128
Losers, 20, 47, 59, 88, 102, 131. *See also specific characters*
Love
  Barton Fink and, 49
  The Big Lebowski and, 91, 94
  Blood Simple and, 3, 4, 10–11
  Burn After Reading and, 168, 173–174

Love (*continued*)
  Fargo and, 78
  The Hudsucker Proxy and, 56, 63
  Intolerable Cruelty and, 126, 127, 130, 131
  The Ladykillers and, 146
  The Man Who Wasn't There and, 118–119
  Miller's Crossing and, 38–39
  Raising Arizona and, 23
Love triangles
  Barton Fink and, 44
  Blood Simple and, 3, 8
  Burn After Reading and, 164
  Intolerable Cruelty and, 126
  The Man Who Wasn't There and, 114, 118, 120
  Miller's Crossing and, 28, 33, 36–37
Loyalty, 27, 31, 32, 33, 35, 36, 38, 39, 40, 41
Lump *(The Ladykillers)*, 140, 147
Lynch, John Carrol, 69

Ma, Tzi, 137
Macdonald, Kelly, 149
MacGuffins, 152, 165. *See also specific MacGuffins*
Mackendrick, Alexander, 139
Macy, William H., 69
Mad Max, 20, 22
Madness
  Barton Fink and, 46, 53
  Blood Simple and, 3–4
  Burn After Reading and, 171
  No Country for Old Men and, 174
Mahoney, John, 43, 55
Major and the Minor (Wilder), 127
Malkovich, John, 163
The Maltese Falcon (Hammett), 3, 52, 93, 134
The Man Who Wasn't There (Coen Brothers), 48, 88, 111–123, 128
Marge Gunderson *(Fargo)*, 69, 70, 71, 73, 75–79, 88, 171–172
Marilyn Rexroth *(Intolerable Cruelty)*, 126, 128

Marriage
  Blood Simple and, 2, 11
  Burn After Reading and, 168, 171
  The Hudsucker Proxy and, 64–65
  Intolerable Cruelty and, 126
  The Man Who Wasn't There and, 113, 116, 118, 119, 121
  Miller's Crossing and, 39–40
  No Country for Old Men and, 160
  O Brother, Where Art Thou? and, 107
  Raising Arizona and, 18, 20, 21
  See also American Dream; Divorce; Family; *Intolerable Cruelty* (Coen Brothers)
Martin Riggs *(Lethal Weapon)*, 76
Marty *(Blood Simple)*, 5–7
Marva Munson *(The Ladykillers)*, 143–145
Marylin Rexroth *(Intolerable Cruelty)*, 131, 132–134
Materialism, 129, 135. *See also* Money
Maude Lebowski *(The Big Lebowski)*, 92, 93
Mayer, Louis B., 53
Mayhew, W.P., 49, 53
McCarthy, Cormac, 149, 149150
McCarthy, Todd, 161
McCrea, Joel, 100
McDormand, Frances, 1, 15, 69, 81, 111, 163
McKinnon, Ray, 97
McMurray, Sam, 15
Men
  Blood Simple and, 2, 3
  Fargo and, 69, 72, 74, 76, 78–79
  The Hudsucker Proxy and, 59
  Intolerable Cruelty and, 131
  The Man Who Wasn't There and, 113, 120, 123
  Miller's Crossing and, 38
  Raising Arizona and, 20, 25
  See also Love; *specific characters*
Metamorphosis (Kafka), 46
Metropolis (Lang), 58, 63
Mike Hammer (Spillane), 86
Mike Yanagita *(Fargo)*, 76

Miles Massey *(Intolerable Cruelty)*, 126, 128, 129–132, 133
Miller's Crossing (Coen Brothers), 3, 27–42, 88, 127, 156
Miscommunication, 2, 3, 4, 9–10, 12. *See also* Communication
Miss Wilberforce *(The Ladykillers)*, 139, 144
Mistrust, 6, 7, 33, 41, 42, 62, 105, 106, 131, 153, 165
Modernity
　The Big Lebowski and, 85
　Burn After Reading and, 165, 170
　Fargo and, 71, 76, 79
　The Ladykillers and, 139, 140, 141, 142, 143, 145, 146
　The Man Who Wasn't There and, 113, 116, 119, 120, 121
　Raising Arizona and, 20
　See also No Country for Old Men (Coen Brothers); Social commentary
Money
　Barton Fink and, 45
　The Big Lebowski and, 86, 94
　Blood Simple and, 4, 7, 11, 12
　Burn After Reading and, 173
　Fargo and, 69, 70, 72, 73, 78
　The Hudsucker Proxy and, 65
　Intolerable Cruelty and, 128
　The Ladykillers and, 138
　The Man Who Wasn't There and, 117
　Miller's Crossing and, 34
　No Country for Old Men and, 152, 154–155, 160
　O Brother, Where Art Thou? and, 107
　Raising Arizona and, 20
　See also Business; Economic violence; Greed; Materialism
Moore, Julianne, 83
Morality
　Barton Fink and, 44
　The Big Lebowski and, 88, 90
　Blood Simple and, 11, 13
　Fargo and, 74, 80
　The Hudsucker Proxy and, 62, 63, 64
　Intolerable Cruelty and, 128, 132
　The Ladykillers and, 144

Miller's Crossing and, 27, 29, 30, 31, 32, 33, 36, 38, 39, 40, 41
No Country for Old Men and, 149, 154–155, 156, 158
O Brother, Where Art Thou? and, 98
Raising Arizona and, 21, 23, 24
Moses *(The Hudsucker Proxy)*, 58, 59, 62, 63, 65–67
Mother Nature, 23
Mothers, 22, 23, 24, 65, 75, 76, 77, 78. 133. 146, 155. *See also* Family
Motivation
　The Big Lebowski and, 88
　Blood Simple and, 2, 3
　Burn After Reading and, 164, 165, 166
　drifters and, 9
　Fargo and, 69–70, 74, 81
　The Hudsucker Proxy and, 60
　Intolerable Cruelty and, 125, 133
　The Ladykillers and, 141, 142
　Miller's Crossing and, 28, 33, 35
　No Country for Old Men and, 156–157, 159
　O Brother, Where Art Thou? and, 99, 100
　Raising Arizona and, 16, 20
　See also specific motives
Movies, 21–22
　See also specific movies
Mr. Deeds Goes to Town (Capra), 58, 62–63
Muni, Paul, 100
Murders
　Barton Fink and, 44, 46, 47
　The Big Lebowski and, 92
　Blood Simple and, 1
　complexity of, 10
　Fargo and, 73
　Intolerable Cruelty and, 128–129
　The Ladykillers and, 141, 146
　The Man Who Wasn't There and, 112, 118, 119
　No Country for Old Men and, 153–154
Music
　The Big Lebowski and, 87
　Blood Simple and, 10

Music (*continued*)
　The Hudsucker Proxy and, 62
　The Man Who Wasn't There and, 121
　Miller's Crossing and, 31
　No Country for Old Men and, 152, 161
　O Brother, Where Art Thou? and, 98, 99, 108, 109
Mussburger, Sidney J. *(The Hudsucker Proxy)*, 64–65
My Blue Heaven (Martin), 27

Nabokov, Vladimir, 114
The Naked City (Dassin), 71
Narration, 28, 63, 65, 116–117, 150, 152, 159
Nature
　Barton Fink and, 47
　Fargo and, 75, 81
　Intolerable Cruelty and, 131
　The Man Who Wasn't There and, 117
　Miller's Crossing and, 34, 35, 37, 39, 40
　Raising Arizona and, 25
Nelson, Tim Blake, 97, 106–107
Neo-noir, 3, 7
Newman, Paul, 55, 64
Night of the Hunter (Laughton), 156
Nihilists *(The Big Lebowski)*, 93
Nixon, Richard, 87
No Country for Old Men (Coen Brothers), 81, 149–161
Normalcy
　Fargo and, 78
　Intolerable Cruelty and, 128, 133
　The Man Who Wasn't There and, 112, 113, 115, 117
　Miller's Crossing and, 34
　No Country for Old Men and, 154, 156, 157
　Raising Arizona and, 22, 23
Norman Bates *(Psycho)*, 156, 167
Norville Barnes *(The Hudsucker Proxy)*, 59–62

O Brother, Where Art Thou? (Coen Brothers), 97–109

O'Connor, Flannery, 17
Odets, Clifford, 48, 53
The Odyssey (Homer), 97, 98, 99, 102, 103
Of Mice and Men (Steinbeck), 17
"Old Man" (Faulkner), 100
Old timey. See *O Brother, Where Art Thou?* (Coen Brothers)
Opening shots
　Barton Fink, 43
　The Big Lebowski, 98
　The Big Lebowski and, 83
　Blood Simple, 4
　Burn After Reading, 163, 166
　Fargo and, 71–72
　Intolerable Cruelty and, 126
　Miller's Crossing, 27
　No Country for Old Men and, 150
　O Brother, Where Art Thou? and, 98
Operation Desert Storm, 85
Opposites, 2, 40, 48, 80, 90, 115, 120, 127, 144. See *also* Alter egos
Oral tradition, 99
Osbourne Cox *(Burn After Reading)*, 164, 166, 167–168, 169–171
Oscars, 28, 81, 158, 161, 174
Othar Munson *(The Ladykillers)*, 144
Outcasts, 35
　Barton Fink and, 53
　The Ladykillers and, 141–142
　Miller's Crossing and, 37
Outlaws, 22, 23–24, 25, 152
Outsiders
　The Big Lebowski and, 88
　Fargo and, 72, 80, 81
　The Man Who Wasn't There and, 113, 116
　No Country for Old Men and, 159
　O Brother, Where Art Thou?, 102

Pappy O'Daniel *(O Brother, Where Art Thou?)*, 97, 98, 100, 108
Paranoia, 113, 163–164
　Burn After Reading and, 165, 166, 167–168, 168–169
Park, Steve, 69

The Past
 The Big Lebowski and, 85, 87, 92–93
 Burn After Reading and, 166, 170, 173
 The Ladykillers and, 139–140, 142
 No Country for Old Men and, 150, 160
 See also Backstories
Penelope *(O Brother, Where Art Thou?)*, 102
Pete Hogwallop *(O Brother, Where Art Thou?)*, 104–106
Philip Marlowe, 84–85, 86, 88, 112
Pickles *(The Ladykillers)*, 144–145
Picture Snatcher, 58
Pitt, Brad, 136, 163
Plot
 The Big Lebowski and, 84
 The Hudsucker Proxy and, 56
 Miller's Crossing and, 28, 33
 Raising Arizona and, 16
Poe, Edgar Allen, 143, 144–145
Polanski, Roman, 46
Politics
 Burn After Reading and, 165
 O Brother, Where Art Thou? and, 108
Polito, Jon, 27, 43, 83, 111
Polyphemus Cyclops, 107
Popeye Doyle, 76
The Postman Always Rings Twice (Cain), 3, 113, 114, 116, 118, 120
 Blood Simple and, 6
Power
 The Big Lebowski and, 92
 Fargo and, 76
 The Hudsucker Proxy and, 66
 Miller's Crossing and, 27, 37, 38, 39, 40
 See also Control
Presnell, Harve, 69
Pride, *O Brother, Where Art Thou?* and, 103, 105
Prison, 20
 Raising Arizona and, 21
Private investigators (detectives), 11, 76
 The Big Lebowski and, 91

clothing and, 89
 Intolerable Cruelty and, 134
 Miller's Crossing and, 30–31
 Raising Arizona and, 20
 See also specific characters
Professionalism, 30, 76, 78, 130, 131, 132, 159, 173
Psychiatry, 8, 168
Psycho (Hitchcock), 10, 115, 156, 167
Psychologists, 20
Psychology, 21, 44. 46, 52, 90, 168
The Public Enemy, 40
Pulp Fiction (Tarantino), 66–67
Purity, 57, 60, 71–72, 79, 81, 122

Race, 65–66, 101, 108, 139, 146
Raimi, Sam, 16
Raising Arizona (Coen Brothers), 15–26, 33, 50, 59, 85, 100, 156
Rasche, David, 163
Rationality, 33, 52, 101, 105, 159. See also Brains
"The Raven" (Poe), 143
Ray *(Blood Simple)*, 9–11, 47
Reagan, Ronald, 20
Reagan, Tom *(Miller's Crossing)*, 31–35, 42, 88
Realism
 Barton Fink and, 43–44, 52
 Fargo and, 70, 71, 73, 74, 76, 77, 79
 The Ladykillers and, 138
 Miller's Crossing and, 37, 42
 No Country for Old Men and, 149, 153
 O Brother, Where Art Thou? and, 99
 settings and, 57
Rebels, 21, 86, 87, 88, 90, 102
Red Harvest (Hammett), 3, 29, 39
Redemption, *Blood Simple* and, 4
Reed, Donna, 76
Region-based films, 17
Reid, Tara, 83
Relationships
 Blood Simple and, 8
 Fargo and, 79
 The Man Who Wasn't There and, 121

Relationships (*continued*)
   See also Divorce; Friendship; Homosexuality; Love triangles; Marriage
Religion
   The Big Lebowski and, 90
   The Ladykillers and, 141, 142–143, 143–144
   O Brother, Where Art Thou? and, 98, 101, 103–104
   See also Faith; The Bible
Repulsion (Polanski), 46
Rio Bravo, 25
The Road Warrior, 29
Robbins, Tim, 55
Rolling Stone (magazine), 84
Root, Stephen, 149
Rudrud, Kristen, 69
Rules, *The Big Lebowski* and, 90
Rush, Geoffrey, 125

Sam Spade *(The Maltese Falcon),* 11, 86, 134
Samuel Gerard *(The Fugitive),* 158
Sarah Sorkin *(Intolerable Cruelty),* 133
Scarface, 28
Schickel, Richard, on *Barton Fink,* 44
Schwarzenegger, Arnold, 19
Scott, A.O., 104
Secrets, 146. See also *Burn After Reading* (Coen Brothers)
Self-examination
   Barton Fink and, 48
   The Big Lebowski and, 89
   Blood Simple and, 5
   The Hudsucker Proxy and, 59
   Miller's Crossing and, 33
Self-preservation, 5, 18
Sellers, Peter, 139
Seesslan, Georg, 4, 13, 18, 27
Setting
   Barton Fink and, 51–52
   Blood Simple and, 4
   Fargo and, 79, 81
   The Hudsucker Proxy and, 56, 57–58, 63
   Miller's Crossing and, 29
   See also specific settings

Seven (Fincher), 76, 156
Sex
   Burn After Reading and, 167, 168
   Intolerable Cruelty and, 132
   The Man Who Wasn't There and, 114, 119, 120, 121–122
   O Brother Where Art Thou? and, 105
Shadow of a Doubt (Hitchcock), 111
Shalhoub, Tony, 43, 111
Sheriff Cooley *(O Brother, Where Art Thou?),* 98, 100, 101, 108–109
Sheriff Ed Tom Bell *(No Country for Old Men),* 151, 152, 158–161
The Shining (Kubrick), 46, 52
Shoes, 52, 60
Sidney J. Mussburger *(The Hudsucker Proxy),* 64–65
Silence of the Lambs (Demme), 156
Silver, Joel, 66, 136
Simmons, J.K., 137, 145, 163
The Simpsons, 104–105, 135
Sleuths. See Private investigators
Slob noir, 85
Smith, Kevin, 25
Smith, Will, 166
Social commentary
   Burn After Reading and, 165, 172–173
   Intolerable Cruelty and, 126, 128, 132
   The Ladykillers and, 140
   The Man Who Wasn't There and, 113, 116
   No Country for Old Men and, 149–150, 153
   O Brother, Where Art Thou? and, 108, 109
Social standards
   The Big Lebowski and, 87
   Blood Simple and, 2, 4
   Fargo and, 80
   O Brother, Where Art Thou? and, 100–101 (*See also* Independence)
   Raising Arizona and, 17, 19–20
Sonnenfeld, Barry, 44
The Sopranos, 40, 123
Souls, 45, 52, 98, 99, 104, 108, 109, 117, 127, 155

Soundtracks. *See* Music
The South, 98–99, 99–100, 104, 105, 108, 143, 146
Space ships, 113, 117
Spock, Benjamin, 18, 23
Spy films, 166
Spy Game, 172
Stallone, Sylvester, 19
State of Grace, 27, 28
Stereotypes, 105, 141, 146. *See also* Characterizations; Clichés
Stevenson, Robert Louis, 17, 21, 46
Stewart, Jimmy, 56
Stormare, Peter, 69, 83
Storytelling, 99
The Strange Case of Dr. Jekyll and Mr. Hyde (Stevenson), 17, 21, 46, 47
"The Stranger" *(The Big Lebowski),* 93
Sturges, Preston, 56, 100
Suicide, 55–67
Sullivan's Travels (Sturges), 100
Sunset Boulevard, 13, 116, 117
Suspense, 4, 85, 166
Swinton, Tilda, 163
Symbols, 30

Tarantino, Quentin, 25, 66–67
Ted *(Burn After Reading),* 173–174
Teeth, 130
Television, 22, 57, 76, 129, 159
The Tenant (Polanski), 46
Texas, 2, 4, 12–13, 150, 152–153, 154, 164
The Third Man, 36
Thornton, Billy Bob, 111, 114, 125, 135, 136
Three Stooges, 101
Time, 58–59, 65, 66
"To Helen" (Poe), 143
To the White Sea (Coen Brothers), 136
Tom Bishop *(Spy Game),* 172
Tom Reagan, 88
Tommy Johnson *(O Brother, Where Art Thou?),* 98, 100, 108
Tony Soprano *(The Sopranos),* 123
Torn Curtain (Hitchcock), 10
Touch of Evil (Welles), 76

Travers, Peter, 123, 147
True-Frost, Jim, 55
Trust, 6, 7, 33, 41, 42, 62, 105, 106, 131, 153, 165
Truth
  Blood Simple and, 10
  Burn After Reading and, 168–169, 170
  Fargo and, 71
  The Hudsucker Proxy and, 62, 63
  Intolerable Cruelty and, 130
  Miller's Crossing and, 29
  O Brother, Where Art Thou? and, 102
  See also Honesty
Turturro, John, 27, 43, 83, 93, 104–106
Twain, Mark, 17
Two-Face *(Batman),* 157

Ulysses Everett McGill *(O Brother, Where Art Thou?),* 101–104
The Unforgiven (Eastwood), 101
The Usual Suspects (Singer), 117

Vanity, 168, 171
Vera Bernbaum *(Miller's Crossing),* 38–40
Vernon Waldrip *(O Brother, Where Art Thou?),* 102–103
Vietnam era, 85, 87, 90, 137, 140, 146–147, 154
Villains, 20, 22, 56, 93, 107, 108–109, 138–139, 152, 156. *See also specific villains*
Violence
  Barton Fink and, 43, 46, 47, 49–50, 53–54
  The Big Lebowski and, 83, 85–86, 87, 88, 89, 91, 93, 94, 95
  Blood Simple and, 2, 5, 6–7, 8, 10
  Burn After Reading and, 164, 167–168, 170, 174
  comedic/realistic, 26
  Fargo and, 69, 70–71, 72–73, 78, 79, 80
  femme fatales and, 7
  The Hudsucker Proxy and, 58, 59, 60, 61, 64

Violence (*continued*)
  Intolerable Cruelty and, 125, 127, 128–129
  The Ladykillers and, 138, 139, 140–141, 143, 147
  The Man Who Wasn't There and, 112, 113, 114–115, 118, 123
  Miller's Crossing and, 30–31, 33, 34, 40–41
  No Country for Old Men and, 149–150, 152, 153, 156–157, 159, 160
  O Brother, Where Art Thou? and, 98, 101, 103, 109
  Raising Arizona and, 15, 17
  See also Economic violence; Murders
Visser, Loren, P.I., 11–14
Voice-overs, 13, 27

Waiting for Lefty (Odets), 48
Wallace, George, 137
Walsh, M. Emmet, 1
Walter *(The Man Who Wasn't There)*, 113
Walter Huff *(Double Indemnity)*, 114, 117, 118
Walter Sobchak *(The Big Lebowski)*, 83, 86, 87, 89–92
War, 129
Warner, Jack, 53
Warner Bros, 66
Wayans, Marlon, 137
Waylon Smithers *(The Simpsons)*, 135

West, Nathaniel, 53
Westerns, 22, 150, 152–153
  See also Cowboys
Wheezy Joe *(Intolerable Cruelty)*, 129
Wilder, Billy, 127
Williams, Samm-Art, 1
Wilson, Trey, 15
The Wizard of Oz, 100
Women
  Fargo and, 76, 78–79
  The Hudsucker Proxy and, 56
  The Man Who Wasn't There and, 114, 116, 119
  No Country for Old Men and, 153
  Raising Arizona and, 22
  See also Femme fatales; *specific characters*
Woody Woodpecker, 21
Work
  Barton Fink and, 44, 48, 49, 53
  The Big Lebowski and, 84, 86
  Burn After Reading and, 169
  Fargo and, 73
  Intolerable Cruelty and, 128
  Miller's Crossing and, 32
  Raising Arizona and, 17, 19, 24, 25
  See also Business; Professionalism
Wrigley *(Intolerable Cruelty)*, 128, 135

Yojimbo (Kurosawa), 29

Zeta-Jones, Catherine, 125

About the Author

RYAN P. DOOM is a freelance writer and teacher. He holds an MFA in creative writing and works as an English instructor for an area community college, where he introduces review techniques to students. Doom presented the essay "A Difference of Character: The Coen Brothers, Noir and the Hardboiled Unusual" at the PCA/ACA conference in Boston in 2007.